D1359634

Ads
Plus

Nate Rosenblatt • Jeff Cramp

Round Lake Publishing

Copyright © 2000 by Round Lake Publishing Co.
All rights reserved. No part of this publication may be reproduced, stored in or introduced into a retrieval system, or transmitted, in any form or by any means now known or hereafter developed (electronic, mechanical, photocopying, recording or otherwise) without the prior written permission of the copyright owner and publisher of this book.

Round Lake Publishing Co.
31 Bailey Avenue
Ridgefield, CT 06877

Printed in the United States of America

0987654321

ISBN 0-929543-61-0

A Note of Thanks from the Publisher

To create this unique book, we called upon the special abilities of a number of unusually talented people, each of whom made an important contribution.

Our deep appreciation goes to Nate Rosenblatt and Jeff Cramp, two of the most gifted copywriters and advertising professionals in the country.

We'd like to thank our graphics designer, Paula Antolini, for the exceptional layouts she so brilliantly executed.

Nancy Boudreau and Bill Hutches used their special skills to create the artwork that made the ads come alive.

Dave Shugarts, our guru of electronic publishing, pulled together the literally thousands of pieces of copy, design and art, into what you see as the finished product.

We were fortunate in working with such a dedicated and talented team.

Table of Contents

CHAPTER 2   BUSINESS CARDS

CHAPTER 3   CLASSIFIED ADS

CHAPTER 4   COVER LETTERS

CHAPTER 5   DIRECT MAIL

CHAPTER 6   FLIERS

Non-Profit

CHAPTER 7   IMAGE BUILDERS

Consumer & Business

CHAPTER 8   NEWSPAPER ADS

Consumer Products

Real Estate

Non-Profit

CHAPTER 9   PRESS RELEASES

Consumer and Business

Professional

Non-Profit

CHAPTER 10   RADIO AND TV COMMERCIALS

Radio Commercials—Consumer

Radio Commercials—Business-to-Business

Radio Commercials—Professional

TV Commercials—Consumer and Business

CHAPTER 11   TRADE ADS

CHAPTER 12   YELLOW PAGES® ADS

What this Book Will Do for You

Imagine that you could have the country's finest copywriters, graphics designers and artists creating powerful, highly effective ads for your business. That's what we've given you in this rich treasury of marketing tools.

An award-winning team of writers, designers and artists developed more than 260 ads to save you and your company the tremendous time and effort of having them created. Of course, developing such a trove of material is far beyond the budgets of most organizations.

The material in this book will provide you with the ability to:

- Increase sales with highly effective ads
- Create superior brochures to promote your business, practice, or organization
- Motivate prospective customers with powerful sales letters
- Put your name before the public with press releases that will get your story across
- Recruit skilled employees using classified ads
- Make your organization more memorable to your target market with business cards and image advertising.
- Prepare fliers to promote timely sales or events

- Create Yellow Pages ads that will generate new business throughout the year
- Plus much more!

Whatever kind of advertising you want, you'll find just what you need in this book:

- Brochures
- Business cards
- Classified ads
- Direct mail
- Fliers
- Image builders
- Newspaper ads
- Press releases
- Radio and TV commercials
- Trade advertising
- Yellow Pages® ads

This book will quickly become your most used valued marketing resource, taking a prominent place on your business bookshelf.

Who Should Use this Book?

This book is an extraordinarily rich resource for any company, organization or individual who needs high quality marketing vehicles to sell virtually any product or service. Here are just a few examples:

- Small businesses that require first class advertising but don't have large-business budgets
- Home-based businesses that want professional looking advertising at a cost that's easily affordable
- Ad agencies of all sizes that can use the examples as a starting point, or use the ads as they are, customizing them for their specific clients.
- Retailers that can use ads from this book instead of having to rely on the tired, old fashioned look of ads supplied by newspapers.
- Real estate brokers who want to generate increased business with attention-getting advertising.
- Manufacturers who can use the ads to promote their products in trade publications or direct to the public.
- Direct marketing companies that are constantly looking for fresh, exciting creative approaches.
- Professional practices that want to boost their revenue with top flight public relations, advertising and direct mail.

- Consultants who wish to develop highly effective brochures and direct mail to build their businesses.
- Corporations that have in-house advertising departments and are constantly looking for innovative promotional concepts.
- Non-profit organizations with limited resources that need to prepare effective fund raising direct mail promotions.

Whatever kind of business you're in, you'll find hundreds of ads and other marketing tools that will improve your sales and impress your customers with your professionalism.

How to Use this Book

This book was designed not only to present more than 260 award-winning ads, but also to make the material extremely easy to use.

Hundreds of sample ads are included, covering virtually every kind of business or organization, from retail to real estate, medical practices to financial planners, and industrial companies to non-profit organizations. If you don't find examples of your own industry or profession here, you're likely to locate ads for similar businesses which you can easily modify to suit your purposes.

How the book is organized

Each chapter contains examples for a wide range of businesses. Ads are arranged by format and media type. For example, all brochures are located in the first chapter, direct mail packages are found in chapter 5, and newspaper ads are placed in chapter 6. The chapters divide the ads further, separating them by the kind of businesses they promote.

Table of contents and indexes

A comprehensive table of contents is located at the beginning of the book. Use this to find the chapter you are looking for. There are two indexes at the end of the book. One lists all the documents by their titles and the other is organized by key word. Use either index or the table of contents to find ads for your specific requirements in just seconds.

How the documents are presented

Each ad is shown first in its entirety. For example, in the brochure chapter, a 3-panel brochure is displayed as it appears when it is printed and folded. The subsequent pages of the brochure show each side in larger size, so you can easily read the text. The same is true of the direct mail chapter. The first page of each direct mail package shows all the pieces of the direct mail package. The next few pages show the individual components in larger size.

Read the helpful hints

At the bottom of each page, you'll find hints that suggest how you can achieve maximum effectiveness for that ad. Be sure to take advantage of these tips.

Getting the best results

You may wish to use the ads exactly as you find them. Another way to create the best ad for your business is to thumb through the ads that appeal to you, and borrow a headline from one, text from another and design and art concepts from yet another. That will give you total flexibility.

If you are competent in desk top publishing, you can produce a desired ad by duplicating what you see in the book. Or you can photocopy the ad and have a graphics designer recreate it for you.

Brochures 1

For all-around usefulness, brochures are probably the most effective marketing devices. A brochure can be used as a "take-one" on a store counter, as a hand-out at your seminar, or as an introduction to your company in a mailing with a brief cover letter. It may also be an integral part of a direct mail package (see the Direct Mail chapter).

A brochure is frequently created from a single sheet of paper. An 8 1/2" x 11" sheet, folded in thirds, produces a 6-panel brochure. That same size paper, folded in half, produces a 4-panel brochure. Examples of each are shown in this chapter.

Cover. Decide on the single most important thing you want the reader to know about your product or service and present that message on the cover. This is referred to as "positioning" and defines how you want your market to think of what you sell and what your company is. For example, if you run a hardware store, any of these could be your positioning: "the best prices in town," "the widest selection of hardware in the county," or "service is our middle name." Incidentally, many people read *only* the cover of a brochure, which underlines the importance of getting your most significant statement right out front.

Inside spread. Once you've captured the reader with your opening appeal, you need to provide copy that will support the positioning on the cover. If you're selling an accounting service, highlight your client list and accomplishments and the in-depth experience of your partners and staff. Whatever you decide, stress the benefits in terms your prospects will relate to. As an ad man once said about selling garden supplies, "Don't tell your customers about *your* grass seed, tell them about *their* lawns."

Use artwork and photographs wherever possible, accompanied by captions, to illustrate your products and services and to introduce yourself and your employees to prospective customers.

Back cover. Here you should reinforce your benefits and restate your offer (if there is one). Be sure to include your address, phone and fax numbers, and office hours, if appropriate.

Graphics and paper. Your brochure will probably be the most important printed promotion you create. Pay careful attention to the typeface, photos and illustrations, layout, paper quality, and printing.

Consistency. Every marketing device you use should have a similar graphic look, copy theme and style, providing a cohesive campaign. Brochures are no exception. Changing the message in midstream confuses your prospects and gives them mixed signals. A consistent strategy builds on all the other marketing messages they receive from you in other media, such as direct mail, newspaper ads and radio advertising.

• Building consumer confidence is an important aspect of selling your services. This 4-panel 8 1/2" x 11" brochure folded in half features testimonials from satisfied users in addition to a description of the award-winning services.

HERE'S WHAT YOUR FRIENDS, NEIGHBORS, AND COLLEAGUES ARE SAYING ABOUT THE BUILDER'S GUILD:

". . . added a beautiful suite for my mother. It was perfect. Now I can keep an eye on mom while she has the dignity and privacy of her own beautiful living space."
- Dale Rohenburg

"Last week I had a one-car garage; this week I have a two-car garage. No one can even tell where the old one ends and the new one begins. Great workmanship."
- Carl Shirkin

"I always think of contractors as people who promise anything to get the job. But The Builder's Guild is a cut above the rest. They showed up on time and finished two days ahead of schedule."
- Allen Bach

Use the home remodeler everyone's talking about.

The Area's
Most Trusted
Home Improvement
Company
214 Landry Ave
Cheyenne, WY 82001
307-555-6460

Member of National Home Remodelers,
Wyoming Home Improvement
Guild Wyoming Remodeling and
Improvement Contractors Association.

The Area's Most Trusted Home Improvement Company

- The front cover design uses "white space" as a design element, refining the message into a few simple but pleasing elements so that "most trusted" is sure to be noticed.

- Testimonials using customers' actual names offer prospects a sense of security about your firm.

THE BUILDER'S GUILD is

a full-service, award-winning construction company that offers many unique features and benefits:

- Over 30 years of experience
- Licensed architect on staff
- Recipient of 13 regional, state, and national awards for excellence
- No up-front charges! You only pay when the work is completed and you're satisfied.
- Start-to-finish supervision, including building permits, architectural plans, and daily on-site inspections
- Member of National Home Remodelers, Wyoming Home Improvement Guild, and Wyoming Remodeling and Improvement Contractors Association

NO JOB TOO BIG
NO JOB TOO SMALL

During our 30 years in business, we've done everything from executing painstaking historic restorations to replacing rotting planking on a deck. We've added mother-in-law suites and turned garages into offices. We've completely rebuilt fire-charred homes and we've replaced windows. Whatever your job, we'd like the opportunity to bid. Here's just a sampling of the projects we can handle:

- Additions
- Kitchens
- Garages
- Windows
- Decks
- Roofing
- Master Bedroom Suites
- Dormers
- Bathrooms
- Doors
- Patios
- Screened porches
- Siding

EVERY JOB IS SUPERVISED

Each job has a foreman, who must have at least five years of exemplary performance with The Builder's Guild. In addition, one of the company principals does an on-site inspection *at least once every day* that a work crew is on your premises. Every job is quality controlled.

REMEMBER: IT COSTS MORE TO MOVE THAN IT DOES TO IMPROVE!

Bathroom   Kitchen   Windows

Here's the document you receive with your home remodeling job. (It's the only one of its kind in this profession!)

- In a competitive marketplace, every point you can make in your company's favor increases the chances you'll be selected to do the job. Pull out all the stops!

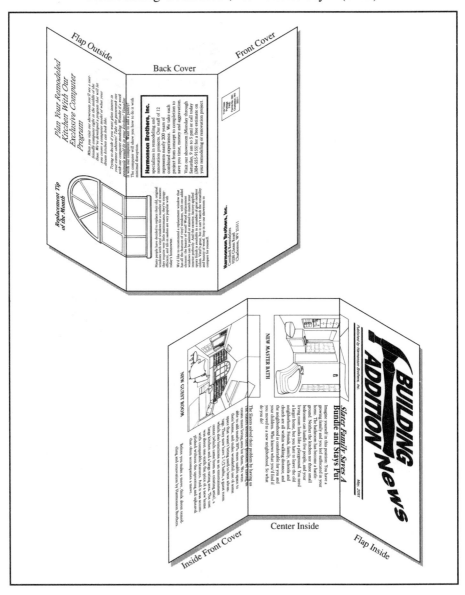

- Newsletter formats get high readership. This 6-panel 8 1/2" x 11" brochure folded in thirds combines a "Tip of the Month," with illustrations of the work that can be accomplished. The reader is left with positive feelings about the company and, hopefully, an interest in getting a quote.

BUILDING ADDITION News

Published by Harmonson Brothers, Inc.   May, 20XX

NEW MASTER BATH

NEW GUEST ROOM

Slater Family Saves A Bundle and Stays Put

Imagine yourself in this position: You have a growing family and you feel suffocated in your home. The bathroom has become a battle-ground. Neither the kitchen nor three small bedrooms can handle five people, and your living room looks like a playground. You need a larger home, but you hate to leave the old neighborhood. Friends, family, schools and church are all within walking distance, and the neighborhood is comfortable for you and your children. Who knows what you'd find if you moved to a new neighborhood. So what do you do?

The Slaters solved their problem by having us create more living area for them. We were able to add nearly 30% more usable space to their home, and make wonderful use of some space that wasn't being used to best advan-tage. They now have 2-1/2 baths, a guest room which also functions as an entertainment center (which came from an existing attic), a large kitchen and a large eating area. The cost was about one-sixth the price of a new home with comparable features. And it was accom-plished without the uprooting and upheaval that often accompanies a move.

Before you make a move, think about remod-eling and renovation by Harmonson Brothers.

- People identify with real-life examples. Use them with or without testimonial quotes to sell your products or services.

- Don't clutter the design of your newsletter. An overwhelming amout of copy and graphics will discourage the prospect from reading your literature.

Replacement Tip of the Month

Many people have decided to replace their old, original windows with vinyl windows for a number of reasons: they require very little maintenance, they're energy-efficient, and tilt-in sashes are very popular with today's homeowner.

We'd like to recommend a replacement window that has all the features of vinyl windows, with one added element: the beauty of wood! Wood replacement windows can be painted or stained to match your interior perfectly. And the exterior, factory-applied epoxy finish is available in a number of great outdoor colors. Vinyl's great, but it can't match the versatility and beauty of wood. Stop in to our showroom to compare for yourself.

Harmonson Brothers, Inc.
Certified Remodelers
9200 Glenn Road
Charleston, WV 25311

Plan Your Remodeled Kitchen With Our Exclusive Computer Program

When you visit our showroom you'll see a user-friendly computer right in the middle of the floor. We've developed a program that will let you create a computer model of what your dream kitchen can look like.

Trying to decide if you want glass inserts in your corner cabinets? Take the guesswork out with our computer modeling. Wonder if a work peninsula would fit in your kitchen? Visualize it with our computer. Want to add a pantry? The computer will show you how to do it with minimal disruption.

Harmonson Brothers, Inc. specializes in remodeling and renovation projects. Our staff of 12 represents nearly 200 years of combined experience. We take each project from concept to completion to save you time, money and aggravation.

Visit our showroom (Monday through Saturday, 9 am to 5 pm) or call today (304-555-9155) for a free estimate on your remodeling or renovation project.

First Class
Postage
PAID
Permit No. 000
Charleston, WV
25311

• Keep the promotional aspect of your mailing to a minimum to maintain the feeling that it's a newsletter.

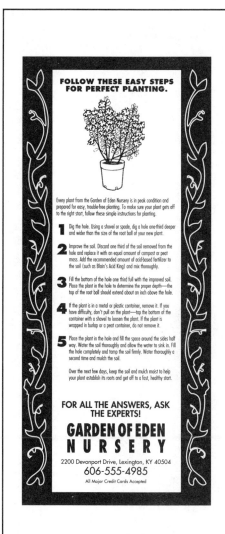

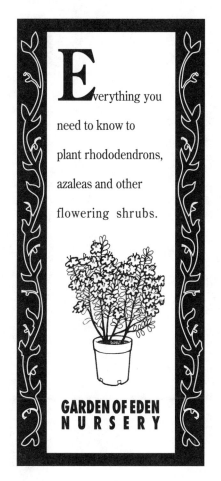

- A brochure can be as simple as a single piece of paper or card stock printed on two sides. This 3 3/4" x 8 1/2" piece has no folds but communicates valuable information along with a clear message that the company knows plants and planting.

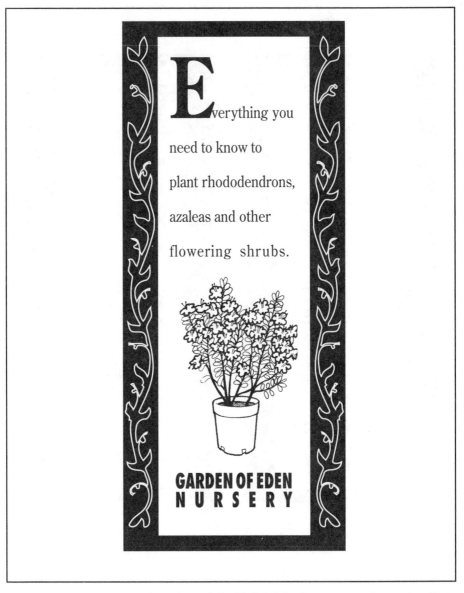

- You can produce a series of brochures full of helpful tips in your area of expertise. Keep the instructions short, simple and easy to follow. If a diagram or drawing will help explain steps, include it.

- This is the perfect size to enclose in a #10 envelope, or for a retail store to distribute at the cash register in a "take one" holder.

- Artwork that reflects what you're offering enhances the strength of the message and increases readership.

- Sometimes, the simplest is best. This 4-panel 7" x 8 1/2" brochure folded in half makes a strong statement about the benefits of the company's services, then backs it up with specifics inside. The "letter" graphic throughout the brochure reinforces the business the company is in while adding interest to what could be a sterile, all-type presentation.

MAIL
MORE
than ever before
AND
SAVE
on postage costs!

BLISS
DIRECT MARKETING

12385 Casa Del Banco Road
Irvine, CA 92714

Phone: 714-555-8798
Fax: 714-555-8704

BLISS
DIRECT MARKETING

Your Mail Manager

• The "stack of letters" artwork makes good use of the brochure's vertical format while communicating the concept of mailings.

• We sort your mail with other mailers to earn you dramatic savings!

• Save up to $44/M on third class/bulk mailing postage costs—no matter how small your mailing!

• Faster, more accurate delivery with no additional work on your end!

• Increased sales because you can afford to do more mailings!

Do you remember your original direct mail advertising budget? The one you threw away when the new postal rates were adopted? Now you can resurrect it because Bliss Direct Marketing can help you slash your postage costs.

Give us a call and we'll show you how we can save you money, even if you mail in small quantities. And you're welcome to visit our facility to see for yourself how our ultra-sophisticated system is programmed to optically read your addresses, search for them in a zip+4 national directory, apply the appropriate barcode, and sort your mail in an automated stream with others to get you the best postage rate possible.

Do it now.
Call 1-714-555-8798.

BLISS DIRECT MARKETING for all your direct mail fulfillment needs

• Literature fulfillment

• Computerized inventory management

• Database management

• Lettershop and list preparation

• Postnet approved bar coding

• Ink jet addressing

• Premium promotions and management

• Inquiry management/Telemarketing

• Warehousing

• Always sell benefits. Tell the customer how they will save money, do their job faster or better, get more customers, etc.

• Offering a plant/facility tour is a way of demonstrating pride and confidence in your company.

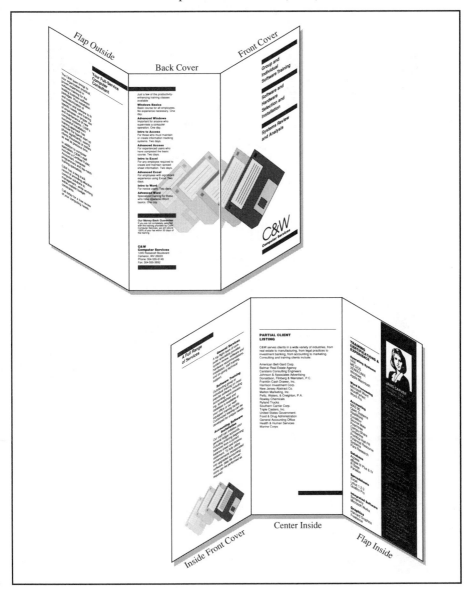

- Building trust is critical when an important part of the prospect's business relies on the services being offered. This 6-panel 8 1/2" x 11" brochure folded in thirds employs two methods to build that trust—a powerful biography of the company president, and an impressive client listing.

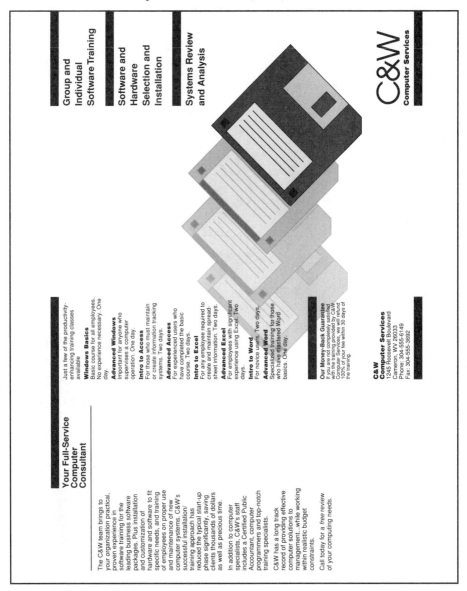

- Don't assume a client or prospect knows every service or product you offer. A company brochure offers a chance to get your *complete* message across.

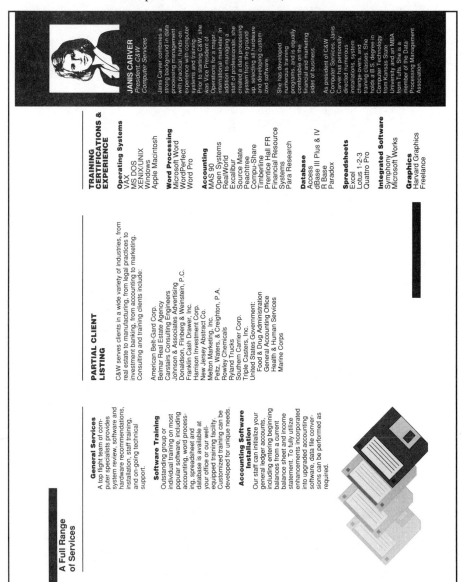

JANIS CARVER
President, C&W
Computer Services

Janis Carver combines a strong background in data processing management with practical, hands-on experience with computer systems and training. Prior to starting C&W, she was Vice President of Operations for a major international marketer. In addition to managing a staff of professionals, she created a data processing system from the ground up, selecting all hardware and developing customized software.

She has developed numerous training programs, and is equally comfortable on the financial and marketing sides of business.

As president of C&W Computer Services, Janis Carver has personally directed numerous installations, system change-overs, and training classes. She holds a B.S. degree in Computer Technology from Kansas State University and an MBA from Tufts. She is a member of the Data Processing Management Association.

TRAINING CERTIFICATIONS & EXPERIENCE

Operating Systems
VAX
MS DOS
XENIX/UNIX
Windows
Apple Macintosh

Word Processing
Microsoft Word
WordPerfect
Word Pro

Accounting
MAS 90
Open Systems
RealWorld
Excalibur
Source Mate
Peachtree
Compu-Share
Timberline
Prentice Hall FR
Financial Resource Systems
Para Research

Database
Access
dBase III Plus & IV
R Base
Paradox

Spreadsheets
Excel
Lotus 1-2-3
Quattro Pro

Integrated Software
Symphony
Microsoft Works

Graphics
Harvard Graphics
Freelance

PARTIAL CLIENT LISTING

C&W serves clients in a wide variety of industries, from real estate to manufacturing, from legal practices to investment banking, from accounting to marketing. Consulting and training clients include:

American Belt-Gard Corp.
Belmar Real Estate Agency
Carstairs Consulting Engineers
Johnson & Associates Advertising
Donaldson, Flinberg & Weinstein, P.C.
Franklin Cash Drawer, Inc.
Harrison Investment Corp.
New Jersey Abstract Co.
Melton Marketing, Inc.
Peltz, Waters, & Creighton, P.A.
Rowley Chemicals
Ryland Trucks
Southern Carrier Corp.
Triple Casters, Inc.
United States Government:
 Food & Drug Administration
 General Accounting Office
 Health & Human Services
 Marine Corps

A Full Range of Services

General Services
A top flight team of computer specialists provides system review, software and hardware recommendations, installation, staff training, and on-going technical support.

Software Training
Outstanding group or individual training on most popular software, including accounting, word processing, spreadsheet and database is available at your office or our well-equipped training facility. Customized training can be developed for unique needs.

Accounting Software Installation
Our staff can initialize your general ledger accounts, including entering beginning balances from a current balance sheet and income statement. To fully utilize enhancements incorporated into upgraded accounting software, data file conversions can be performed as required.

• Providing a list of your clients gives prospects confidence in doing business with your company. If you can, list both large and small businesses and cover a wide range of industries, to demonstrate your experience with a diverse group of clients.

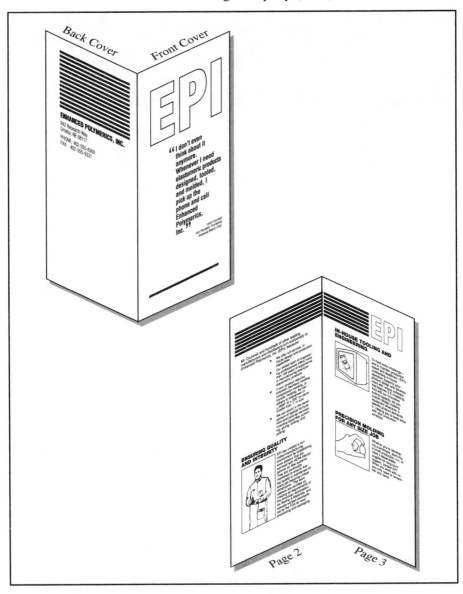

- Industrial companies face the challenge of making their brochures interesting to look at, while imparting information about their products and services. This 8 1/2" x 11" brochure folded in half uses illustrations with captions to provide necessary information about the company's areas of expertise.

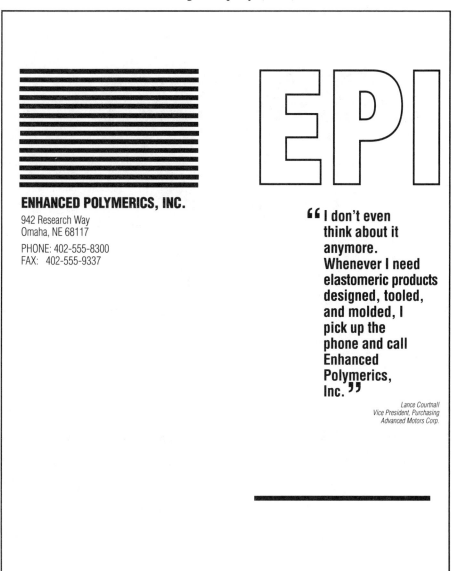

ENHANCED POLYMERICS, INC.

942 Research Way
Omaha, NE 68117

PHONE: 402-555-8300
FAX: 402-555-9337

❝ I don't even think about it anymore. Whenever I need elastomeric products designed, tooled, and molded, I pick up the phone and call Enhanced Polymerics, Inc. ❞

Lance Courtnall
Vice President, Purchasing
Advanced Motors Corp.

• Customer testimonials assure prospects that your services are effective.

Mr. Courtnall and hundreds of other leading manufacturers and distributors turn exclusively to Enhanced Polymerics, Inc. (EPI), because:

- We offer full-service, in-house design and production capabilities.
- Our skilled team of engineering professionals offers more than 100 years of experience in manufacturing precision elastomeric products.
- If your product requires precision flashless molding, compression molding, or transfer molding, we can adhere to tolerances of ±.0008" to ±.005" on parts smaller than 1" in size.
- We can assist in the development of special formulations and post-op services including assembly, punching, gluing, drilling, and potting.

ENSURING QUALITY AND INTEGRITY

EPI has created a controlled manufacturing environment by establishing work stations that are serviced with HEPA-filtered laminar air flow systems. They are continually monitored to ensure that top quality is maintained on every job requiring critical dimensions. The work stations are certified as meeting all requirements of the American Association for Testing & Materials, and actually exceed standards set by the FDA for food processing and packaging.

IN-HOUSE TOOLING AND ENGINEERING

To meet every challenge—and to maintain production speed and deadlines—EPI's outstanding in-house operation supports your product design and development with unique software that features 3-D modeling. And with our innovative tooling capacity, we can custom-design molding equipment whenever a specific product demands it...helping you to keep pace with your production schedule.

PRECISION MOLDING FOR ANY SIZE JOB

Whether you're developing a prototype, planning a small production run, or need a dependable supplier for long-term support, contact EPI. When you work with us, you only need to remember one name.

- Use headlines to lead into key paragraphs. They help focus the reader on what follows...and improve the design by breaking up large blocks of type.

• The many services offered by a conference center add up to a powerful statement about what it can do for a client. This 8" x 8 1/2" brochure folded in half features illustrations showing not only a meeting room, but the recreational facilities and room amenities.

THE
A T R I U M
Hotel & Conference Center
Manitou Island on White Bear Lake

THE
A T R I U M
Hotel & Conference Center
Manitou Island on White Bear Lake

1100 Siblet Highway
White Bear Lake, MN 55110
Phone: 612-555-8000
Fax: 612-555-5744

1100 Siblet Highway
White Bear Lake, MN 55110
Phone: 612-555-8000
Fax: 612-555-5744

- If you're selling something that's visually attractive, let the pictures speak for themselves.

- The drawing is carried across the front and back covers, and the company information is repeated.

THE
A T R I U M

The Atrium wasn't created by architects and engineers. It was conceived by meeting planners and participants, executives and managers, salespeople and speakers, and by lodgers and diners. We asked thousands of them what they wanted in a hotel/conference center...and then we built what many people acknowledge as the best in the business.

Every detail has been attended to, from room lighting to meeting room arrangement and comfort; from recreational facilities that most health clubs only dream about to dining and room service amenities; from bed size to desk space, and hundreds of other details that you would have asked for yourself. Plus an experienced staff to assist you every step of the way.

THE
A T R I U M

CONFERENCE FACILITIES

- 5 meeting rooms for up to 30 people each
- 2 meeting rooms for up to 100 people each
- Auditorium for up to 400 people
- Private dining facilities for groups from 10-400
- Complete buisiness center, including computers, modems, copiers and fax service

Each meeting room is equipped with television, VCR, 16mm projector, sound equipment, retractable screen, whiteboards, orthopedically-designed chairs to ease muscle and mental fatigue, in-room cold beverages, and coffee service, and private bathrooms.

RECREATIONAL FACILITIES

Full-service gymnasium with treadmills, bicycles, power steps, Nautilus and free weights. Olympic swimming pool, whirlpool, sauna and steam room, and complete locker facilities. Spectacular game room with 22 of the newest electronic arcade games. Championship golf course within 5 minutes.

LODGING

King-size beds for full comfort. Large desk for conference homework or business catch-up. Phones at desk, bed, and bathroom. Remote control television with cable and two premium movie channels. Private bar. Shower massage. Safety-first card access to rooms. Lighting designed to ease eye strain. Two fine restaurants and friendly lounge.

- Always put the focus on customer needs and concerns. Assure them that everything has been planned to create a totally positive experience.

- Illustrating a technology that isn't particularly glamorous is a job best left to an innovative graphic designer. This 8 1/2" x 11" brochure folded in thirds uses an intriguing graphic to grab the reader's interest while relating it directly to the company's main service.

- A brochure announcing your merger should detail your combined services. Send it to existing customers to advise them of additional services now available and to prospects to tell them about your full range of capabilities.

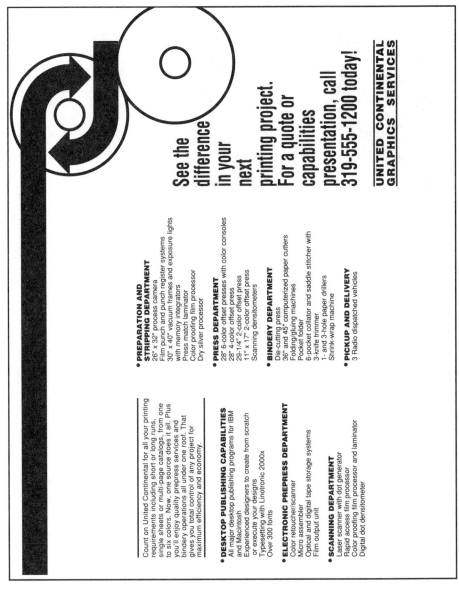

Count on United Continental for all your printing requirements including short or long runs, single sheets or multi-page catalogs, from one to six colors. Now, one source does it all. Plus you'll enjoy quality prepress services and bindery operations all under one roof. That gives you total control of any project for maximum efficiency and economy.

• DESKTOP PUBLISHING CAPABILITIES
All major desktop publishing programs for IBM and Macintosh
Experienced designers to create from scratch or execute your designs
Typesetting with Linotronic 2000x
Over 300 fonts

• ELECTRONIC PREPRESS DEPARTMENT
Color retoucher/scanner
Micro assembler
Optical and digital tape storage systems
Film output unit

• SCANNING DEPARTMENT
Laser scanner with dot generator
Rapid access film processor
Color proofing film processor and laminator
Digital dot densitometer

• PREPARATION AND STRIPPING DEPARTMENT
26" x 32" process camera
Film punch and punch register systems
30" x 40" vacuum frames and exposure lights with memory integrators
Press match laminator
Color proofing film processor
Dry silver processor

• PRESS DEPARTMENT
28" 6-color offset presses with color consoles
28" 4-color offset press
29-1/4" 2-color offset press
11" x 17" 2-color offset press
Scanning densitometers

• BINDERY DEPARTMENT
Die-cutting press
36" and 45" computerized paper cutters
Folding/gluing machines
Pocket folder
6-pocket collator and saddle stitcher with 3-knife trimmer
1- and 3-hole paper drillers
Shrink-wrap machine

• PICKUP AND DELIVERY
3 Radio dispatched vehicles

See the difference in your next printing project.
For a quote or capabilities presentation, call 319-555-1200 today!

UNITED CONTINENTAL GRAPHICS SERVICES

• Keep reinforcing the concept that your newly merged companies will provide even better service than before.

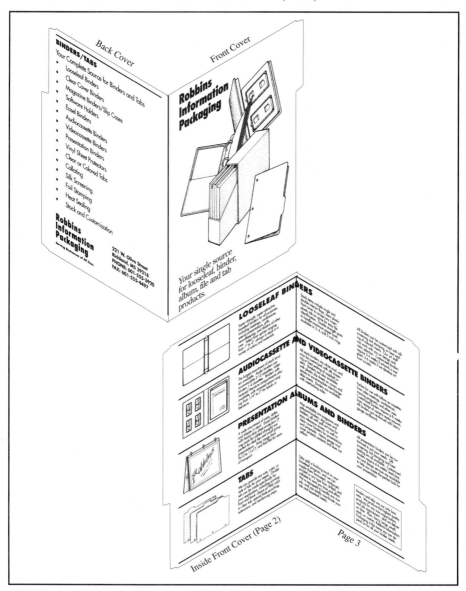

- This brochure uses an innovative format to sell its product line. The file-folder size brochure, die-cut to be an actual file folder, is not only imaginative and eye-catching but can be placed in a file drawer for future reference.

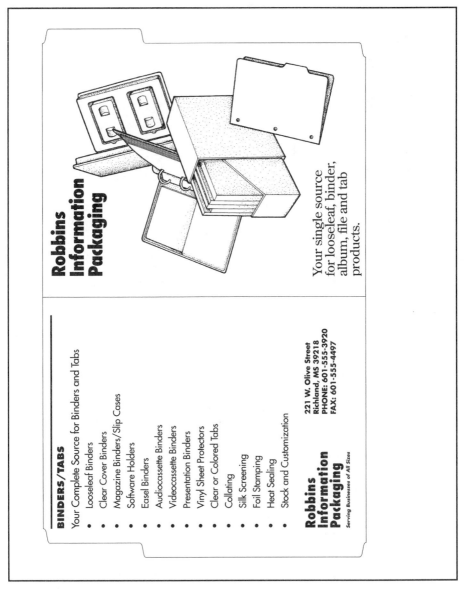

Robbins
Information
Packaging

Your single source
for looseleaf, binder,
album, file and tab
products.

BINDERS/TABS

Your Complete Source for Binders and Tabs

- Looseleaf Binders
- Clear Cover Binders
- Magazine Binders/Slip Cases
- Software Holders
- Easel Binders
- Audiocassette Binders
- Videocassette Binders
- Presentation Binders
- Vinyl Sheet Protectors
- Clear or Colored Tabs
- Collating
- Silk Screening
- Foil Stamping
- Heat Sealing
- Stock and Customization

Robbins
Information
Packaging

Serving Businesses of All Sizes

221 W. Olive Street
Richland, MS 39218
PHONE: 601-555-3920
FAX: 601-555-4497

- Present photos or artwork to show how your products look—and to give recipients ideas for how they can use your products in their own businesses.

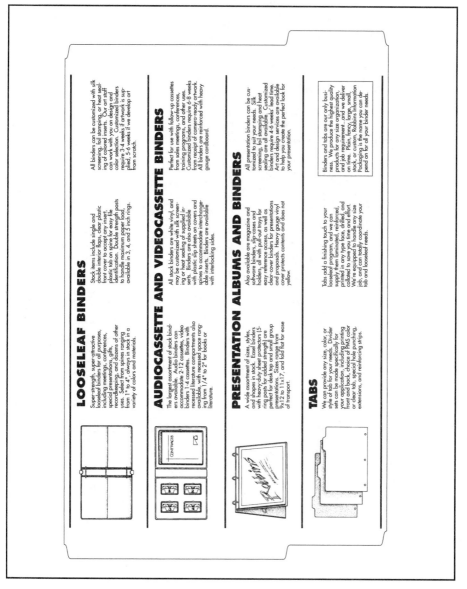

LOOSELEAF BINDERS

Super-strength, super-attractive looseleaf binders for all purposes, including meetings, conferences, special presentations, gifts, recordkeeping, and dozens of other uses. Select from spines ranging from 1" to 4", always in stock in a variety of colors and materials.

Stock items include single and double interior flaps, clear plastic front cover to accept any insert, plastic tab on spine for easy file identification. Double strength posts to handle maximum paper load, available in 3, 4, and 5 inch rings.

All binders can be customized with silk screening, foil stamping, or heat sealing of colored inserts. Our art staff can work with you on design and color selection. Customized binders require 3-4 weeks if artwork is supplied, 5-6 weeks if we develop art from scratch.

AUDIOCASSETTE AND VIDEOCASSETTE BINDERS

The largest assortment of stock binders available. Audio binders can accommodate 2-12 cassettes, video binders 1-4 cassettes. Binders with recessed literature compartments also available, with recessed space ranging from 1/4" to 2" for books or literature.

All stock binders are white vinyl, and may be customized with silk screening or heat sealing of supplied inserts. Binders are also available with plastic slip sheets on covers and spines to accommodate interchangeable inserts. Binders are available with interlocking sides.

Perfect for use with follow-up cassettes from sales meetings, conferences, training programs, and other uses. Customized binders require 6-8 weeks from receipt of camera-ready artwork. All binders are reinforced with heavy gauge cardboard.

PRESENTATION ALBUMS AND BINDERS

A wide assortment of sizes, styles, and shapes in stock. Easel binders with heavy-duty sheet protectors (5-ring posts for added strength) are perfect for desk top and small group presentations. Sizes range from 9x12 to 11x17, and fold flat for ease of transport.

Also available are magazine and software binders, slip-cases and holders, all with pull-out trays for easy reference access, as well as clear-cover binders for presentations and proposals. Heavy gauge vinyl cover protects contents and does not yellow.

All presentation binders can be customized to suit your needs. Silk screening, foil stamping and heat sealing are all available. Customized binders require 4-6 weeks' lead time. Art and design services are available to help you create the perfect look for your presentation.

TABS

We can provide any size, color, or style of tab for your needs. Divider sets can be made specifically for your application, including printing front and back, choice of PMS color or clear tab, special hole punching, extensions, and reinforcing strips.

Tabs add a finishing touch to your looseleaf program, and we can supply them laminated, reinforced, printed in any type face, drilled, and collated to save you time and effort. We're equipped to handle any size job, and can totally coordinate your tab and looseleaf needs.

Binders and tabs are our only business. We produce the highest quality products for any size organization, and job requirement...and we deliver on time. Plain, fancy, large, small, stock, or custom, Robbins Information Packaging is the name you can depend on for all your binder needs.

- Don't print pricing on a piece you want the client to keep for a long time. It will be outdated as soon as prices change. It's better to include a separate sheet that lists complete size and cost specs.

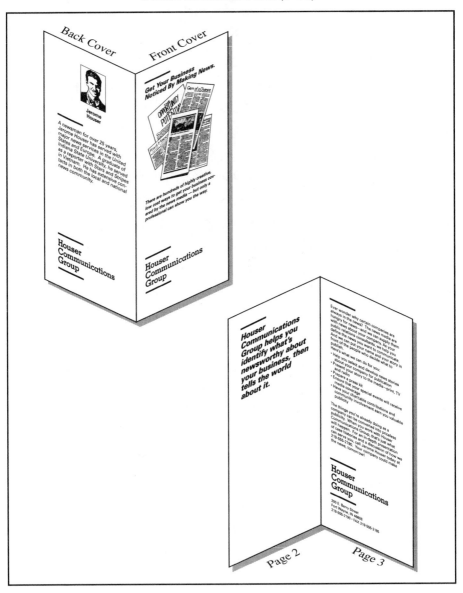

- Brochures that demonstrate the company's product or services are highly effective. This 8" x 8 1/2" brochure folded in half contains examples of news stories generated by the company with copy that actually can be read by the prospect.

**Jerome
Houser**

A newsman for over 25 years, Jerome Houser has served with major news services in the United States and Europe. A graduate of Indiana State University, he served as a reporter with Stars and Stripes in Vietnam. He has extensive contacts in both the local and national news community.

Get Your Business Noticed By Making News.

There are hundreds of highly creative, low cost ways to get your business covered by the news media — but only a professional can show you the way.

Houser Communications Group

Houser Communications Group

- The front cover shows a montage of news articles generated as a result of the company's public relations services. The back cover highlights the background and experience of a principal in the business. This format can be adapted by many firms.

Houser Communications Group helps you identify what's newsworthy about your business, then tells the world about it.

Ever wonder why certain companies are always in the news? The news media are hungry for news—and we can supply them with news about your company. As your public relations consultants, we help you define the news you want to communicate. And we can put your name and your story in front of the people who decide what to publish.

Here's what we can do for you:

- Help you select and develop news stories about your company for publication
- Present your story to the media—print, TV and radio
- Prepare a press kit
- Ensure that your special events will receive media coverage
- Have your charitable contributions and community involvement earn you valuable publicity

The things you're already doing as a company can be converted into priceless publicity. When you work with Houser Communications Group, that's just what will happen. For an in-depth presentation of case histories and a discussion of how we can serve you, call Jerome Houser today at 219-555-2190. Your company could make the news, tomorrow!

Houser Communications Group

200 E. Berry Street
Fort Wayne, IN 46808
219-555-2190 • FAX 219-555-2185

- Promise prospects that they'll receive valuable ideas they'd never think of themselves.

- This brochure features an unusual graphic tied to the services offered. The 8 1/2" x 11" brochure folded in thirds is guaranteed to grab the reader's attention. Concise yet comprehensive biographies of the principals build a sense of trust in the company.

ROSS, ALLEN & ALTMAN, C.P.A.

CPA

Certified Public Accountants

Ross, Allen & Altman, P.A.
Certified Public Accountants
1360 State Street/Suite 2F
Chicago, IL 60607

Phone: 312-555-7557
Fax: 312-555-5829

A
Tradition
of
Personalized
Service

From our inception in 1976, Ross, Allen & Altman, P.A., has been a full-service CPA firm, providing accounting, auditing, tax planning and preparation, financial planning and computer consulting.

Our firm strongly believes in maintaining close partner contact with clients to achieve the highest level of financial and tax strategies.

Our partners bring unique perspectives to this client-oriented organization. Two of the partners offer the viewpoint of the corporate financial executive, having served as top financial officers for private firms before specializing in public accounting. The third partner is an attorney specializing in corporate, partnership, fiduciary, and individual taxation.

- Focus on one theme and follow that theme through the entire brochure. In this brochure, it's the unique skills and experience of the principals.

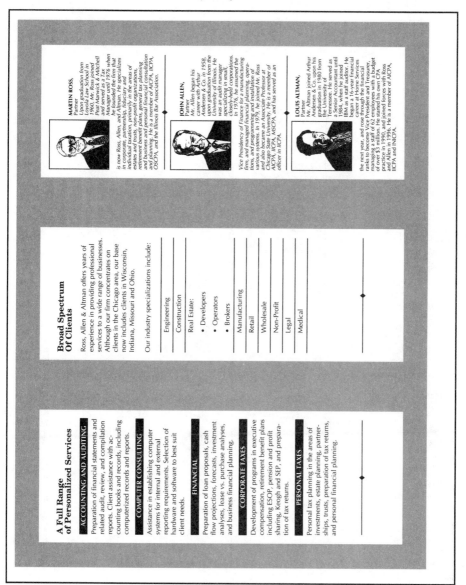

A Full Range of Personalized Services

ACCOUNTING AND AUDITING

Preparation of financial statements and related audit, review, and compilation reports. Client assistance with accounting books and records, including computerized records and reports.

COMPUTER CONSULTING

Assistance in establishing computer systems for internal and external reporting requirements. Selection of hardware and software to best suit client needs.

FINANCIAL

Preparation of loan proposals, cash flow projections, forecasts, investment analyses, lease vs. purchase analyses, and business financial planning.

CORPORATE TAXES

Development of programs in executive compensation, retirement benefit plans including ESOP, pension and profit sharing, Keogh and SEP, and preparation of tax returns.

PERSONAL TAXES

Personal tax planning in the areas of investments, estate planning, partnerships, trusts, preparation of tax returns, and personal financial planning.

Broad Spectrum Of Clients

Ross, Allen & Altman offers years of experience in providing professional services to a wide range of businesses. Although our firm concentrates on clients in the Chicago area, our base now includes clients in Wisconsin, Indiana, Missouri and Ohio.

Our industry specializations include:

Engineering

Construction

Real Estate:
- Developers
- Operators
- Brokers

Manufacturing

Retail

Wholesale

Non-Profit

Legal

Medical

MARTIN ROSS,
Partner
Upon graduation from Loyola Law School in 1960, Mr. Ross joined Peat Marwick & Mitchell and served as a Tax Manager until 1976 when he founded the firm that is now Ross, Allen, and Altman. He specializes in corporate, partnership, fiduciary and individual taxation, primarily in the areas of estates and trusts, non-profit organizations, retirement benefit plans, general tax planning and business and personal financial consultation and planning. He is a member of AICPA, IICPA, OSCPA, and the Illinois Bar Association.

JOHN ALLEN,
Partner
Mr. Allen began his career with Arthur Andersen & Co. in 1958, upon graduation from the University of Illinois. He was an audit manager specializing in small, closely-held corporations. In 1976, he assumed the Vice Presidency of Finance for a manufacturing firm, and managed financial planning, operations, and programming and installation of various systems. In 1979, he joined Ross and also became an Associate Professor at Chicago State University. He is a member of AICPA, IICPA, MSCPA, and has served as an officer in IICPA.

LOUIS ALTMAN,
Partner
Mr. Altman joined Arthur Andersen & Co. upon his graduation in 1980 from the University of Tennessee. He served as a Senior Accountant until 1984, when he joined IBM as a staff auditor. He began a 16-year financial career at Home Services the next year, and rose through the financial ranks to become Vice President and Treasurer, managing a staff of 62 employees with a budget of over $3 million. He started his own CPA practice in 1990, and joined forces with Ross and Allen in 1996. He is a member of AICPA, IICPA and INICPA.

• Spell out the categories of services you provide, as well as the types of industries served, so that your firm is seen as one that can help virtually any client.

- All-type brochures can be effective when their purpose is purely informational and the desired image is "no-nonsense." This 8" x 8 1/2" brochure folded in half focuses on the kinds of cases in which the attorney specializes and tells how the prospect will benefit from calling.

SPECIALISTS

in

**PERSONAL
INJURY
CLAIMS**

- Automobile Accidents
- Work-Related Accidents
- Medical Malpractice
- Animal Bites/Attacks
- Swimming Pool Accidents
- Brain Injuries
- Wrongful Deaths
- Head/Spinal Cord Injuries

Also Practicing Divorce and
Bankruptcy Law

**There's no substitute
for experience**

CANIFF & TAYLOR
12 Central Court Place
Binghamton, NY 13904

Phone: 607-555-1801
Fax: 607-555-9230

*Specializing in Personal Injury Claims •
Divorce • Bankruptcy • Licensed in New
York, Pennsylvania and New Jersey*

The Law Firm of
CANIFF & TAYLOR
Since 1972

- List as many items as you feel best describe your practice. The one you leave out may
  be the one a prospective client is searching for.

CALL US AND GET THE ANSWERS TO ALL YOUR QUESTIONS

1. We'll tell you if you have a good case.

2. We'll explain what benefits may be available to you now and in the future.

3. We'll offer an opinion as to what is recoverable in terms of disability, property damages, lost income and medical expenses.

More than 20 Years Devoted to Serving the Community

We have extensive experience working with accident victims and understanding their needs. We'll meet with you for a FREE consultation any day of the week—and virtually any time of day—in your home or hospital room. We're here when you need us.

OUR GUARANTEE TO YOU

All claims are investigated at our expense, and you are <u>never</u> charged for any costs or legal fees unless we are successful in recovering money to cover them.

**William Caniff, Esq.
Barbara Taylor, Esq.**

WE'RE HERE WHEN YOU NEED US
Call 7 Days a Week,
24 Hours a Day
Phone 607-555-1801
Fax 607-555-9230

12 Central Court Place
Binghamton, NY 13904

• In a personal service profession, it's particularly important to make your hours convenient—and to display them clearly in your advertising.

The doctor will see you now.

Or whenever you have the need . . . 24 hours a day . . . 365 days a year, there's a qualified physician on duty.

For all your family medical needs
Never an appointment necessary

SPRINGFIELD FAMILY MEDICAL CENTER

548 Quail Nest Road
Springfield, MA 01111
413-555-0101

Depend on Springfield Family Medical Center for urgent medical care and everyday needs too.

- Walk-in urgent patient treatment
- Physical exams for employment, sports, school, etc.
- Full lab and X-ray on premises
- X-ray, laboratory, EKG testing on site
- Transportation available
- Specialists for
  - Allergy
  - Cardiology
  - Dermatology
  - Ear, Nose & Throat
  - Gastroenterology
  - Geriatrics
  - Gynecology & Obstetrics
  - Orthopedics
  - Pediatrics
  - Pulmonary Diseases
  - Urology

Accepting all major credit cards, Medicare, Workers' Compensation and most health insurance.

Clip & save for emergencies:

SPRINGFIELD FAMILY MEDICAL CENTER
For all your family medical needs
Never an appointment necessary
548 Quail Nest Road
Springfield, MA 01111
413-555-0101

- Well designed brochures can be used many different ways. This 4" x 8 1/2" two-sided brochure is usable as a component in a direct mail program (it can easily fit into a No. 10 envelope), as a "take-one" on a counter, in a neighborhood coupon mailing, or as a hanger on a front doorknob (with the addition of a diecut hole at the top).

The doctor will see you now.

Or whenever you have the need . . . 24 hours a day . . . 365 days a year, there's a qualified physician on duty.

For all your family medical needs
Never an appointment necessary

**SPRINGFIELD FAMILY
MEDICAL CENTER**

548 Quail Nest Road
Springfield, MA 01111

413-555-0101

- If you are located in an attractive building, and your customers (in this case, patients) will be visiting you, incorporate a photograph or artwork of your facility both to identify it for ease of finding and to show it off.

Depend on Springfield Family Medical Center for urgent medical care and everyday needs too.

- Walk-in urgent patient treatment
- Physical exams for employment, sports, school, etc.
- Full lab and X-ray on premises
- X-ray, laboratory, EKG testing on site
- Transportation available
- Specialists for
  - Allergy
  - Cardiology
  - Dermatology
  - Ear, Nose & Throat
  - Gastroenterology
  - Geriatrics
  - Gynecology & Obstetrics
  - Orthopedics
  - Pediatrics
  - Pulmonary Diseases
  - Urology

Accepting all major credit cards, Medicare, Workers' Compensation and most health insurance.

Clip & save for emergencies:

SPRINGFIELD FAMILY MEDICAL CENTER

For all your family medical needs
Never an appointment necessary

548 Quail Nest Road
Springfield, MA 01111
413-555-0101

- Print your name, address, and phone number on the back of the brochure to act as a business card/phone reference. Use a dotted line to prompt recipients to clip and save it for future use.

- Real estate brochures displaying the properties being offered produce strong response. This 8 1/2" x 11" brochure folded in thirds employs attractive illustrations of the properties with compelling copy describing the natural environments in which the properties are located.

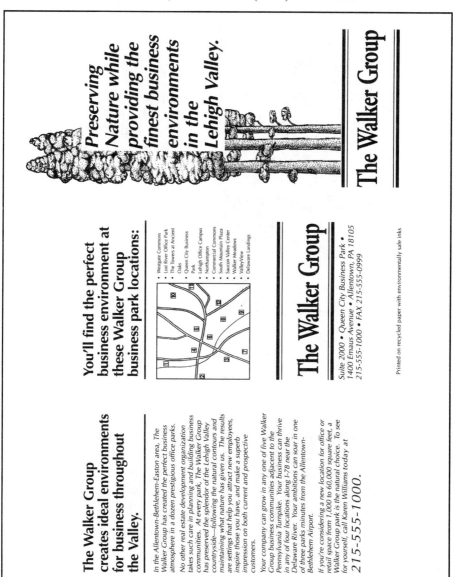

The Walker Group

Preserving Nature while providing the finest business environments in the Lehigh Valley.

The Walker Group creates ideal environments for business throughout the Valley.

In the Allentown-Bethlehem-Easton area, The Walker Group has created the perfect business atmosphere in a dozen prestigious office parks.

No other real estate development organization takes such care in planning and building business communities. At every park, The Walker Group has preserved the splendor of the Lehigh Valley countryside—following the natural contours and maintaining what nature has given us. The results are settings that help you attract new employees, inspire those you have, and make a superb impression on both current and prospective customers.

Your company can grow in any one of five Walker Group business communities adjacent to the Pennsylvania Turnpike. Your business can thrive in any of four locations along I-78 near the Delaware River. Your ambitions can soar in one of three parks minutes from the Allentown-Bethlehem Airport.

If you're considering a new location for office or retail space from 1,000 to 60,000 square feet, a Walker Group park is the natural choice. To see for yourself, call Karen Williams today at

215-555-1000.

You'll find the perfect business environment at these Walker Group business park locations:

- Westgate Commons
- Lost River Office Park
- The Towers at Ancient Oaks
- Queen City Business Park
- Lehigh Office Campus
- Northampton
- Commercial Commons
- South Mountain Plaza
- Saucon Valley Center
- Walker Meadows
- ValleyView
- Delaware Landings

The Walker Group

Suite 2000 • Queen City Business Park •
1400 Emaus Avenue • Allentown, PA 18105
215-555-1000 • FAX 215-555-0999

Printed on recycled paper with environmentally safe inks

• If your company is environmentally active, by all means mention it in your advertising. Be sure to show that your environmental efforts are also good for business. Reinforce your image by printing on recycled paper, and state so in your brochure.

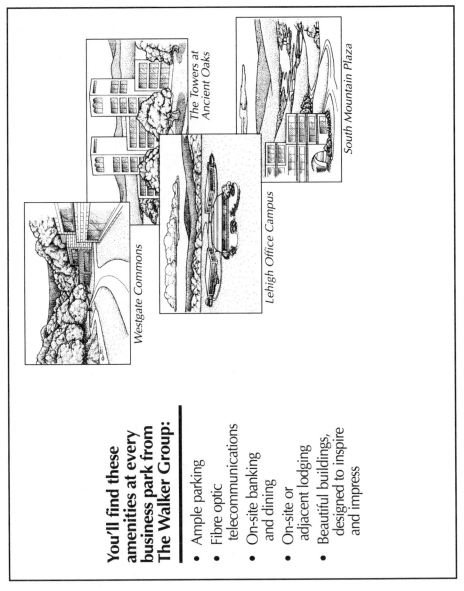

The Towers at Ancient Oaks

South Mountain Plaza

Westgate Commons

Lehigh Office Campus

You'll find these amenities at every business park from The Walker Group:

- Ample parking
- Fibre optic telecommunications
- On-site banking and dining
- On-site or adjacent lodging
- Beautiful buildings, designed to inspire and impress

- Keep in mind that a strong brochure tells a story, with each section expanding on a single theme, in this case environmental awareness.

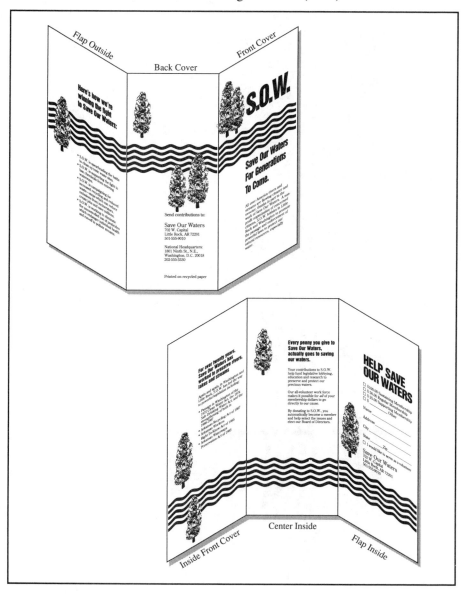

- Brochures for non-profit organizations need not be any less attractive than those for businesses. This 8 1/2" x 11" brochure folded in thirds uses two art elements to produce a striking effect.

- The use of two graphics, one for trees and one for water, not only creates an attractive look but is an effective reminder of what the organization stands for.

HELP SAVE OUR WATERS

Every penny you give to Save Our Waters, actually goes to saving our waters.

Your contributions to S.O.W. help fund legislative lobbying, education and research to preserve and protect our precious waters.

Our all-volunteer work force makes it possible for *all* of your membership dollars to go directly to our cause.

By donating to S.O.W., you automatically become a member and help select the issues and elect our Board of Directors.

For over twenty years, Save Our Waters has worked to preserve rivers, lakes and streams

Again and again, in Washington and Little Rock, S.O.W. has led the way to powerful legislation including:

• Passage in Washington of the 1972 Clean Water Act, the 1974 Safe Drinking Water Act, and the strengthening of both in 1986-1987
• Arkansas Recycling Act of 1987
• Arkansas Workers Right-To-Know Act of 1985
• Arkansas Waterways Preservation Act of 1983

☐ $100.00 Sustaining Membership
☐ $ 50.00 Regular Membership
☐ $ 25.00 Supporting Membership
☐ $_____ Other

Name _____

Address _____

City _____

State _____ Zip _____

☐ I would like to serve as a volunteer

Save Our Waters
702 W. Capital
Little Rock, AR 72201
501-555-9010

• Many organizations are in need of people to volunteer almost as much as they are in need of funds. The response panel of this brochure solicits both.

Business Cards 2

Business cards can be an extremely versatile component of your advertising and marketing programs. In addition to handing them out to prospects, you may give them to associates to use in referrals, employ them as part of a mailing with a catalog or sales letter, place them in a tray on a retailer's check-out counter, and offer them as hand-outs after a seminar or speech.

Have you ever been handed a business card that impressed you? Perhaps it was the embossing (raised type) that made you admire it. Perhaps it was the clever graphics or descriptive copy. Maybe a unique typeface or a particularly attractive paper stock or color that caught your eye. Chances are you'll remember the company which gave you that distinctive card.

While most people spend considerable time and effort in choosing the layout, copy, graphics, and size of their advertisements, they may not think twice about their business cards. But business cards are really advertisements that your potential clients keep on file.

To create a card that says something positive about you and your company, have it reflect your image. A few elements to consider:

Size and format. Most business cards are the same size, for practical reasons (they fit wallets and card files), but there are still possibilities for creativity. A double-sized card can be folded to regulation size, yet it gives you the chance to say more and be unique. Die-cuts can change the edges or appearance of a card, even creating tabbed cards that can fit a Rolodex®.

Content. In addition to listing your company name, address, phone and fax numbers, add a line describing your business if it is not clear from your company name what you do. Length of time in business can be included if it's an impressive number of years.

Graphics. A visual representation of your business in the form of an illustration or logo will help people remember you, your company, and your service. Your graphic image can set a mood. Be sure it is consistent with your other advertising materials. The logo and type style you use on your business card should be the same one that appears on your stationery, in your ads, and in your direct mail. The more consistent the theme in all of your advertising (including your business card), the more successful you will be in generating a positive image for your business.

Paper stock. You don't have to lock yourself into a "standard" white business card stock. There are literally thousands of stock and color combinations that provide an unlimited opportunity to make your business card stand out. Current technology allows cards to be printed on papers that not only look impressive, but feel good as well. And more exotic materials now can be used, such as plastics.

Make your business card part of your marketing team.

- A distinctive visual symbol will cause people to remember your card, increasing patronage.

- If you use a slogan in your advertising, put it on your business card for added impact.

**ANIMAL & BIRD
VETERINARY
CLINIC AND HOSPITAL**

Jennifer Feldman, V.M.D.
Bird Specialist
745 Altamonte Road
Fairport, Kansas 67665
Phone: (913) 555-2200

- Give careful thought to the title you use on your card. Sometimes you may benefit by using something other than your professional title if it's more descriptive or informative (in this case "Bird Specialist").

- Well executed graphics can enhance your message and deliver a good feeling about your company/practice.

LUXURY BATHS AT AFFORDABLE PRICES

GALLERY BATH

- Vanities - Toilets
- Whirlpool Tubs and Spas
- Custom Showers
- Skylights - Stained Glass

*Customized Bathrooms for the
Physically Impaired*

FREE ESTIMATES • FREE DESIGN SERVICE

765 Avian Plaza, Suite 610
Cleveland, OH 44117

Phone: (216) 555-1993

RICHARD T. HARRIS
President

- Use your card to sell, but watch out for clutter.

- The more you tell people about unique services, the better the chance of being called.

ROBERT LAKE
Phone: 415-555-7810

PAINTING CONTRACTOR

Residential	
Commercial	
11 Eden Drive	
Belmont, CA 94002	

- If color is important to your business (e.g., painter, printer, art gallery, florist), using a second color or printing on colored paper will enhance your image. This card could use a blue or red ink on the type in the "paint" area.

- If you have a logo, use it on your business card to develop continuity between all your printed materials.

- This is the outside spread of a tent-fold, or fold-over business card. The inside spread is shown on the following page.

A History of Fine Dining:

Exquisitely maintained for more than 200 years, the tavern was constructed by the Bayer family (distant relatives of Benjamin Franklin). Enjoy fine dining with many of the same delicious dishes (and libations) that gratified post-revolutionary America.

ELIZABETH AND DAVID WARD
Your hosts

333 Main Street,
Lancaster, PA 17603

(215) 555-5600

- The fold-over format gives you an opportunity to provide information about your business and make a lasting impression.

- Depending on your business, you can show your building, products you manufacture, an illustration of your services, etc.

COVERED BRIDGE ANTIQUES

73 Cedar Grove Lane
Brandywine, MD 20613
301-555-7118

- With computer-generated typesetting, you can create virtually any style that seems appropriate (such as the arched type over the artwork). Don't be afraid to experiment.

- Emphasize one of your company's unique features (e.g., name, location, etc.), and you'll reinforce recall.

Brian Holcomb
Sales Associate

AUBURN ASSOCIATES
Providence's #1 Realtor

556 Brighton Road
Providence, RI 02886
(401) 555-7333

- In a business where personal contact is important, photographs give a very personalized, distinctive look to a business card.

- Use the services of a competent photographer to assure a high quality photograph.

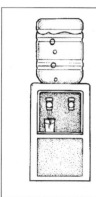

Serving Salt Lake City Since 1948

CLEARWATER
INCORPORATED

Pure spring water for your office and home

FRANK GREEN
SALES REPRESENTATIVE

909 Chesapeake Road
Salt Lake City, UT 84101

801-555-1117

FREE DELIVERY TO HOME OR OFFICE

• When length of service is notable, include it on your business card.

• A special service (in this case, free delivery) can help a potential buyer select your service over others.

IAN BRANDON
Sales Representative

4400 LEMON AVE
AUGUSTA, ME 04330
207-555-0800
FAX: 207-555-1195

PROGRAMMING/CONSULTING

- Use a strong graphic related to your field to make your card memorable. Your logo is fine to use, if it meets this criterion. If it doesn't, consider designing a new one that reflects your business in an effective way.

- A tone of gray or a second color makes your card look special.

• This is the outside spread of a tent-fold, or fold-over business card. The inside spread is shown on the following page.

YOU DO!
WHEN YOU WANT TO . . .

Impress the boss • Entertain a roomful of 4-year olds • Have a $30,000 wedding on a $15,000 budget • Throw a family reunion • Host a Christmas party • Create the ultimate Bar Mitzvah • Have a hauntingly different Halloween party • Have all the glory and none of the work.

Carole Kaye
Consultant

Site Selection
Invitations
Theme Creation
Catering/Service
Music and Talent Selection
Floral Selection
Customized Centerpieces
Balloons and Favors
Clean-Up
Thank You Notes

CELEBRATIONS 615 E. Orange St., Bartlett, TN 38134
901-555-5045

- A fold-over business card can tell a complete story and generate business.

- Develop a theme and follow it throughout the card—just as you would in a brochure.

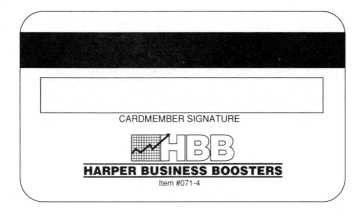

• A sure way to be remembered is to have your business card represent your product or service. This card, for instance, would have maximum impact if done in plastic, in the shape of a credit card. Or a flooring company could print a wood pattern background. The possibilities are endless. Turn your business card into a promotion piece.

STEEN

SECURITY
SERVICES
Since 1971

Call Us for a
FREE EVALUATION
of Your Security Needs

- Bodyguards
- Undercover and
  Uniformed Operations
- Special Events
- K-9 Patrols
- Internal Investigations

24 HOURS A DAY
7 DAYS A WEEK
Serving construction sites, hospitals, offices, warehouses, residences, and apartment complexes.

14 Allison Avenue, Louisville, KY 40207

LICENSED AND BONDED
All employees thoroughly background-checked and drug tested

CALL 1-502-555-4860
for information or an appointment for your FREE security analysis.

- With unusual services, indicate how they can be used.

- Free evaluations generate response. Use them whenever they are appropriate.

**PACKAGING–
PLASTICS**

1-501-555-8784

Injection-molded
cases and boxes
for all your
merchandising and
packaging needs

• All sizes
• All shapes
• Decorative
  inserts available

Jim Hanifan
Sales

Convey Plastics, Inc.
1818 Market Street
Little Rock, AR 72201

FAX: 501-555-9385

• Consider a business card in the shape of a Rolodex® card. It costs more, but it's seen on a daily basis.

• Put your service or specialty on the tab. It's easier for customers to find than your name.

Data Retrieval
The Computer Problem-Solver

Larry G. Ferguson
Systems Analyst

22 Progress Drive
Las Vegas, NV 89117
Tel: 702-555-2200 • Fax: 702-555-3749

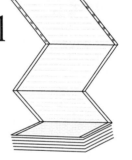

- Adding a tagline (for example, "The Computer Problem-Solver") that indicates what your company actually does will pay off in increased sales.

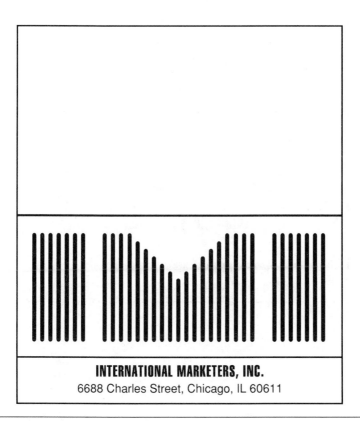

• If "image" is important, consider a fold-over business card. It will always earn a second look.

Marketing Innovations
Since 1960

Atlanta, GA:
Call: 404-555-1718
Fax: 404-555-8642

Chicago, IL:
Call: 312-555-0700
Fax: 312-555-3572

Jeanette Thomason
Marketing Representative

INTERNATIONAL MARKETERS, INC.
6688 Charles Street, Chicago, IL 60611

- It gives the potential buyer a sense of confidence to know how long you've been in business.

- Any information you can provide to help a prospect or customer contact you easily should be displayed prominently.

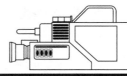

CORPORATE VIDEO

Sales • Marketing • Training
430 Mount Airy Boulevard
Longwood, Florida 32750
Phone: (407) 555-8000
Fax: (407) 555-8148

TONY DAZEN, *Producer*

• Bold graphics can dramatically enhance the look of a business card and tell the customer quickly what your business is.

• List your key points; help the customer remember what you do.

• If you've won prestigious awards, include them on your card.

• If you serve several markets, consider using several cards—each targeted to a specific audience.

Classified Ads 3

Classified ads ("want ads") often fail to do the job for which they're intended—producing suitable applicants. Take a little extra time to profile your needs and the required qualifications for the prospective applicants. This will create an automatic screening process and give you the best possible chance of attracting qualified respondents.

Planning steps

1. Separate the skills that are absolutely necessary from skills that are merely desirable. Don't overstate skill requirements. You may scare off prospects.
2. Be specific about what the job entails and you'll avoid dealing with unqualified applicants. Use technical terms to eliminate novices.
3. If communication skills are important, ask for a cover letter. You'll save countless interview hours by having the chance to see how well someone uses words in advance of your meeting.
4. If compensation is based on commissions, be straightforward about it. You'll avoid misunderstandings and wasted time.
5. Don't oversell the position. You'll be setting yourself up for a disappointed applicant.
6. Don't shortchange the job description to save a line or two of ad space. It costs far more in lost time than it would have cost to run the ad with the correct information.
7. Sell your organization (growth, success, profitability, location, awards, etc.). Most classifieds don't give a sense of how the company feels about itself. Enthusiasm attracts enthusiastic people.

Selecting the media. Many potential sources for recruitment are often unused. In addition to your daily or weekly newspaper, local business, trade, and professional associations often have publications that reach specific audiences. Business schools and colleges provide job location services. Many churches and community centers offer employment information.

Make it a point to give as much thought to your classifieds as you do to your general advertising and you'll dramatically increase your recruiting success rate.

CONTROLLER

International publisher (NYSE) has a once-in-a-lifetime opening for a management accountant who looks at travel as an opportunity, not a chore. (You'll be working with our offices and joint venture partners all over the world.) If you have at least 5-10 years of corporate financial experience (no public accountants, please), knowledge of SEC regulations and international tax implications, and possess strong budget management and monitoring credentials, you may be perfect for us. High salary and travel allowance, outstanding benefits and bonuses. Report directly to the VP of Finance. Send resume, along with a cover letter that sells you and your qualifications, to: CFO, Burris International Group, 1 Federal Plaza, New York, NY 10022. All replies strictly confidential.

- For executive positions, it's worth the cost of an ad that's large enough to spell out your needs and preferences.

- When searching for top level people, it's best to have resumes sent to an executive in the company rather than to "Human Resources Dept."

ADMINISTRATIVE ASSISTANT

If you like a fast pace, can handle diversity (and adversity), enjoy the give-and-take of creative work teams, and want the chance to learn advertising from the ground up, you'll want to talk to us. And if you have basic keyboard skills, an associate degree or better, and a positive outlook on life and work, we want to talk to you, too. This is a career opportunity with great benefits. Send cover letter, resume, and salary requirements to: Wynne, Blaise and Barton Advertising, 44 Wainscot Crossing, Fayetteville, AR 72701. No calls, please.

- If the job requires written skills, ask for a cover letter to accompany the resume. It will speak volumes about the applicant.

- Be specific about the work involved and the skills required, to avoid getting applicants who don't fit the requirements.

MASCOT, TN (Near Knoxville)
Walking distance to Main Street

FIRST MONTH
RENT FREE!

Great suburban location, quiet neighborhood, within 15 minutes of shops and movie theater. Private entrance in a converted Victorian building, near train and bus. Affordable, convenient, and spacious for $625 + electric. Senior citizen discount.

- Large 1 bedroom apartment
- Washer/dryer
- Kitchen with all major appliances
- Large storage area
- First month RENT FREE plus reduced security deposit.

Brentwood Realty
232 Grove Street,
Knoxville, TN 37929.
Call 615-555-0903.

- Location and proximity to major landmarks (schools, shopping, city, etc.) are often as important as price.

- What you omit is often as meaningful as what you include. For example, no mention of schools, and inclusion of senior citizen discount telegraphs an apartment appropriate for older adults.

BUYING OR SELLING A BUSINESS?

Talk to us first.

Nobody knows the Laredo market better than Larson & Smith. We can provide valuation services, locate financing, handle merger arrangements. Specializing in retail, service, manufacturing and distribution. Hundreds of opportunities available right now.

Call

512-555-5120

Ask for Mr. Taylor

Larson & Smith

BUSINESS BROKERS

21 Mesa Blvd. Laredo, TX 78041

- Be direct, aiming your headline at your prospects.

- Keep your message brief but include enough information to state your capabilities and special areas of expertise.

- Using different people's names as contacts in your ads lets you track where the inquiry was generated—for example, classified vs. yellow pages.

Art Director (3-05)

ART DIRECTOR

Our company prepares a 48-page catalog four times a year containing 1,000 dental supply items. If you work quickly, have a sharp eye for detail and have 3-5 years of experience in catalog art direction, we've got a challenging position for you. Salary commensurate with experience. Good benefits and work environment. Send resume with salary requirements and samples to IMAGES, 450 Sydney St., Peoria, IL 61645. No phone calls please.

- Many want ads paint too rosy a picture of the job. An ad such as this brings more qualified candidates because it accurately describes the challenge.

- To make sure you get only written responses, include a statement advising applicants not to call.

MEDICAL RECEPTIONIST
Full time non-smoker with
strong work ethic to work full-
time for busy medical practice. Professional demeanor
and patient-handling skills a
must. Experience with computerized record-keeping and
medical insurance a plus. Top
dollar for the right person.
Resume: Dr. H.W. Walston,
906 N. 2nd Street, Portland,
OR 97204. No phone calls.

- Clearly distinguish between your absolute requirements ("must-have") and your preferences ("would like to have"). Otherwise you might lose some excellent candidates.

- If you offer a particularly good salary or benefits, refer to it in the ad.

Sales Trainer (3-07)

TELECOMMUNICATIONS
SALES TRAINER
If you combine technical knowledge of ISDN, Centrex, Voice Mail, and Digital Wireless with proven sales training experience, we want you on our team. In addition to training prospective salespeople, you'll assist in launching new high-tech products, and help conduct/ organize major client presentations. We offer an excellent incentive compensation package, and outstanding benefits including medical, dental, life, and 401K. Mail your resume to:
AMERICAN TELECOMMUNICATIONS, INC.
2122 Greenwood, Box 61
West Monroe, LA 61291

- If technical knowledge is required, be specific.

- Describe your benefits package; it may be the key to drawing the best applicants.

> **BOOKKEEPER**
> Take-charge person for thriving kitchen wholesaler. Experience required in all phases of A/R, A/P, GL, payroll. Knowledge of Excel a must. Growth opportunity. Full benefits. Competitive salary. Resume only to: ABC Kitchen Supplies, P.O. Box 747, Trenton, NJ 08677.

• Look at the ad two ways: with and without the first sentence. If you need a leader, the first sentence is important. If you need a follower, it isn't. Be sure to say what you mean.

• It's okay to use jargon (A/R, A/P, etc.). It saves money and eliminates "rookies."

TRACTOR TRAILER DRIVER

If you have a CDL Class A or B license, want to work within a 400-mile radius (home on weekends and some week-nights), and have strong refer-ences, this is the job you've always hoped for. Outstand-ing opportunity, compensation and benefits with Missouri Transport. Call 314-555-5800.

- By spelling out job requirements, you'll weed out most unqualified people.

- Even though every word costs money, it's worth it to list benefits that will attract the kind of applicant you want (in this case, people who want to be home on weekends.)

SALES
SOFTWARE SALES

We're a national leader in commercial financial software development, and we're not satisfied with our 5-year average growth of 50% per year! If you're aggressive enough to help us reach our goal of 100% growth, we want you on board right away! We require a college degree, at least 5 years of software application sales success, strong communication skills, and a desire to earn well into six figures (excellent salary and commission). Rush your resume to:

FSI
1221 City Line Avenue
Box 932
Phoenix AZ 85004
FAX 602-555-2544.
All replies strictly
confidential.

- The tone of your ad dictates the type of response you'll receive. Words such as "not satisfied," "aggressive," and "right away," will appeal to more extroverted personalities.

- Always indicate if compensation includes commission or bonus. Top sales earners want strong commission plans.

Attorney (3-11)

ENVIRONMENTAL ATTORNEY

Immediate opening for staff attorney with at least 3-5 years experience in environmental law and a working knowledge of commercial and contract law. Candidate must possess excellent communication, interpersonal and negotiating skills to represent our interests at consumer meetings, review and standards boards, and government agencies. Must be able to adapt to changing rules and regulations, have the freedom to travel internationally on short notice, and have the stamina to work long hours. Winning candidate will be well compensated. Send detailed resume and salary requirements to:

JOHN KELLEHER
GENERAL COUNSEL

Proteus Chemical Products
Route 10, Proteus Building #3
Mountain View, CA 94040

- The more specific you are about working environment (e.g., long hours, travel), the more qualified your applicants will be.

- For key positions, it's better to invest in a few extra words and spell out job requirements, than to skimp on an ad and find out later that applicants are unable to perform the necessary responsibilities.

Cover Letters 4

Many businesspeople devote considerable time, effort, and expense to developing handsome brochures and direct mail promotions. And while it's true that a quality brochure or mailer is important, it's equally true that a good cover letter will enhance response. In fact, most direct mail experts will tell you that a good letter will have greater impact than a good brochure. And when you combine the two, you generate optimum response.

Here are the major elements that make an effective cover letter:

Appearance. Short paragraphs look better than long paragraphs and are more appealing to the reader. The shortest paragraphs should be the first and the last.

Content. Even though cover letters may be form letters, they can create a favorable tone or mood. Don't just repeat what's in the brochure; point out important sections that you feel should be read.

Graphic devices. Highlight key points by numbering or bulleting them. Underlining will always draw the reader's attention, and so will centering a line of type.

Call to action. A cover letter should direct the reader to do something: complete a response card, make a phone call, place an order.

Freshness. Avoid clichés and old fashioned language. Saying "Enclosed herein is the material you requested," is akin to saying "This is a boring, dull letter." Write as you would speak; with enthusiasm and contemporary language.

The P.S. The part of the letter most likely to be read is the P.S. This is where you can restate your offer, request a specific action, or make a special offer ("P.S. Act today and receive two free widgets").

A cover letter will set the stage for whatever else is included in your mailing. It requires every bit as much planning and thoughtfulness as your more colorful enclosures. And it will pay off in increased inquiries and orders.

Golf Equipment Dealer (4-01)

Company Name
Address
City, State Zip

Dear Golf Pro:

There's probably no sport that has changed and improved its equipment as much as golf. From the early feather-stuffed ball to today's rubberized ball; from soft wood heads to harder woods to iron; from tree branch shafts to high carbon steel, to fiberglass, aluminum, and graphite.

One thing remains constant about golf equipment, however. When there's an innovation to be considered, an improvement to be made, a reliability factor to be mastered, Wrightson Industries will be the manufacturer to lead the way—just as we've done since we crafted the first steel-shafted club in 1911.

When you review the enclosed catalog to select your Spring purchases, consider the tradition and standards of golf. And consider that Wrightson has consistently been in the forefront of every major change that has benefited our great game.

When you select golf equipment for your club, go for the standard bearer. Put the Wrightson logo in your shop.

Sincerely,

Arthur J. Wrightson IV

Chairman

P.S. To pay homage to our great traditions, we've included in our line, for the first time, replicas of early balls and clubs. They will make proud gifts and mementos for all golfers.

- In industries where history and tradition count, make it a point to display your own contributions.

- A "P.S." is an effective way to introduce a new product or concept. It's also the part of the letter that's read most.

Insurance Agency (4-02)

Company Name
Address
City, State Zip

Date

Mr. Matthew Semmel
3490 Fairfield Way
Springdale, AK 72764

Dear Matt:

When I put all the positives together—your age, excellent health and non-smoking status, plus good job with lots of growth potential—it seems obvious that you'd benefit most from our Premium Protector whole life insurance.

Here's why I'm recommending this particular policy:

1. Your age (24) and health qualify you for our <u>lowest</u> annual premium. The timing couldn't be better for you to start with this kind of program.

2. Given your current salary level, you'll hardly notice what amounts to $10 a week in premiums.

3. You're building a cash reserve that's always available to you, and that grows dramatically as you move into your 30's. Basically, you're investing in yourself and protecting your family at the same time.

4. If anything unforeseen happens to you, your family will be compensated at a minimum of $50,000.

Please take a few days to review the enclosed numbers. I think they represent the perfect package for you, your wife, and your upcoming addition. I'll call you Thursday evening to answer any questions that may remain.

Cordially,

Chad Smith

- Present your recommendations in the most positive way so your clients understand the full benefit of what you're selling.

- Offer to follow-up, and then be sure to do it.

Attorney (4-03)

Company Name
Address
City, State Zip

Date

Mr. Lewis DeSuma
7021 Kindred Street
Elmsford, NY 10523

Dear Mr. DeSuma:

I appreciate your considering us to represent you in your proposed suit against the Elmsford Cab Company. I'm sure Jack Grossman, who referred you to us, told you that we were able to negotiate a substantial settlement for him in a similar case.

As I explained during our phone conversation, we'll handle your case on a 25% contingency basis. That means we're paid 25% of any award—but won't receive any compensation if we are not successful on your behalf. You have no other cost or expense.

I've enclosed a brochure that offers some insights into our legal specialties and philosophy. I hope you'll find it of value.

I'm looking forward to hearing from you.

Very truly yours,

- If there was a referral, mention it. And if the person who made the referral is a client, mention that as well.

- Since many people are uncomfortable asking about fees, make it a point to explain them yourself. This will eliminate uncertainty.

Medical Practice Consultant (4-04)

Company Name
Address
City, State Zip

Date

Charles Yarmouth, M.D.
Cape Elizabeth Medical Associates
938 W. Highway 76
Cape Elizabeth, ME 04107

Dear Dr. Yarmouth:

If you're like most physicians, what you enjoy doing most is practicing your profession. But in these days of increasing regulations, computerization, personnel issues, and other non-medical demands, you probably find yourself up to your neck in paperwork and procedures. And that limits your time and energy for your first love, medicine.

That's where we come in.

As professional practice managers, we can put you back where you want to be: with your patients. That's because we can handle virtually everything else. Interviewing, hiring, firing, customer service training, inventory control, and accounts payable and receivable.

If you're looking for a way to enhance your practice and your profitability, we should talk. The enclosed brochure will demonstrate how we've turned practices that were in disarray into smoothly functioning operations, and how we've made good practices even better.

By combining talents, we have a lot to offer each other. I'll be in touch in a few days to discuss this with you.

Sincerely,

Carmen Cosenza

- A cover letter must sell benefits (e.g., free your time, make you more money, etc.) to earn readership of the accompanying brochure.

- Short paragraphs aid readability.

Company Name
Address
City, State Zip

Dear Meeting Planner:

We're pleased to enclose our brochure containing the information you requested about our conference center and hotel (numbers of rooms, meeting capacity, accessibility, equipment, amenities, and so forth).

I'd like to point out, however, a couple of "little" things that really make a difference at our facility.

Most hotels have inadequate lighting that's off to one side of the bed, making it difficult to read. All of our lodging rooms have direct lighting over the bed headboard. (Studies show that guests prefer to read in bed, even if desks are provided.)

Each of our conference rooms has cushioned chairs that were designed by orthopedic specialists to enhance comfort, and dramatically reduce the back and leg discomfort associated with long meeting hours. Your participants will be more alert, and more interested in the proceedings. And that will make your conference more successful.

When you add all the "little" things together (and there are far too many to mention in this letter), they add up to big successes...for you and for your conference participants. May I have the pleasure of giving you a tour of our facilities so you can see all of our unique features—the grand touches as well as the more subtle ones? And then I'd like you and a guest to join me and my staff for lunch or dinner.

We'll call to arrange for a visit. Thanks for your inquiry.

Cordially,

Henry Martin

- Avoid cold openings ("Enclosed please find..." or "This is sent in response to your inquiry..."). A fresh approach sets a better mood for what follows.

- Reinforce, whenever possible, the message that your service will make the reader look good.

Mailing Services (4-06)

Company Name
Address
City, State Zip

Date

Ms. Althea Washington
Discount Carpeting
4200 Levitan Boulevard, Suite 601
Laguna Hills, CA 92653

Dear Ms. Washington:

Chances are you'd love to do more mailings. But the cost of postage has been so high—even for bulk mail—that you haven't done as many mailings as you'd like. You'll be pleased to know, however, that things have changed.

Now you can save hundreds or thousands of dollars
on every mailing by using
the exciting new technology of commingling

We're one of a handful of select mailers in the entire country who have been authorized by the U. S. Postal Service to offer this postage-saving option. The enclosed brochure explains the mechanics of how we combine your promotion with those of others into a single bar-coded mailing. That not only saves you dollars, but reduces your time of delivery because you've become part of an automated stream.

If you want to spread the word about your product or service, we can do it for you at reduced postage rates. Call me at (714) 555-8798 and I'll answer all your questions.

Sincerely,

Patti Worley
VP, Sales

- Emphasize your key selling point.

- Don't get technical in the cover letter. The technology may fascinate you, but it may turn others off.

- State the action you want the reader to take.

Company Name
Address
City, State Zip

Date

Mr. David Michaels
President
Archer Electronics
3212 Route 38
Caldwell, ID 83605

Dear Mr. Michaels:

We asked CEO's what they value most in their relationship with an accounting firm.
The overwhelming answer, based on a recent survey of our clients, was <u>personal
service from a partner</u>.

Think about that for a minute. They could have checked items such as size of the firm,
number of accountants on staff, or many other pertinent responses. But what they
valued most was knowing that they have the ear of one of our three partners, that every
bit of advice and counsel originates with one of us.

If you'd like the opportunity to have your financial needs handled by someone equal to
your level of expertise and experience, call us. We'll show you the difference that
personal service can make in your company's profitability and growth.

Sincerely,

Martin Ross   John Allen   Louis Altman
Partner   Partner   Partner

- Tie in the cover letter with the focus of your brochure. Be consistent in your approach.

- Survey results (or testimonials) based on peer group response are powerful motivators.

Computer Consultant (4-08)

Company Name
Address
City, State Zip

To: Everyone Who Has A Computer in the Office

From: Janis Carver, President

Subject: Computer Training

It doesn't matter if your employees are seasoned computer professionals, novices, or somewhere in between. C&W training can make a substantial improvement in their productivity.

We've had the opportunity to train people in nearly every field: manufacturing, marketing, finance and accounting, trucking, government, engineering and real estate. And we've trained them to be more proficient in every phase of computer technology: operating systems, word processing, spreadsheets, integrated software, graphics, accounting and database management.

We'd like to work with your company, too. You'll find that C&W makes it particularly attractive for you to use our services:

1. Our rates are extremely competitive.
2. Our trainers are among the most knowledgeable in the area.
3. Our results are *outstanding*. We deliver what we promise.

In the attached brochure you'll find a listing of training classes. You'll also find a partial list of our clients. And you'll see our 100% satisfaction guarantee: If you're not completely satisfied with our training, we'll give you your money back!

Please complete and return the enclosed postage paid card to reserve seats in our classes. Or call 304-555-6149 to discuss custom training and in-house programs. We'd also be happy to discuss our consulting services.

Let us show you why we've become the solution to so many companies' computer challenges.

• When making cold mailings, a cover letter greatly improves the reception of your brochure.

• Your brochure will cover many of your company's services. Focus on just one in your cover letter. You can vary the focus depending on who you're mailing to.

• Make it easy for the reader to respond by providing the means (a reply card and phone number).

Direct Mail 5

While direct mail is one of the most expensive ways to sell, it is also one of the most effective. It permits you to narrowly target your market and thus avoid wasted advertising dollars. In contrast to such media as newspaper and broadcast advertising, which are considered "shotgun" methods, direct mail is thought of as a "rifle" approach, where the advertiser takes narrow aim at his intended market. This targeting makes direct mail an excellent medium for reaching prospects when you can accurately determine precisely who you want to reach. List brokers, companies that rent the tens of thousands of mailing lists that are available, will be happy to guide you in selecting the right ones for your purposes. For the names of list brokers you can consult the Direct Marketing Market Place directory, available in the reference department of larger libraries.

There are two basic direct mail formats. The standard package contains several components: the outer envelope, sales letter, brochure, order card, and business reply envelope. The self-mailer is traditionally a brochure with a built-in postpaid order card, though it may contain a postpaid envelope glued or stapled into the center of the brochure.

Standard Direct Mail Package

Outer envelope. In addition to its obvious function as the container for the direct mail components, the outer envelope's main purpose is to get the recipient to look into the package. This can be done with "teaser" copy which doesn't reveal the offer inside but piques the recipient's curiosity. Or it can be done with "benefit" copy designed to appeal to the recipient. Benefit words that always are effective are "Free," "New," and "Save."

Sales letter. The sales letter is generally considered the most important component in a direct mail package. It is usually 1, 2 or 4 pages. A good letter will start with an opening sentence that grabs the reader and gets him to read the entire letter. Short sentences and paragraphs, with crisp to-the-point writing, heavy with benefits to the reader, will keep the recipient reading. Research has long shown that a P.S. at the end of a letter is usually the most frequently read part of the letter. That is why it is an excellent place to repeat the offer, state a time limit for responding, or offer a special bonus for responding.

Brochure. The front of the brochure should contain your sales message and be enticing enough to get the recipient to open it up. Appealing graphics and attractive type help in getting the reader into the brochure.

Where possible, inside the brochure use photos or illustrations with captions to describe your product or service. A photo of the president of the company, or some other pertinent executive, adds credibility to your presentation.

Order card. This device, used to generate an order or a qualified inquiry too frequently is given the least attention by direct mailers. But a weak order card can lose the sale—and a good one can make the sale. Construct the card with the user in mind, making sure it 1) contains all the ordering information necessary, 2) encourages the respondent to mail it in quickly (an order delayed is frequently an order forgotten), and 3) helps your order processing department to read and understand what the person ordering wishes, where it is to be sent, and how it is to be paid for.

Business reply envelope. Make sure that the envelope is postpaid, to achieve maximum response. And, while this sounds so obvious that it needn't be mentioned, *make sure the envelope is large enough to accommodate the order card.* It's truly amazing how often this simple rule isn't followed.

Self-Mailer

The self-mailer consists of a brochure, frequently an 8 1/2" x 11" sheet folded in half or in thirds, with one section of the outside containing the recipient's name and address. The fill-in section of an order card is usually found inside, while the other side of the card is frequently a postpaid business reply card.

Self-mailers rely on strong headlines and graphics on the outside to grab the reader's attention, along with a strong offer. The challenge is to get the recipient to open up the self-mailer and fill out the order card.

As a general rule, business mailings sent in a business envelope will generate more response than a self-mailer, so the increase in response from an envelope mailing may more than offset the increased costs. The way to find out which is more cost effective for your needs is to test the standard format against the self-mailer, and let the results decide.

Read the introduction to the Brochures chapter (Chapter 1) for a discussion of "positioning," which discusses how to select the most important benefits of your product or service to feature in your direct mail.

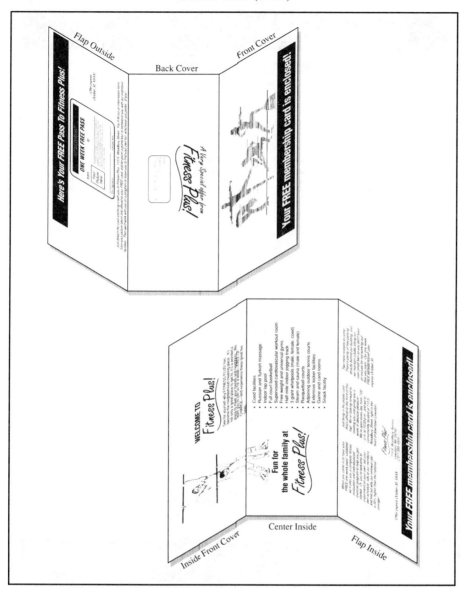

- Direct mail is the ideal medium to reach prospects with highly definable characteristics. This 8 1/2" x 11" self-mailer folded in thirds is targeted to women between the ages of 18 and 50. Mailing lists are readily available from list brokers throughout the country.

Here's Your FREE Pass To Fitness Plus!

FITNESS PLUS!

ONE WEEK FREE PASS

from_____ to _____

| Your Picture Here | is extended all privileges, including use of racquetball and basketball courts, swimming pool, whirlpools, steam and sauna, universal and free weight gyms, running track, locker and recreational facilities, and all other services to which members are entitled. |

Your Signature   Validate Here

(Offer expires October 30. XXXX)

Just detach the card and bring it with you to Fitness Plus, 113 S. Woodbury Street. You'll fill out an information form, have your picture taken and affixed to your FREE card, and be given a grand tour to familiarize you with our extensive facilities. Then we'll work with you on a program or leave you to find your own fun, whichever you prefer. Enjoy!

Your FREE membership card is enclosed!

- A free pass (card, ticket, coupon, etc.) will motivate people to try something they ordinarily would not.

- Don't leave the offer open-ended. Without a time limit, many people will procrastinate, and lose the impulse that a time frame creates.

**Fun for
the whole family at**

Fitness Plus!

WELCOME TO

Fitness Plus!

See for yourself why FITNESS PLUS! has become the neighborhood meeting place. It's not only a great place to get fit, it's a wonderful place to meet your friends and neighbors. We want you to join us for a week—FREE OF CHARGE—and experience these great features:

- Coed facilities
- Russian and Turkish massage
- Indoor lap pool
- Full court basketball
- Supervised cardiovascular workout room
- Free weight and universal gyms
- Half-mile indoor jogging track
- 3 giant whirlpools (male, female, coed)
- Steam and sauna (male and female)
- Racquetball courts
- Adjoining outdoor tennis courts
- Extensive locker facilities
- Game and card rooms
- Snack facility

When you come in to have your FREE one-week pass* validated, we'll offer you a complete fitness evaluation and individualized exercise program to help you get started. Or, you're welcome to experiment on your own, set your own schedule, talk to our members and find out why our renewal rate is 50% higher than the national average!

Just bring in the plastic card that's affixed to the front of this flap! We're looking forward to meeting you and giving you a week of absolute pleasure. We're open every day from 7:00 a.m. to 10:00 p.m., and we're conveniently located at 113 S. Woodbury Street, right in the heart of downtown Lewiston.

Two more reasons to come: There's plenty of free parking directly behind our building, and we maintain a baby sitting service (small fee) so you don't have an excuse for not working out! See you soon. Our one-week FREE MEMBERSHIP offer expires October 30.

Fitness Plus!

113 S. Woodbury Avenue
Lewiston, ME 04240
(207) 555-4004

*Offer expires October 30, XXXX

Your FREE membership card is enclosed!

- Although fitness clubs gladly accommodate individual memberships, this brochure stresses attractions for the entire family, a sound marketing strategy.

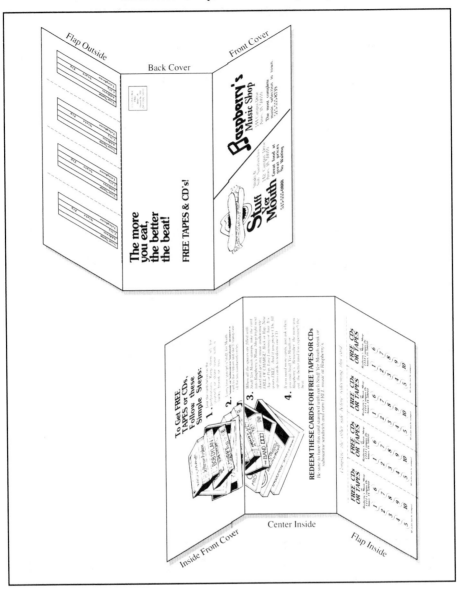

- Promotions conducted by two complementary businesses can be highly effective. This 8 1/2" x 11" self-mailer, aimed at young people, offers exciting discounts in areas that particularly interest this market.

The more
you eat,
the better
the beat!

FREE TAPES & CD's!

U.S. POSTAGE
PAID
Ames. IA
Permit No. 000
ZIP CODE 50010

Stuff Yer Mouth

515-555-0888

Steaks &
Sub Sandwiches
142 Campus Drive
Ames. IA 50010
**Great food at
great prices
No Waiting**

Raspberry's *Music Shop*

144 Campus Drive
Ames. IA 50010

**The most complete
music selection in town.**
515-555-8739

• Joint merchant promotions can help stimulate business for both companies, and keep costs manageable for advertising and promotional campaigns.

• In any giveaway, be sure to obtain the names for future mailings.

To Get FREE TAPES or CDs, Follow these Simple Steps:

1. Tear the cards below on the perforations. Keep them all for yourself or share some with a lucky friend or two.

2. Every time you get a Stuff Yer Mouth Steak or Submarine Sandwich, present a card to the cashier and she'll stamp one of the ten numbered circles.

3. When all the spaces are filled with Stuff Yer Mouth stamps, take the card into Raspberry's Music Shop (right next door) and get any music audiocassette FREE OF CHARGE! Rock or Rap, New Age or Pop, Easy Listening or Jazz. It's yours FREE. And if you prefer CDs, fill up two cards to redeem one CD.

4. If you need more cards, just ask when you visit Stuff Yer Mouth or Raspberry's. Remember: the more you eat, the better (and less expensive!) the beat.

REDEEM THESE CARDS FOR FREE TAPES OR CDs

Be sure to have this card stamped with each Stuff Yer Mouth steak or submarine sandwich and earn FREE music at Raspberry's.

Complete the other side before redeeming this card.

FREE CDs OR TAPES	FREE CDs OR TAPES	FREE CDs OR TAPES	FREE CDs OR TAPES
at Rasberry's Music Shop 1444 Campus Dr. Aimer, IA 50010	at Rasberry's Music Shop 1444 Campus Dr. Aimer, IA 50010	at Rasberry's Music Shop 1444 Campus Dr. Aimer, IA 50010	at Rasberry's Music Shop 1444 Campus Dr. Aimer, IA 50010
① ⑥ ② ⑦ ③ ⑧ ④ ⑨ ⑤ ⑩	① ⑥ ② ⑦ ③ ⑧ ④ ⑨ ⑤ ⑩	① ⑥ ② ⑦ ③ ⑧ ④ ⑨ ⑤ ⑩	① ⑥ ② ⑦ ③ ⑧ ④ ⑨ ⑤ ⑩
All circles mst be stamped	All circles mst be stamped	All circles mst be stamped	All circles mst be stamped

- This brochure will work best when printed on a light-weight card stock, with perforations made by the print shop. However, it can also be printed on a heavy text stock, and the customer can be instructed to fold and tear along the dashed lines.

- Direct mail is ideal for reaching your existing customers (every business should maintain a current customer list) as well as new prospects. This 8 1/2" x 3 3/4" postcard dramatically announces a new, larger facility in a memorable way.

- When you improve your business in a significant way, use the news to create a special promotion.

- Type selection and layout can help deliver your message better than a lot of words.

U.S. POSTAGE
PAID
Atlanta, GA
Permit No. 000
ZIP CODE 30305

CARVELLI'S
Ristorante & Catering Hall
3314 W. Highway 88
Atlanta, GA 30305

• Put your name prominently on the address side so customers will recognize who has sent the mailing, increasing the likelihood that they will read the message on the back.

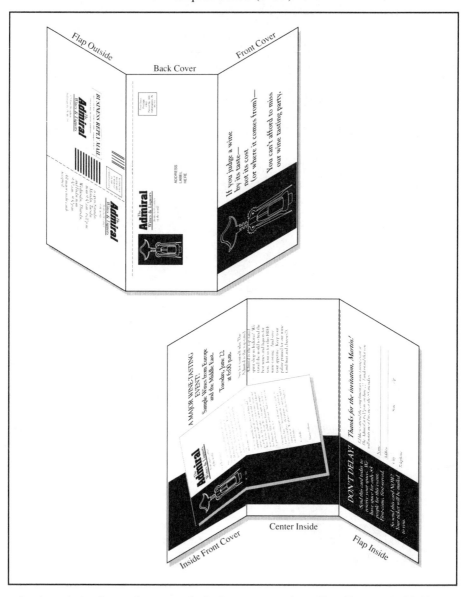

- 4-color printing is not always required. One or two-color self-mailers can be highly effective. A dark ink for the left panel and logo—black or blue, for example—creates a dramatic look for this 8 1/2" x 11" self-mailer while keeping printing costs low.

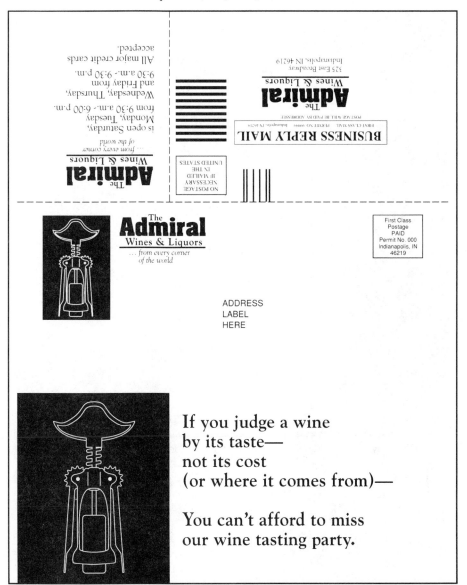

The
Admiral
Wines & Liquors
... from every corner of the world

ADDRESS
LABEL
HERE

First Class
Postage
PAID
Permit No. 000
Indianapolis, IN
46219

If you judge a wine
by its taste—
not its cost
(or where it comes from)—

You can't afford to miss
our wine tasting party.

• Printed on light weight card stock, this brochure includes a business reply card, perforated so that it can be separated and dropped in the mail. Response rates increase dramatically when you provide an easy, prepaid method like this.

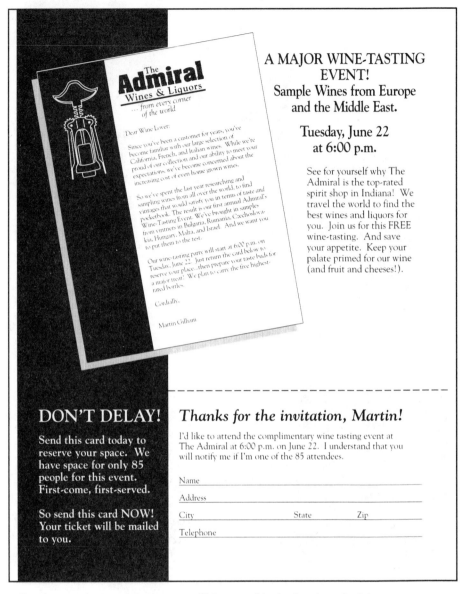

The Admiral
Wines & Liquors
...from every corner of the world

Dear Wine Lover:

Since you've been a customer for years, you've become familiar with our large selection of California, French, and Italian wines. While we're proud of our collection and our ability to meet your expectations, we've become concerned about the increasing cost of even home grown wines.

So we've spent the last year researching and sampling wines from all over the world, to find vintages that would satisfy you in terms of taste and pocketbook. The result is our first annual Admiral's Wine-Tasting Event. We've brought in samples from vintners in Bulgaria, Rumania, Czechoslovakia, Hungary, Malta, and Israel. And we want you to put them to the test.

Our wine-tasting party will start at 6:00 p.m. on Tuesday, June 22. Just return the card below to reserve your place...then prepare your taste buds for a major treat! We plan to carry the five highest-rated bottles.

Cordially,

Martin Gillam

A MAJOR WINE-TASTING EVENT!
Sample Wines from Europe and the Middle East.

Tuesday, June 22 at 6:00 p.m.

See for yourself why The Admiral is the top-rated spirit shop in Indiana! We travel the world to find the best wines and liquors for you. Join us for this FREE wine-tasting. And save your appetite. Keep your palate primed for our wine (and fruit and cheeses!).

DON'T DELAY!

Send this card today to reserve your space. We have space for only 85 people for this event. First-come, first-served.

So send this card NOW! Your ticket will be mailed to you.

Thanks for the invitation, Martin!

I'd like to attend the complimentary wine tasting event at The Admiral at 6:00 p.m. on June 22. I understand that you will notify me if I'm one of the 85 attendees.

Name _____

Address _____

City _____ State _____ Zip _____

Telephone _____

• Customers enjoy special treatment. This type of invitation does the job.

• This mailer could easily be adapted to any kind of open house or special event.

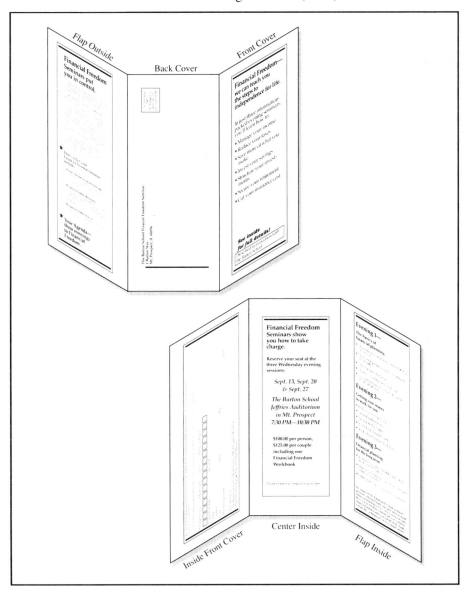

- Seminar promotions require sufficient explanatory copy to describe the subject matter. The concise but thorough descriptions in this 8 1/2" x 11" self-mailer provide adequate information for the recipient to make an informed decision regarding attendance.

Financial Freedom— we can teach you the steps to independence for life.

In just three information-packed evening seminars, you'll learn how to:

- Manage your income
- Reduce your taxes
- Save more of what you make
- Invest your savings
- Structure your investments
- Secure your retirement
- Cut your insurance cost

See inside for full details!

Presented in association with the Barton School

U.S. POSTAGE
PAID
Mt. Prospect, IL
Permit No. 000
ZIP CODE 60056

The Barton School Financial Freedom Seminar
1 Barton Way
Mt. Prospect, IL 60056

Financial Freedom Seminars put you in control.

Whether you work full-time or part-time, are self-employed or work for someone else, and regardless of your income, you need to learn financial planning.

In three evenings, Financial Freedom Seminars can help you take command. Even if you've never invested a dime before, you can learn how to start out small and grow. You'll be introduced to a wide range of investment opportunities...and learn their benefits and risks. You'll discover how to make informed decisions on everything from savings accounts to life insurance to retirement funds. You'll find out where to invest your money safely, yet receive maximum return.

And most important, you'll enjoy discovering these steps with Financial Freedom Seminars. For the first time in your life, you'll really know how to control your financial destiny.

★ Here's what your Financial Freedom Seminar includes:

• **Three information-packed evenings**— three hours each. You'll meet people who share your interest at these informative classroom sessions.

• **Financial Freedom Workbook**
You'll receive a workbook with over 200 pages of examples and worksheets that will help you put your new knowledge to work, securing your financial freedom.

• **Financial Freedom Profile**
Use this handy worksheet to structure your personal financial plan

★ Your Agenda— three evenings to Financial Freedom.

- For self-mailing brochures, the panels should be planned so that the last fold forms the bottom edge of the mail piece, in order to allow postal machines to process the mailing.

Evening 1—

**The basics of
financial planning**

- What financial planning is and what it can do for you
- Why some people succeed and others fail financially
- The dangers of inflation
- Taxes— avoiding them at all cost
- Investment menu— a taste of various financial options

Evening 2—

**Getting your money
to work for you**

- Reducing your taxes, legally
- Limited partnerships
- Tax deferred annuities
- Investing in tangible assets
- Stocks, bonds and mutual funds

Evening 3—

**Financial planning
for the long term**

- Securing your retirement through IRAs, 401K and SEP plans
- Managing insurance— what you need and when you need it
- Estate planning. . . pass it on, your way

Developer of the Financial Freedom Seminars program, Donald Naples has provided in-depth financial planning services for over two decades. He is a registered investment advisor, certified financial planner and is president of the Naples Group, Inc., a financial services organization.

**Financial Freedom
Seminars show
you how to take
charge.**

Reserve your seat at the three Wednesday evening sessions:

*Sept. 13, Sept. 20
& Sept. 27*

*The Barton School
Jeffries Auditorium
in Mt. Prospect
7:30 PM—10:30 PM*

$100.00 per person,
$125.00 per couple
including one
Financial Freedom
Workbook

Payment must accompany registration

Yes, I wish to register for your financial seminar. I understand the fee is $100. *(Registrations must be received by September 1.)*

— I've enclosed a check for $100 *(make check payable to Barton Financial Freedom Seminars)*

Charge to my ☐ American Express ☐ Visa ☐ Mastercard

☐☐☐☐☐☐☐☐☐☐☐☐☐☐☐☐

Expiration date _____ Signature _____

Name _____

Address _____

City _____ State _____ Zip _____ mail

Daytime phone# _____

Fax or mail to:
The Barton School, 1 Barton Way, Mt. Prospect, IL 60056
(708) 555-5520 Fax • (708) 555-5500 Phone

- Affiliating your seminar program with a school or college can give you instant credibility as well as access to facilities equipped to serve a large group of attendees.

- If you're sending separate mailings offering seminars at different locations, consider color-coding your reply cards for different dates. If that's not possible, be sure to print the specific date on the reply card for easier record keeping.

- Nostalgia is a powerful theme, particularly when tied in with a promotion that supports the concept, such as this one that offers "prices from the good old days." This mailing package uses the nostalgia motif throughout—in the headline, graphics and merchandise.

TURN BACK THE CLOCK

WITH POWELL'S GREAT

TIME TRAVEL SALE!

You'll feel like a time traveler when you see the price tags on our great new collection of men's and boys' Fall outerwear! Modern value and styling with 20-year-old pricing!

Seeing is believing! Take a look at our special group of leather-like aviator jackets with pop-up collars, cuffs and waists. You'd expect to pay up to $79.95...at Powell's you pay only $39.95!

This is a once-in-a-lifetime buy! We have all sizes now but they won't last long. When this inventory goes, that's it! FIRST COME, FIRST SERVED! NO RAIN CHECKS for this special sale.

Sale Begins Friday, September 17 at 9:00 a.m. and continues on Saturday, September 18 and Sunday, September 19.

POWELL'S DEPARTMENT STORE

"The People Place"

230 West Central Avenue
Anchorage, AK 99502
907-555-9330

All major credit cards accepted.
Open 7 days a week:
Mon, Tues, and Thurs 9:00 a.m. - 7:00 p.m.
Wed, Fri, and Sat 9:00 a.m. - 9:00 p.m.
Sun Noon - 6:00 p.m.

SPECIAL BUY!
MEN'S AVIATOR JACKETS
Value to $79.95: Powell's Price only $39.95. Just like the good old days!

Also sale-priced:
our entire collection of men's outerwear, including waist-length and 3/4 length coats. Savings of up to 50% on everything in stock!

SPECIAL TIME TRAVEL GIVEAWAY
See details on enclosed card.

- Show the merchandise. Don't make the mistake of assuming customers will know what it looks like.

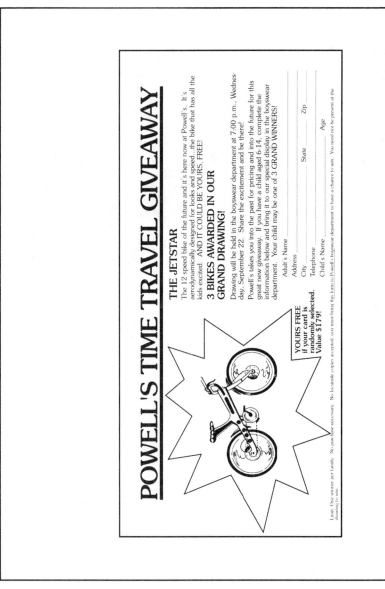

POWELL'S TIME TRAVEL GIVEAWAY

THE JETSTAR

The 12-speed bike of the future and it's here now at Powell's. It's aerodynamically designed for looks and speed...the bike that has all the kids excited. AND IT COULD BE YOURS, FREE!

3 BIKES AWARDED IN OUR GRAND DRAWING!

Drawing will be held in the boyswear department at 7:00 p.m., Wednesday, September 22. Share the excitement and be there!

Powell's takes you into the past for pricing and into the future for this great new giveaway. If you have a child aged 6-14, complete the information below and bring it to our special display in the boyswear department. Your child may be one of 3 GRAND WINNERS!

Adult's Name _____

Address _____

City _____ State _____ Zip _____

Telephone _____

Child's Name _____ Age _____

**YOURS FREE
if your card is
randomly selected.
Value $179!**

Limit: One winner per family. No facsimile copies accepted. You must bring this form to Powell's boyswear department to have a chance to win. You need not be present at the drawing to win.

- Giveaways boost store traffic. The prizes don't have to be very expensive, as long as they relate to what you're promoting and appeal to your customers.

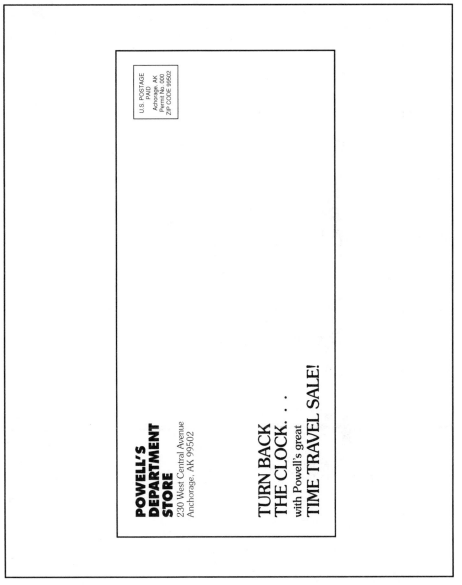

- The bulk rate indicia allows for a lower postal rate so long as certain postal service stipulations are met. It requires that you purchase a low-cost permit, good for one year, and that you sort the addressed pieces according to a strict set of rules.

GLENVILLE
MANAGEMENT CORP.
7607 Fairchild Boulevard
Green Bay, WI 54304

U.S. POSTAGE
PAID
Ames, IA
Permit No. 000
ZIP CODE 50010

"I don't have to think about leaky
faucets, cracks in the foundation,
tenant complaints or maintenance
problems any more."

Why should I worry?
The property management pros at
GLENVILLE MANAGEMENT
do it all for me.

25 years of helping property owners.
GLENVILLE MANAGEMENT CORPORATION
7607 Fairchild Boulevard
Green Bay, WI 54304
Phone: 414-555-8900

GLENVILLE
Management
Corporation

- A postcard format can be highly effective if it catches the reader's attention. This simple mailing talks to retirees who own rental property by picturing a typical retirement activity with a caption that expresses a common sentiment.

GLENVILLE
MANAGEMENT CORP.
7607 Fairchild Boulevard
Green Bay, WI 54304

U.S. POSTAGE
PAID
Ames, IA
Permit No. 000
ZIP CODE 50010

"I don't have to think about leaky faucets, cracks in the foundation, tenant complaints or maintenance problems any more."

• A strong ad series will include some promotions that highlight benefits and some that highlight features. This mailing features a benefit (relaxation).

Why should I worry?
The property management pros at
GLENVILLE MANAGEMENT
do it all for me.

25 years of helping property owners.
GLENVILLE MANAGEMENT CORPORATION
7607 Fairchild Boulevard
Green Bay, WI 54304
Phone: 414-555-8900

GLENVILLE
Management
Corporation

• A series of inexpensive mailers won't tax your ad budget, but will create an awareness in your prospect's mind.

Pueblo Chiropractic Care
1411 Cerveza Drive
Pueblo, CO 81008

U.S. POSTAGE
PAID
Pueblo, CO
Permit No. 000
ZIP CODE 81008

HELPFUL HINT #11
FOR YOUR BETTER HEALTH

HELPFUL HINT #11

Figure A

Figure B

If you'd like to stay out of our office, don't sit like figure A.

Proper back maintenance means you should push your spine against the chair, and hold yourself erect, just like figure B.

Brought to you as a community service.

Another HELPFUL HINT from
Pueblo Chiropractic Care.
We're the people you want to see first for:

- Auto and Whiplash Injury
- Lower Back and Leg Pain
- Neck, Shoulder, and Arm Pain
- Gentle Spinal Corrections
- Sports Injuries
- Pain Control

Most Insurance Accepted

INITIAL CONSULTATION FREE

**24 HOUR EMERGENCY CARE
CALL: 719-555-2100**

PUEBLO CHIROPRACTIC CARE
1411 Cerveza Drive (Across from Gaetano's Diner) Pueblo, CO 81008

• A mailing that contains helpful information will get read. Larger than normal, this 8 1/2" x 5" postcard is sure to be noticed in a stack of mail.

Pueblo Chiropractic Care

1411 Cerveza Drive
Pueblo, CO 81008

U.S. POSTAGE
PAID
Pueblo, CO
Permit No. 000
ZIP CODE 81008

**HELPFUL HINT #11
FOR YOUR BETTER HEALTH**

• Put a compelling headline on the address side so the reader is sure to turn it over and see your sales message.

HELPFUL HINT #11

Figure A

If you'd like to stay out of our office, don't sit like figure A.

Proper back maintenance means you should push your spine against the chair, and hold yourself erect, just like figure B.

Figure B

Brought to you as a community service.

Another HELPFUL HINT from
Pueblo Chiropractic Care.
We're the people you want to see first for:

- Auto and Whiplash Injury
- Lower Back and Leg Pain
- Neck, Shoulder, and Arm Pain
- Gentle Spinal Corrections
- Sports Injuries
- Pain Control

Most Insurance Accepted

INITIAL CONSULTATION FREE

24 HOUR EMERGENCY CARE
CALL: 719-555-2100

PUEBLO CHIROPRACTIC CARE
1411 Cerveza Drive (Across from Gaetano's Diner) Pueblo, CO 81008

- Creating a series of "helpful hints" mailers is an excellent strategy for virtually any business that's service/care oriented.

- Repeating the message that "We Care" has a cumulative effect that will result in business when your service is required.

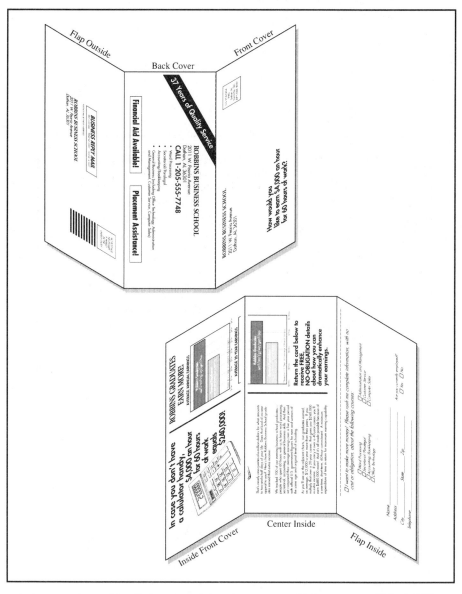

- A strong customer benefit is a powerful tool to generate high response. This 8 1/2" x 11" self-mailer focuses on how much more a business school graduate makes on average than someone without such education.

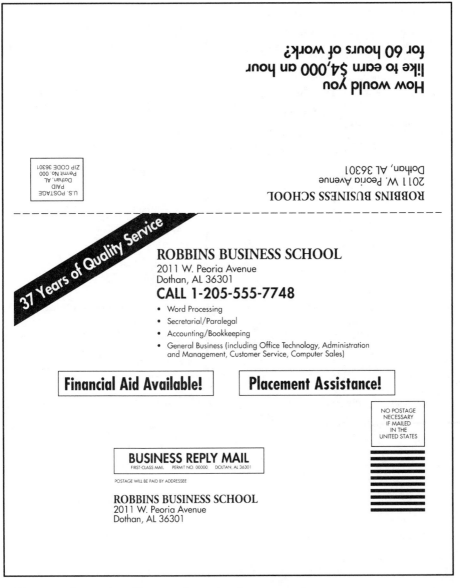

How would you
like to earn $4,000 an hour
for 60 hours of work?

ROBBINS BUSINESS SCHOOL
2011 W. Peoria Avenue
Dothan, AL 36301

U.S. POSTAGE
PAID
Dothan, AL
Permit No. 000
ZIP CODE 36301

37 Years of Quality Service

ROBBINS BUSINESS SCHOOL
2011 W. Peoria Avenue
Dothan, AL 36301
CALL 1-205-555-7748

- Word Processing
- Secretarial/Paralegal
- Accounting/Bookkeeping
- General Business (including Office Technology, Administration and Management, Customer Service, Computer Sales)

Financial Aid Available!   **Placement Assistance!**

NO POSTAGE
NECESSARY
IF MAILED
IN THE
UNITED STATES

BUSINESS REPLY MAIL
FIRST-CLASS MAIL   PERMIT NO. 00000   DOLTAN, AL 36301

POSTAGE WILL BE PAID BY ADDRESSEE

ROBBINS BUSINESS SCHOOL
2011 W. Peoria Avenue
Dothan, AL 36301

- Use a question on the address portion to involve your readers.

- The mailing panel forms the "front cover" of this brochure, and there also is a business-reply mailing panel on the other side of the response form.

In case you don't have a calulator handy,

$4,000 an hour for 60 hours of work equals $240,000!

ROBBINS GRADUATES EARN MORE!

AVERAGE ANNUAL EARNINGS

Robbins Graduates
sec'l/acc't'g/wp/gen'l bus

General Population*

*Based on U.S. Dept. of Commerce, Office of Statistics

$10m $15m $20m $25m $30m $35m $40m $45m

AVERAGE 20 YEAR EARNINGS

Robbins Graduates
sec'l/acc't'g/wp/gen'l bus

*Based on U.S. Dept. of Commerce, Office of Statistics

$200m $250m $500m $750m $1,000m

That's nearly one-quarter-of-a-million-dollars for what amounts to two-and-a-half days of your life. Does that kind of income appeal to you? Here's how Robbins Business School graduates earned that extra income:

We tracked 100 of our evening business school graduates—people who spent 60 hours with us to learn word processing, secretarial, accounting, or general business skills. And then we compared their average earnings over a five year period with official U.S. government figures for men and women of the same age and original level of schooling.

As you'll see on the adjacent charts, our graduates earned, on average, $12,000 a year more than their peers. If you multiply that over a 20-year career, that gives you $240,000 in extra income. If you carry it over a 40-year career, you'll earn $480,000 more! And it's all made possible because of a one-time, short-term, 60-hour commitment. A minimum expenditure of time in return for maximum earning capability.

Return the card below to receive FREE, NO-OBLIGATION details about how you can dramatically enhance your earnings.

☐ I want to make more money! Please rush me complete information, with no cost or obligation, about the following courses:

☐ Word Processing
☐ Secretarial/Paralegal
☐ Accounting/Bookkeeping
☐ Office Technology

☐ Administration and Management
☐ Customer Service
☐ Computer Sales

Name _____

Address _____

City _____ State _____ Zip _____

Telephone _____

Are you currently employed?
☐ Yes   ☐ No

• Charts and graphs lend credibility to a promotion and visually drive your point home.

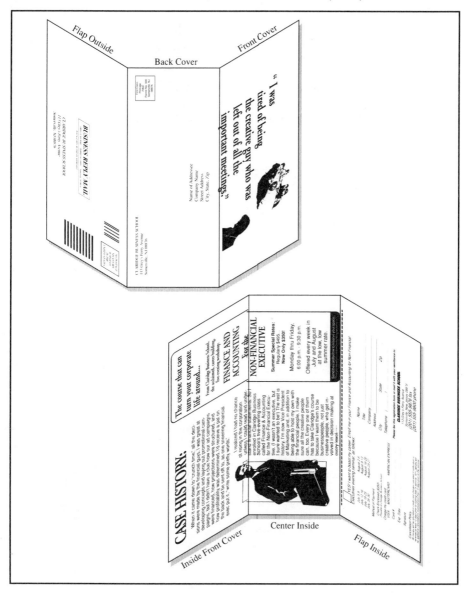

- Testimonials and case histories are powerful techniques for building impact with your prospects. This 8 1/2" x 11" self-mailer combines a case history with attention-getting graphics and a theme that readers can relate to.

" I was
tired of being
the creative guy who was
left out of all the
important meetings."

Name of Addressee
Company Name
Street Address
City, State, Zip

First Class
Postage
PAID
Permit No. 000
Somerville, NJ
08876

CLARIDGE BUSINESS SCHOOL
113 Grey's Ferry Avenue
Somerville, NJ 08876

NO POSTAGE
NECESSARY
IF MAILED
IN THE
UNITED STATES

BUSINESS REPLY MAIL
FIRST-CLASS MAIL   PERMIT NO. 99999   Somerville, NJ 08876

POSTAGE WILL BE PAID BY ADDRESSEE

CLARIDGE BUSINESS SCHOOL
113 Grey's Ferry Avenue
Somerville, NJ 08876

- A statement your market will immediately relate to provides a compelling reason for the recipient to open the mailing.

- Use strong artwork to support the copy.

CASE HISTORY:

When it came down to "crunch time," all the decisions were made by the financial guys. I was great at developing concepts and laying out promotional campaigns, but I didn't have a clue how our ad campaigns were financed, how projections were structured, and how profitability was determined. I'd receive a pat on the back and be sent off to, as one sneering financial exec put it, "write some pretty words."

I realized I had no chance of rising in the corporation unless I could read and understand financial statements. So I enrolled in Claridge Business School's five-evening class called Finance & Accounting for the Non-Financial Executive. (I wasn't an executive, but I sure wanted to be!) The rest is history. I'm now Vice President of Marketing and, in addition to being able to hold my own with the financial people, I make sure all the creative people can, too. Every one of them has to take Claridge's course because I want them to be businesspeople, not just creative people, who get involved in decision making at every level.

The course that can turn your corporate life around...

From Claridge Business School, the acclaimed, career-building, five-evening workshop:

FINANCE AND ACCOUNTING
For the
NON-FINANCIAL EXECUTIVE

Summer Special Rates:
Regularly $495...
Now Only $350!

Monday thru Friday,
6:00 p.m. - 9:30 p.m.

Offered every week in
July and August
at the low, low
summer rate.

Send the card below to reserve your space.
Reservations must be received by June 1.

☐ YES! I want to boost my career. Enroll me in your Finance and Accounting for Non-Financial Executives evening seminar, as follows:

July 5-9   August 2-6
July 12-16 August 9-13
July 19-23 August 16-20
July 26-30 August 23-27

Method of Payment:

☐ Check Enclosed ($350)
(Payable to Claridge Business School)
☐ Charge my credit card:
    VISA   MASTERCARD   AMERICAN EXPRESS

Card # _____

Exp. Date _____

Signature _____

Cancellation Policy:
All money will be refunded or credit card charges canceled if notification is received at least 10 days prior to starting date of seminar. 50% penalty will be applied to cancellations received less than 10 days prior to the seminar.

Name _____

Title _____

Company _____

Address _____

City _____ State _____ Zip _____

Telephone (_____) _____

Please fax this registration form or mail it with your remittance to:
CLARIDGE BUSINESS SCHOOL
113 Grey's Ferry Avenue
Somerville, New Jersey 08876
(201) 555-9876 fax
(201) 555-9800 phone

- For greatest success, tailor your appeal to a specific audience. This one would be mailed to people in advertising, marketing, promotion and design for maximum impact.

- Case histories really get the reader involved, and involvement increases response.

- There is no rule about how many components direct mail must have. This effective mailing contains just two 8 1/2" x 11" sheets—one is a sales letter and the other a service agreement—and a mailing envelope.

DEACON BROTHERS, INC.
Heating, Ventilating, and Air Conditioning
Service and Installation

1401 S. First Street
Casper, WY 82601

Dear Homeowner:

You may not recognize our name, but we're the contractor that originally installed the complete heating and air conditioning system in your home. Because we know your system, and because we'd like to see it continue to serve you well, we've designed an exclusive service program for you. It's so valuable, we call it our Platinum Maintenance Service.

Here's how we'll keep your heating and air conditioning system running economically and lasting far beyond manufacturer expectations. You'll receive expert Spring and Fall inspection and service that includes:

- Cleaning of all operating parts in your system (thermostat, too!)
- Replacement of all filters
- Lubrication of all moving parts

What this means is <u>no surprises</u>! When the weather gets hot, your air conditioner will be ready to cool your home more efficiently than ever before. . . and when the weather turns cold, your heating system won't let you and your family down for even a minute.

We've enclosed a sample of our Platinum Maintenance Service Agreement so you can see how simple it is. Proper maintenance means savings and peace of mind. Call us today at 307-555-2090.

Warmly,

Jack Hessian
Owner and Manager

P.S. If you call by February 15, you'll be eligible for our Early Bird Discount. That means you can take 10% off the cost of our Platinum Maintenance service just by dialing now (307-555-2090)

- Even if your company didn't sell the customer directly, offering them a service contract is an excellent way to generate sales. This letter, along with a sample service contract, is mailed shortly after the installation is completed.

- The Early Bird Discount in the P.S. is a powerful inducement for the customer to buy now.

DB DEACON BROTHERS, INC.
1401 S. First Street
Casper, WY 82601

PLATINUM MAINTENANCE
SERVICE AGREEMENT

For:_____

Proper maintenance means enhanced product operating
performance and life.

Your Platinum Service includes:

Spring Inspection and Service:
Performed between March 1 and April 30

Deacon Brothers will thoroughly check and clean all operating
parts of your heating system, air conditioner, and thermostat. We
will replace all system filters and lubricate moving parts, as required. We will evaluate and report to you the condition of your
complete HEATING AND AIR CONDITIONING system at no
additional charge.

Fall Inspection and Service:
Performed between September 1 and October 31

Deacon Brothers will thoroughly check and clean all operating
parts of your heater, air conditioner, and thermostat. We will
replace all system filters and lubricate moving parts, as required.
We will evaluate and report to you the condition of your complete
heating and air conditioning system at no additional charge.

Annual Fee: _____ Name _____

Address _____

10% Early
Bird Discount: _____ City _____ State___ Zip_____

TOTAL: _____ Phone _____

Agreed:_____ Date _____
(Signature)

- You should consult an attorney to create any sort of agreement for yourself and your
company. The one provided here is simply meant to provide a style that may be
adapted.

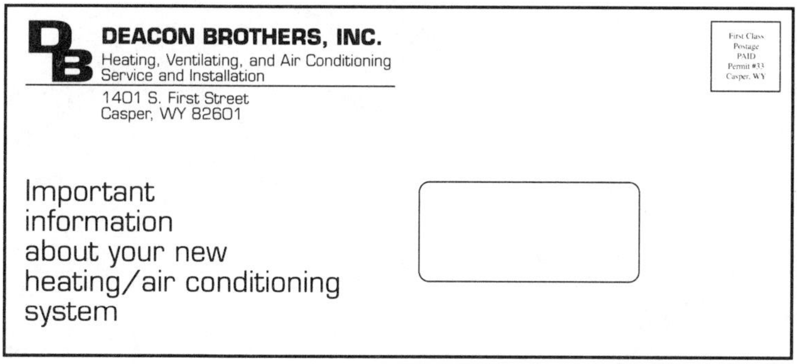

DEACON BROTHERS, INC.
Heating, Ventilating, and Air Conditioning
Service and Installation
1401 S. First Street
Casper, WY 82601

First Class
Postage
PAID
Permit #33
Casper, WY

Important
information
about your new
heating/air conditioning
system

• Envelope copy alerts the recipient that something important about their recent purchase is inside.

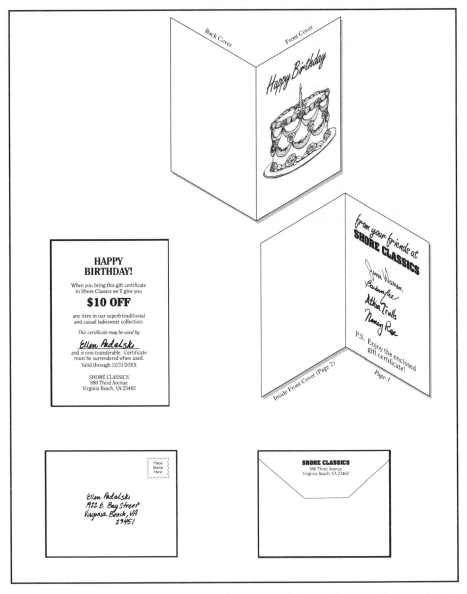

- Who can resist a birthday present? This birthday card/gift certificate mailing consists of an 8 1/2" x 5 1/2" invitation folded in half and and a savings certificate the same size, inserted into a 5 3/4" x 4 1/2" envelope, hand addressed.

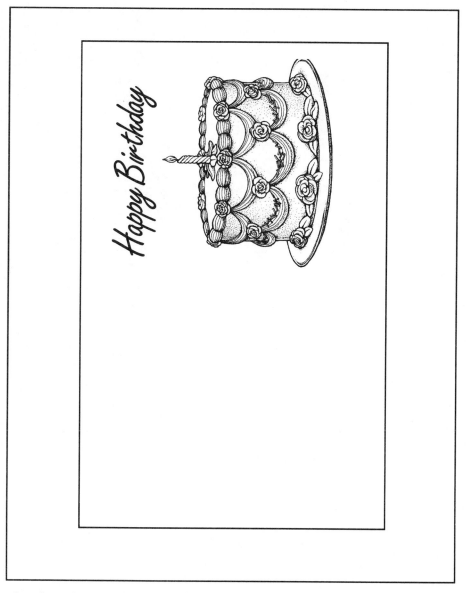

• In order to develop data for birthday mailings, have customers fill out an information
  card with their name, address and birthday month when they visit your store.

- The message is simple, but it includes the signatures of the staff for a very personal touch.

HAPPY BIRTHDAY!

When you bring this gift certificate to Shore Classics we'll give you

$10 OFF

any item in our superb traditional and casual ladieswear collection.

This certificate may be used by

Ellen Padalski

and is non-transferable. Certificate must be surrendered when used.
Valid through 12/31/20XX

SHORE CLASSICS
880 Third Avenue
Virginia Beach, VA 23462

• Birthday promotions provide excellent opportunities to show customers that you make the extra effort to keep them coming back. And, in spite of knowing that it's done for commercial reasons, people are flattered that their birthdays are remembered.

- Personal touches earn points. First-class stamps, hand-addressed envelopes, and signed cards speak volumes about your personal service.

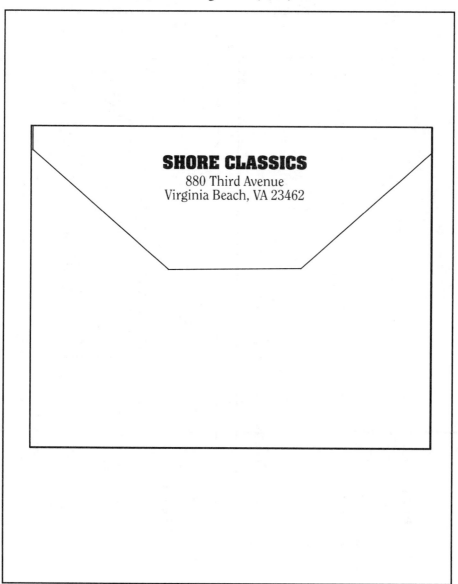

SHORE CLASSICS
880 Third Avenue
Virginia Beach, VA 23462

• Traditionally, an invitation envelope has the return address on the back flap.

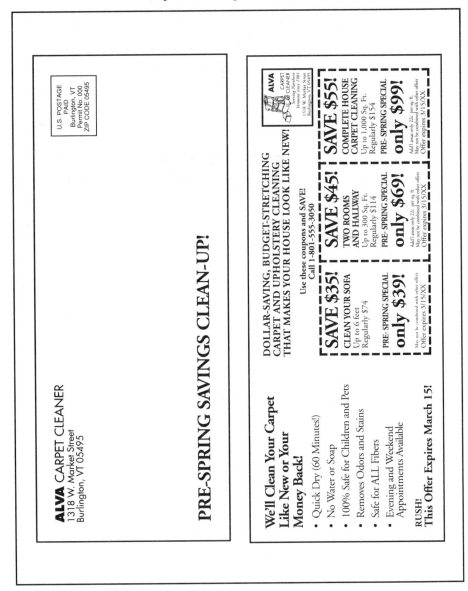

- Discount coupons are an excellent way to drive up sales during a quiet season. This 8 1/2" x 3 1/2" card contains several money-saving coupons emphasizing significant savings in highly visible bold type.

• This 8 1/2" x 3 1/2" card can be mailed by itself, or it can be put into a business envelope.

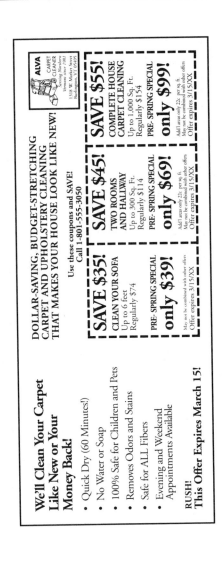

- It's possible to get across a message of big savings even if your ad budget is small. Coupons don't require a lot of space to indicate great value.

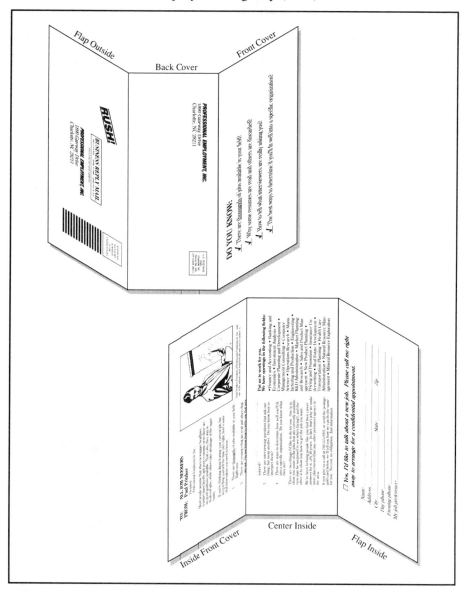

- Asking provocative questions that your company can answer effectively is a sure-fire way to entice prospects to read your mailing—and respond. This 8 1/2" x 11" self-mailer folded into thirds does just that, starting on the outside panel and continuing inside.

DO YOU KNOW:

✓ There are thousands of jobs available in your field?

✓ Why some resumes are read and others are discarded?

✓ How to tell what interviewers are really asking you?

✓ The best ways to determine if you'll fit well into a specific organization?

PROFESSIONAL EMPLOYMENT, INC.
1890 Gateway Drive
Charlotte, NC 28211

U.S. POSTAGE
PAID
Charlotte, NC
Permit No. 000
ZIP CODE 28211

NO POSTAGE
NECESSARY
IF MAILED
IN THE
UNITED STATES

BUSINESS REPLY MAIL
FIRST-CLASS MAIL   PERMIT NO. 00000   CHARLOTTE, NC 28211

POSTAGE WILL BE PAID BY ADDRESSEE

PROFESSIONAL EMPLOYMENT, INC.
1890 Gateway Drive
Charlotte, NC 28211

• The word "RUSH" makes the customer feel the communication is much more important than an "ordinary" business reply card, increasing the chance that he will read it.

TO: **ALL JOB SEEKERS**
FROM: **Paul Pritzker**
President
Professional Employment, Inc.

Most people assume that when newspaper headlines trumpet mass layoffs and poor economic news there are no good positions available. That's why they stay in dead-end jobs, while others take advantage of the opportunity.

If you're thinking about leaving your current job, but keep telling yourself the time isn't right, here's some vital information you need to know:

1. There are <u>thousands</u> of jobs available in your field. Right now.

2. There are resumes that are read and others that are not. Do you know how to write one that gets noticed?

3. There are interviewing questions that ask one thing, but mean another. Do you know how to interpret them?

4. There are ways to determine how well you'll fit into a specific organization. Do you know what they are?

There are two things I'd like to do for you. One is to show you some of the jobs that are currently available (you may be surprised to see who's hiring!), and the other is to show you how to get the job you want.

We've been helping people like you find their career answers for nearly 30 years. In fact, that's why we make more placements than any other personnel agency in the area.

If you give us a call at 704-555-9292, or send the postage-paid card below, we'll tell you how we can do the same for you. No cost, no obligation. Just information.

Paul Pritzker, President of Professional Employment, Inc., and one of the nation's most respected job and career counselors.

Put us to work for you.
We have openings in the following fields:

•Finance and Accounting • Banking and Economics • Investment Analysis • Corporate Planning and Development • Management Consulting • Computer Science • Operations Research • Manufacturing and Production • Engineering • R&D Administration • Market Planning and Research • Sales and Product Management • New Product Planning • Pricing and Promotion • Insurance Underwriting • Real Estate Development • Transportation Planning • Health Care Administration • Natural Resource Management • Mineral Resource Exploration

---

☐ **Yes, I'd like to talk about a new job. Please call me right away to arrange for a confidential appointment.**

Name _____

Address _____

City _____ State _____ Zip _____

Day phone _____

Evening phone _____

My job preference: _____

• This mailing can be tailored easily for a booming economy with a simple copy change in the first paragraph: "With lots of jobs available in today's booming market, we can help you land the job that's just right for you...and at the highest possible salary."

• A letter from the president gives the mailing a personal touch.

Place
stamp
here

It's that time of year!

DENTAL HEALTH BULLETIN FOR:

Arthur Teasdale

It's time for your 6-month check-up. Stop tooth decay and gum disease before they occur. Call us at 406-555-3984 and we'll arrange an appointment that fits your busy schedule.

Hours:
MONDAY–FRIDAY
8:00 a.m. - 5:00 p.m.

SATURDAY
9:00 a.m. - 1:00 p.m.

Looking forward to seeing you soon.

Jay Smith

Jay Smith, DDS
710 E. Seventh Avenue
Missoula, MT 59802
406-555-3984

• Postcards are well suited to a wide variety of purposes, from announcing sales to informing customers of a change of location to reminding patients of their appointments. This postcard is oversized (5" x 7") and can be printed on colored card stock for extra visibility.

• Make sure the message on the address side encourages the recipient to turn the card over. When your mailings repeat a familiar graphic or logo, the reader will know it is in his best interest to read on.

DENTAL HEALTH BULLETIN FOR:

Arthur Teasdale

It's time for your 6-month check-up. Stop tooth decay and gum disease before they occur. Call us at 406-555-3984 and we'll arrange an appointment that fits your busy schedule.

Hours:
MONDAY–FRIDAY
8:00 a.m. - 5:00 p.m.

SATURDAY
9:00 a.m. - 1:00 p.m.

Looking forward to seeing you soon.

Jay Smith

Jay Smith, DDS
710 E. Seventh Avenue
Missoula, MT 59802
406-555-3984

- Be sure to include all the information the reader will need to take an action or make a decision. That way you'll avoid having to answer "informational calls" which put an extra burden on your staff.

- Any time you can add a personal touch to a mailing, the impact will be increased. In this case, having the patient's name inserted into this "bulletin" makes the difference.

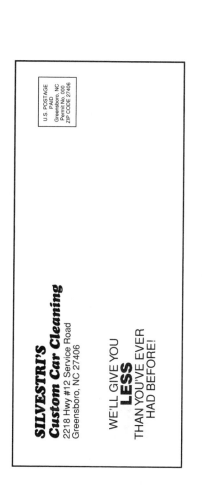

- Introduce your products or services to new customers in an innovative way. This unusually sized postcard (8 1/2" x 3 3/4") with an intriguing message should generate a good deal of interest.

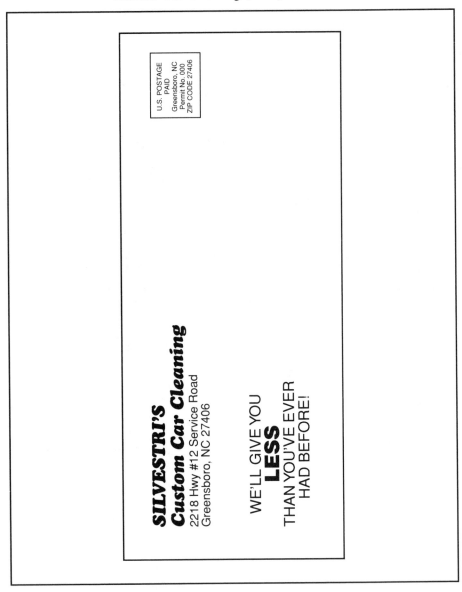

- This can be used as a stand-alone mailer or may be resized for inclusion in local shoppers' guides, coupon mailings, etc.

- The message on the address side uses the "less is more" theory to pique interest in your company.

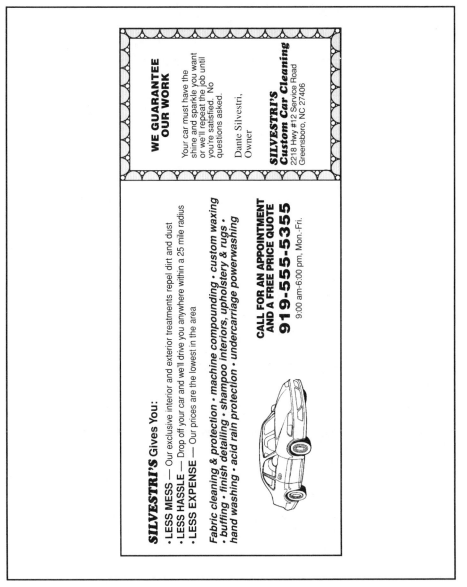

- Back up your promise with details of your offer, and encourage the customer to call or come in.

- Offering a guarantee reassures the customer that you'll be good to your word.

Wesley Parett
Quality Menswear
79 East Barber Street
Hilo, HI 96720

Place
Stamp
Here

PRIVATE SALE
FOR PREFERRED CUSTOMERS ONLY

Bring this special invitation for admittance to our unique, after-hours sale event. You're invited to purchase any red-tagged item—at remarkable savings—before it's made available to the general public.

You'll get first choice of Perry Valentine suits, regularly $850...yours for just $450! You can walk away with Marc Ravenol slacks, regularly $125...yours for only $65! Purchase the Nathaniel Worthington jacket you've always wanted, regularly $400...yours for just $275.

Look for our red-tag on these famous makers: Willy Tufton * Paul Primos * Gordon Archer * Aldo Montagnaro * Arden Fox

Join us for wine, champagne, hors d'oeuvres, and sensational sale pricing on the finest men's clothing. One night only.

Thursday, July 22 from 7:00 p.m. - 10:00 p.m.

No one admitted without this card. Sale prices are limited to red-tagged merchandise. Not all sizes are available in every category of clothing.

Wesley Parett
Quality Menswear

79 East Barber Street
Hilo, HI 96720 (808)-555-6400

• Sale announcements, sent to customers at regular intervals, maintain a positive impression of your company and keep your name before them. This 5 1/2" x 4 1/4" card is exactly one-fourth of a letter-sized sheet. It can be printed "four-up" (four to a sheet) at virtually any printing shop, for an economical print run.

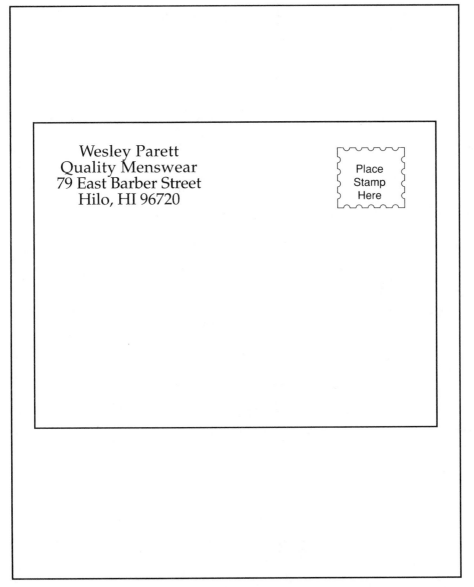

• Card stock is available in a wide range of colors, finishes and weights. Choose a style that complements the image you're trying to promote.

PRIVATE SALE
FOR PREFERRED CUSTOMERS ONLY

Bring this special invitation for admittance to our unique, after-hours sale event. You're invited to purchase any red-tagged item—at remarkable savings—before it's made available to the general public.

You'll get first choice of Perry Valentine suits, regularly $850...yours for just $450! You can walk away with Marc Ravenol slacks, regularly $125...yours for only $65! Purchase the Nathaniel Worthington jacket you've always wanted, regularly $400...yours for just $275.

Look for our red-tag on these famous makers: Willy Tufton * Paul Primos * Gordon Archer * Aldo Montagnaro * Arden Fox

Join us for wine, champagne, hors d'oeuvres, and sensational sale pricing on the finest men's clothing. One night only.

Thursday, July 22 from 7:00 p.m. - 10:00 p.m.

No one admitted without this card. Sale prices are limited to red-tagged merchandise. Not all sizes are available in every category of clothing.

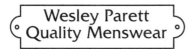

Wesley Parett
Quality Menswear

79 East Barber Street
Hilo, HI 96720 (808)-555-6400

- Build a loyal customer base by offering something special to "preferred customers."

- Using the card as the "price of admission" dramatizes the fact that this event really is exclusive.

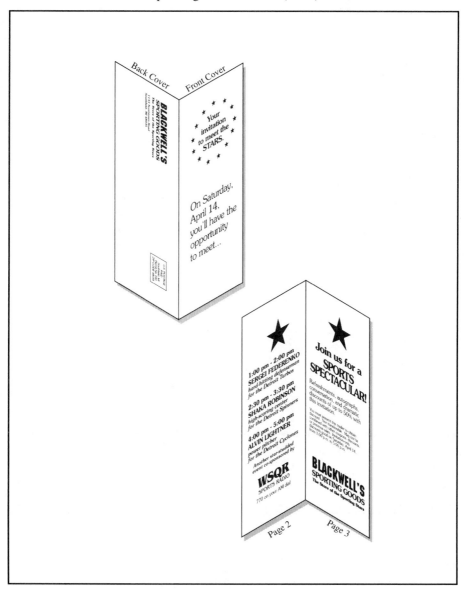

- 8" x 8 1/2" paper or card stock, folded in half, gives you a convenient four-sided brochure. The design can be either horizontal or vertical, or may change direction from panel to panel if that suits your purposes.

- This design may be used as a stand-alone mailer, or inserted into a business envelope, or delivered as a newspaper insert.

1:00 pm - 2:00 pm
SERGEI FEDERENKO
hard-hitting defenseman
for the Detroit Turbos

2:30 pm - 3:30 pm
SHAKA ROBINSON
high-scoring center
for the Detroit Spinners

4:00 pm - 5:00 pm
ALVIN LIGHTNER
power pitcher
for the Detroit Cyclones

Another star-studded
event co-sponsored by

WSQR
SPORTS RADIO

770 on your AM dial

Join us for a
SPORTS
SPECTACULAR!

Refreshments, autographs,
conversation, and dramatic
discounts of up to 50% with
this invitation.

You must present this mailer to obtain
discount. Not transferable. May not be
combined with other coupons, discounts,
or previous sales. Invitation-only
discounts good on Saturday, April 14,
from 1:00 p.m. to 5:00 p.m.

BLACKWELL'S
SPORTING GOODS
The Store of the Sporting Stars

- In-store events with special offerings "by invitation only" make a strong impression on customers—and increase store traffic.

- Use artwork to establish the theme of a mailing. This 5 1/2" x 4 1/4" card can be mailed to an existing customer base, or may be sent to a list of people in specific zip codes to prospect for new customers.

Margie's Menagerie
2801 Little Cross Corner Center
Alexandria, LA 71307

U.S. POSTAGE
PAID
Alexandria, LA
Permit No. 000
ZIP CODE 71307

Your Invitation to a Great Louisiana Holiday Tradition

- Start your appeal on the address side of the card. Don't waste the space with just an address.

- You can vary the color of the cards you send to reflect seasonal offers.

OPEN HOUSE

Margie's Menagerie
at Little Cross Corner

Here's a special invitation for you and your family to attend our third annual Open House to usher in the holiday season. Please stop in and delight to our brand-new Christmas and seasonal dolls and decorations from all over the world. Refreshments will be served.

OPEN HOUSE HOURS
Friday, November 20, 6:00 - 9:30 p.m.
Saturday, November 21, 10:00 a.m. - 8:00 p.m.
Sunday, November 22, 12:00 noon - 6:00 p.m.

FREE GIFT FOR YOUR CHILD
During our Open House hours, Santa's helpers will be on hand to give a Christmas gift to every child accompanied by an adult.

Stop in at:
Margie's Menagerie, 2801 Little Cross Corner Mall, Alexandria, LA 71307, 318-555-7978.

- Keep the design simple and avoid clutter. You want the reader to be drawn into your message at first glance.

- Highlight any special offer, such as "free gift."

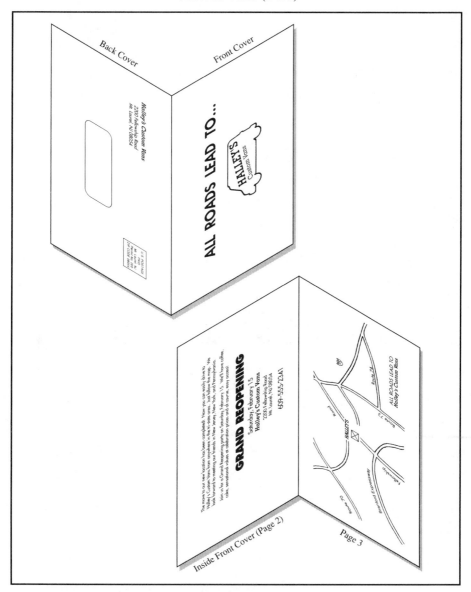

- Sometimes a postcard doesn't allow for quite enough space to get your message across. In such cases, a simple self-mailer may be just right. This 4-panel piece is created by folding an 8" x 8 1/2" sheet or card in half.

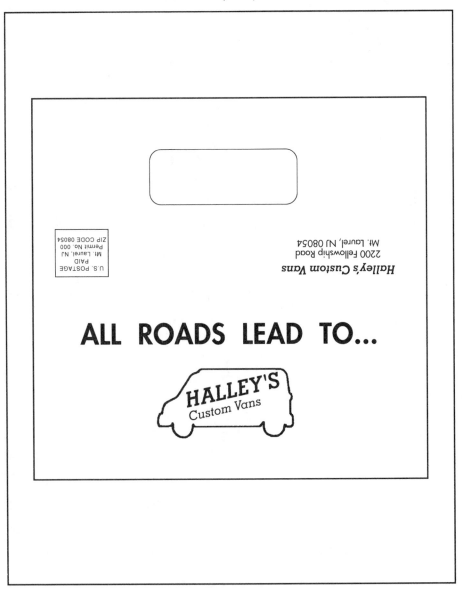

- It's a good idea to develop a slogan that you can use in all your advertising. In this case it's "All Roads Lead To...Halley's."

- Adhesive backed, pre-printed address labels may be easily affixed to this mailer. You can be preparing the labels even before the brochure is back from the printer, or you might wish to have the labels outsourced.

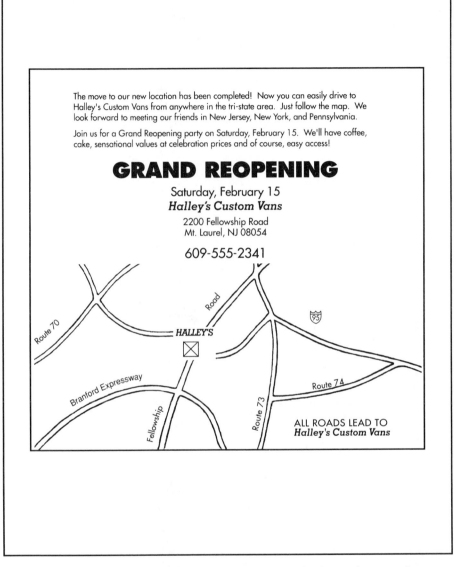

- Special events bring customers. Everything from remodeling/expansion to anniversaries can be used as rationales for special promotions.

- A map is particularly useful when you're announcing a relocation. Stress how easy it is to reach your business from a wide geographic area.

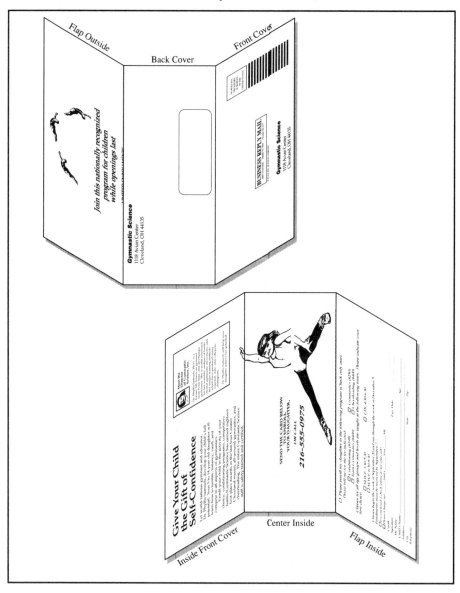

- A 6-panel self-mailer, including a registration form, is perfect for offering classes and seminars. This mailer is created by folding an 8 1/2" x 11" paper or card stock in thirds.

**Join this nationally recognized
program for children
while openings last**

LIMITED ENROLLMENTS
NOW BEING ACCEPTED!

- -

Gymnastic Science
1118 Avian Center
Cleveland, OH 44135

- -

NO POSTAGE
NECESSARY
IF MAILED
IN THE
UNITED STATES

BUSINESS REPLY MAIL
FIRST-CLASS MAIL   PERMIT NO. 0000   Cleveland, OH 44135

POSTAGE WILL BE PAID BY ADDRESSEE

Gymnastic Science
1118 Avian Center
Cleveland, OH 44135

- A strong headline, coupled with eye-catching graphics, make the outside panel of the self-mailer hard to avoid reading.

Give Your Child the Gift of Self-Confidence

Meet the Director of Gymnastic Science, Inc.

Dr. Phyllis Samuels, Ph.D., is a former All-American gymnast from Penn State, and an Olympic performer. She is world-renowned for her scientific analysis of fundamental gymnastic movements, and her unique training methods which have produced many regional, state, and collegiate champions.

Dr. Phyllis Samuels will help your daughter achieve her potential.

Let world-famous gymnast and educator, Dr. Phyllis Samuels, develop your child's full potential. Your 5 to 14 year old daughter will learn how to tumble, balance, vault, and compete in all aspects of gymnastics.

Enroll your child in the activity of your choice: conditioning programs, competitive teams (Gymnastic Science has earned eighteen first-place awards in the last four Greater Cleveland meets), all-around gymnastics, and cheerleading. The entire Gymnastic Science staff is safety trained and certified.

SEND THE CARD BELOW TO ENROLL YOUR DAUGHTER, OR CALL

216-555-0975

☐ Please enroll my daughter in the following program (Check only one).
Please bill me for the fee indicated:

☐ Conditioning ($195) ☐ Gymnastics ($250)
☐ Team Gymnastics ($400) ☐ Cheerleading ($400)

Classes for all age groups and levels are taught at the following times. Please indicate your first choice.

☐ M,W,F: 3:30-5:30 ☐ T,Th: 4:30-6:30
☐ M,W,F: 6:30-8:30

Classes begin the week of September 20 and run through the week of December 5. Enrollments must be received by September 7.

☐ I've enclosed a check *(please do not send cash)*
☐ Please Charge my _____AmEx _____Visa _____MC

Card# _____
Signature _____ Exp. Date _____
My Name _____
Child's Name _____Age _____
Address _____
City _____ State _____ Zip _____
Telephone _____

- Let parents know that enrollment is not open-ended and state when the deadline is.

- The caliber of person running skill centers (art, dance, gymnastics, etc.) is important. Emphasize the credentials of the owner/director.

Brian Holcomb has sold more homes this year than anyone in Providence.

Isn't that the kind of agent you'd like to have working for you and your family?

"I believe I've achieved the #1 position because I'm <u>always</u> available. If a client wants to see your home at 8:00 in the morning or 10:00 at night (and you're agreeable), I'll be there. By shaping my schedule to theirs (and yours), I never miss an opportunity to get you what you deserve."
— Brian Holcomb

Send the enclosed reply card as your first step to getting the price you want for your home.

AUBURN ASSOCIATES
Providence's #1 Realtor

556 Brighton Road
Providence, RI 02886
(401) 555-7333

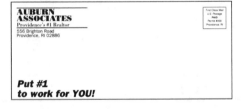

AUBURN ASSOCIATES
Providence's #1 Realtor
556 Brighton Road
Providence, RI 02886

First Class Mail
U.S. Postage
PAID
Permit #000
Providence, RI

Put #1 to work for YOU!

BUSINESS REPLY MAIL
FIRST CLASS MAIL   PERMIT NO. 0000   Providence, RI 02886
POSTAGE WILL BE PAID BY ADDRESSEE

AUBURN ASSOCIATES
Providence's #1 Realtor
556 Brighton Road
Providence, RI 02886

NO POSTAGE
NECESSARY
IF MAILED
IN THE
UNITED STATES

Okay, Brian, I'm interested in having the #1 real estate salesperson help me market my home. Give me a call and we'll set up an appointment for you to visit.

Name _____
Address _____
City _____ State _____ Zip _____
Telephone _____
Best time to call _____

• Lead generation (as opposed to selling) is frequently the objective of a mailing. This package, seeking people who are interested in selling their homes, consists of an 8" x 10" flier, a business reply card and a No. 10 mailing envelope that carries the other pieces and begins the sales message.

Brian Holcomb has sold more homes this year than anyone in Providence.

Isn't that the kind of agent you'd like to have working for you and your family?

"I believe I've achieved the #1 position because I'm <u>always</u> available. If a client wants to see your home at 8:00 in the morning or 10:00 at night (and you're agreeable), I'll be there. By shaping my schedule to theirs (and yours), I never miss an opportunity to get you what you deserve."
— **Brian Holcomb**

Send the enclosed reply card as your first step to getting the price you want for your home.

AUBURN ASSOCIATES
Providence's #1 Realtor

556 Brighton Road
Providence, RI 02886
(401) 555-7333

- A photograph of an individual adds a personal touch to your mailing, and gives the prospective client a feeling of familiarity when they actually meet your staff in the flesh.

- A personal statement from a sales professional tells the client about the service they can expect.

BUSINESS REPLY MAIL

FIRST-CLASS MAIL   PERMIT NO. 99999   Providence, RI 02886

POSTAGE WILL BE PAID BY ADDRESSEE

AUBURN ASSOCIATES
Providence's #1 Realtor

556 Brighton Road
Providence, RI 02886

NO POSTAGE
NECESSARY
IF MAILED
IN THE
UNITED STATES

- It only takes a little bit of extra effort to "dress up" the business reply card with the company logo and slogan.

- This business reply card is the minimum size of 5" x 3 1/2" inches.

Okay, Brian, I'm interested in having the #1 real estate salesperson help me market my home. Give me a call and we'll set up an appointment for you to visit.

Name _____

Address _____

City _____ **State** _____ **Zip** _____

Telephone _____

Best time to call _____

- It's good business to give the respondent some control over the timing of the sales call and it helps ensure that they'll make themselves available when you do call.

**AUBURN
ASSOCIATES**
Providence's #1 Realtor

556 Brighton Road
Providence, RI 02886

First Class Mail
U.S. Postage
PAID
Permit #000
Providence, RI

*Put #1
to work for YOU!*

- Envelope copy can heighten a reader's interest in the contents. This "teaser" copy will help get them inside.

- A question and answer approach works well on two sides of a postcard. This card is somewhat oversized at 8 1/2" x 5 1/2", which is exactly half of a letter-sized sheet. It's convenient and economical to print "two-up" (two to a sheet) at your local print shop.

• The jigsaw puzzle graphic links effectively with the copy which asks "are you puzzled?"

- Since the housing market is constantly changing, most homeowners would find it intriguing to know just what their property is worth, even if they're not considering selling at the present time.

- Once you establish a positive contact with a homeowner, they're more likely to turn to you when they are ready to sell.

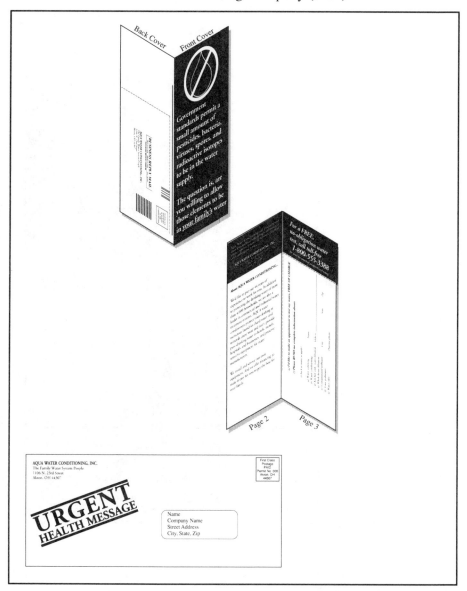

• The same "take-one" brochure that attracts attention in a stand-up display at a trade show or on your business countertop can be used as a strong mailing piece. This dramatic mailing consists of a 4-panel brochure, created by folding a piece of 8" x 8 1/2" paper or card stock in half, and inserting it into a No. 10 envelope.

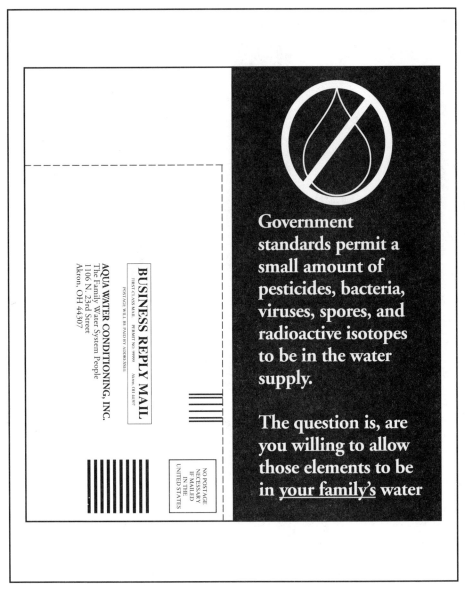

- You don't need a lot of copy to get an important concept across. In fact, powerful short copy will keep a reader focused on your key message.

- A bold graphic draws the reader's attention to your message and reinforces the concept.

Aqua Water Conditioning will produce purer water for your household through an innovative reverse osmosis system that removes dissolved solids and organic wastes.

AQUA WATER CONDITIONING, INC.
The Family Water System People
1106 N. 23rd Street
Akron, OH 44307

For a FREE,
no-obligation water
test, call toll-free
1-800-555-3388

Or mail the attached postpaid card today!

About AQUA WATER CONDITIONING...

We'd like to put our 44 years of experience to work for you. In addition to protecting the drinking water of more than 4,000 households, we are also a leader in commercial and industrial water treatment systems. AQUA water conditioners protect your clothing at numerous laundries (hard water and minerals cause wear and tear), provide pure drinking water to hotels, motels, hospitals, and businesses, and preserve sensitive equipment for many manufacturers.

We install and service our own equipment. And we offer financing to make it easy for you to get the best for your family.

☐ **I'd like to make an appointment to test my water, FREE OF CHARGE**

☐ **Please RUSH me complete information about:**

(Check as many as apply)

☐ Water softening
☐ Water conditioning
☐ Kitchen-only water filtration
☐ Whole-house filtration
☐ Contaminated wellwater
☐ Toxic pollutants
☐ Water odor

Name _____
Address _____
City _____ State _____ Zip _____
Daytime phone _____

• The business reply section can be separated at the perforations and mailed, leaving your company's name and phone number on your promotion for future reference.

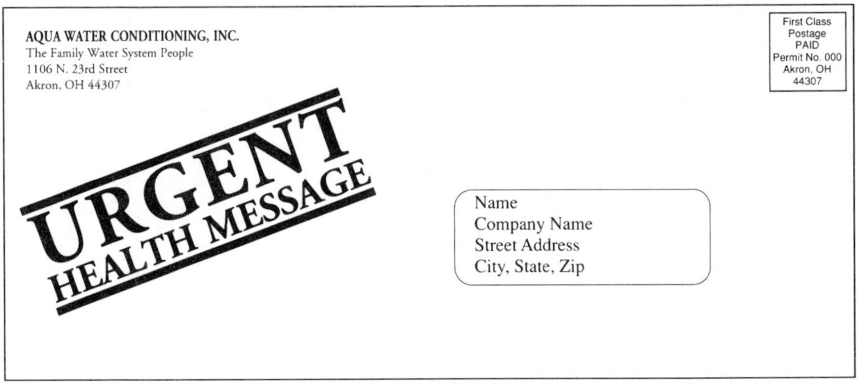

AQUA WATER CONDITIONING, INC.
The Family Water System People
1106 N. 23rd Street
Akron, OH 44307

First Class
Postage
PAID
Permit No. 000
Akron, OH
44307

URGENT
HEALTH MESSAGE

Name
Company Name
Street Address
City, State, Zip

- The word "URGENT" is likely to provoke the reader to open your package. Be sure you don't irritate the prospect by making an outrageous claim in your copy. In this case, valuable health information is actually offered.

Mahaffey Insurance Brokerage
1229 Robbins Street
Warwick, RI 02886

Do you know . . .

. . . that the size of insurance claims paid to homeowners for burglary and theft has actually dropped...while the number of burglary and theft crimes has dramatically risen?

. . . that unless you have at least 80% replacement value built into your homeowner's policy, chances are you'll never recover full value in the event of a fire or other disaster?

. . . under what conditions your insurer can cancel your disability insurance? No? Then, you'd better not get hurt or sick.

For your own peace of mind, take the following 2-minute test to discover what you don't know about your insurance. And then get the answers you need.

Jack Mahaffey

P.S. If you want an insurance agent who will give you the answers you need to be fully protected, call me at 401-555-0944. It won't cost you a penny. Since I'm a broker for numerous insurance companies, I will give you an honest, no-strings appraisal.

The 10-Question Insurance Audit
Prepared by Jack Mahaffey

1. Do you rely on automatic increases in property coverage that are added by your agent or company?
   ☐ YES ☐ NO ☐ I DON'T KNOW
2. Does your fire policy cover only damage done by the flames?
   ☐ YES ☐ NO ☐ I DON'T KNOW
3. If your home has to be demolished because of damage, would your policy cover the total loss, or only the loss caused by the flames?
   ☐ YES ☐ NO ☐ I DON'T KNOW
4. If you're in an automobile accident, and the court awards $250,000 to the person you struck, will your insurance cover the award and legal fees, court costs, and other expenses?
   ☐ YES ☐ NO ☐ I DON'T KNOW
5. If a visitor to your home falls down your stairs, and sues you for medical expenses, pain, suffering, and loss of wages, will your insurance company cover it?
   ☐ YES ☐ NO ☐ I DON'T KNOW
6. If you're part of a two-income family, do you have spouse insurance to compensate for what could be the loss of half the family income?
   ☐ YES ☐ NO ☐ I DON'T KNOW
7. Is term life insurance better for you than whole life insurance?
   ☐ YES ☐ NO ☐ I DON'T KNOW
8. Will you have to wait more than one month after being unable to work before your disability policy coverage begins?
   ☐ YES ☐ NO ☐ I DON'T KNOW
9. If your insurance company doesn't send you a premium reminder and your policy lapses, is the insurer still responsible for any claims?
   ☐ YES ☐ NO ☐ I DON'T KNOW
10. Will your health care plan cover you adequately in a medical emergency?
    ☐ YES ☐ NO ☐ I DON'T KNOW

If you're like most people, you probably don't know the answers to most of these questions...and you're not happy with the answers you gave to the ones you do know. Get the answers you need and the coverage you require. Call Jack Mahaffey at 401-555-0944 for a no-cost, no-obligation review of all of your insurance, or mail the enclosed card.

Mahaffey Insurance Brokerage
1229 Robbins Street
Warwick, RI 02886

U.S. POSTAGE
PAID
Warwick, RI
Permit No. 000
ZIP CODE 02886

**"Taking this
2-minute test
could save you
hundreds of
dollars!"**

NO POSTAGE
NECESSARY
IF MAILED
IN THE
UNITED STATES

Jack Mahaffey
Mahaffey Insurance Brokerage
1229 Robbins Street
Warwick, RI 02886

☐ **Yes. I want to protect my family and conserve my assets. Please call me for a no-obligation review of my insurance program.**

Name _____
Address _____
City _____ State _____ Zip _____
Telephone: _____ (_ Home _ Business)

Best time to call: ____ a.m. ____ p.m.

- It's not necessary to use visual devices in every mailing. Sometimes an all-type presentation is more appropriate, as in this questionnaire mailing. The package consists of a sales letter (4 1/4" x 5 1/2"), the questionnaire (5 1/2" x 8 1/2", folded in half), a business reply card (5 1/2" x 4"), and a mailing envelope (5 3/4" x 4 1/2").

Mahaffey Insurance Brokerage
1229 Robbins Street
Warwick, RI 02886

Do you know . . .

. . . that the size of insurance claims paid to homeowners for burglary and theft has actually dropped...while the number of burglary and theft crimes has dramatically risen?

. . . that unless you have at least 80% replacement value built into your homeowner's policy, chances are you'll never recover full value in the event of a fire or other disaster?

. . . under what conditions your insurer can cancel your disability insurance? No? Then, you'd better not get hurt or sick.

For your own peace of mind, take the following 2-minute test to discover what you don't know about your insurance. And then get the answers you need.

Jack Mahaffey

P.S. If you want an insurance agent who will give you the answers you need to be fully protected, call me at 401-555-0944. It won't cost you a penny. Since I'm a broker for numerous insurance companies, I will give you an honest, no-strings appraisal.

- Some of the most successful direct mail promotions are those that have a personal look (e.g., typewriter style type face).

- The P.S. is the most read section of a sales letter. Use it to make a special offer or restate an important selling point.

The 10-Question Insurance Audit
Prepared by Jack Mahaffey

---

1. Do you rely on automatic increases in property coverage that are added by your agent or company?
   ☐ YES ☐ NO ☐ I DON'T KNOW

2. Does your fire policy cover only damage done by the flames?
   ☐ YES ☐ NO ☐ I DON'T KNOW

3. If your home has to be demolished because of damage, would your policy cover the total loss, or only the loss caused by the flames?
   ☐ YES ☐ NO ☐ I DON'T KNOW

4. If you're in an automobile accident, and the court awards $250,000 to the person you struck, will your insurance cover the award *and* legal fees, court costs, and other expenses?
   ☐ YES ☐ NO ☐ I DON'T KNOW

5. If a visitor to your home falls down your stairs, and sues you for medical expenses, pain, suffering, and loss of wages, will your insurance company cover it?
   ☐ YES ☐ NO ☐ I DON'T KNOW

6. If you're part of a two-income family, do you have spouse insurance to compensate for what could be the loss of half the family income?
   ☐ YES ☐ NO ☐ I DON'T KNOW

7. Is term life insurance better for you than whole life insurance?
   ☐ YES ☐ NO ☐ I DON'T KNOW

8. Will you have to wait more than one month after being unable to work before your disability policy coverage begins?
   ☐ YES ☐ NO ☐ I DON'T KNOW

9. If your insurance company doesn't send you a premium reminder and your policy lapses, is the insurer still responsible for any claims?
   ☐ YES ☐ NO ☐ I DON'T KNOW

10. Will your health care plan cover you adequately in a medical emergency?
    ☐ YES ☐ NO ☐ I DON'T KNOW

If you're like most people, you probably don't know the answers to most of these questions...and you're not happy with the answers you gave to the ones you do know. Get the answers you need and the coverage you require. Call Jack Mahaffey at 401-555-0944 for a no-cost, no-obligation review of all of your insurance, or mail the enclosed card.

• People like *short* questionnaires, and will respond to them in large numbers. Questions can be prepared for virtually any product or service.

NO POSTAGE
NECESSARY
IF MAILED
IN THE
UNITED STATES

Jack Mahaffey
Mahaffey Insurance Brokerage
1229 Robbins Street
Warwick, RI 02886

☐ **Yes. I want to protect my family and conserve my assets. Please call me for a no-obligation review of my insurance program.**

Name _____

Address _____

City _____ State _____ Zip _____

Telephone:_____ (__Home __Business)

Best time to call: ____ a.m. ____ p.m.

• Consumers are barraged with telephone solicitations, many of which come at the most inconvenient times. Since your prospect has an interest in hearing what you have to say, extend them the courtesy of letting them decide when they would welcome your call.

Mahaffey Insurance Brokerage
1229 Robbins Street
Warwick, RI 02886

U.S. POSTAGE
PAID
Warwick, RI
Permit No. 000
ZIP CODE 02886

"Taking this 2-minute test could save you hundreds of dollars!"

• The envelope copy will encourage recipients to look inside.

OFFICE SPACE-SAVERS
1422 S. Patterson Street
Wichita, KS 67202

U.S. POSTAGE
PAID
Wichita, KS
Permit No. 000
ZIP CODE 67202

OUR EXPERTS WILL TURN YOUR OFFICE CHAOS INTO THE ORGANIZED WORKSPACE OF YOUR DREAMS

Just when you think you're over the edge, the space savers at OFFICE SPACE-SAVERS can throw you a lifeline. We sell and install innovative shelving, modular systems, file cabinets and other unique storage systems to help you reorganize and de-clutter!

Let us create a system that works for you. Visit our Office Planning Center today. No appointment necessary.

OFFICE SPACE-SAVERS
1422 S. Patterson Street
Wichita, KS 67202

316-555-0255

Open Monday-Saturday, 10:00-6:00

- Postcards printed in large volume provide a cost effective way to do a bulk mailing and reach a vast market. This card measures 6" x 4" and can be printed on brightly colored card stock.

- You can repeat the same mailing every three to six months. It may be wise to print enough cards for multiple mailings, to reduce your unit cost of the cards.

OFFICE SPACE-SAVERS
1422 S. Patterson Street
Wichita, KS 67202

U.S. POSTAGE
PAID
Wichita, KS
Permit No. 000
ZIP CODE 67202

• Readership surveys consistently show that cartoons generate tremendous interest and will help get your message read— but be sure the cartoon relates directly to your product or service.

OUR EXPERTS WILL TURN YOUR OFFICE CHAOS INTO THE ORGANIZED WORKSPACE OF YOUR DREAMS

Just when you think you're over the edge, the space savers at OFFICE SPACE-SAVERS can throw you a lifeline. We sell and install innovative shelving, modular systems, file cabinets and other unique storage systems to help you reorganize and de-clutter!

Let us create a system that works for you. Visit our Office Planning Center today. No appointment necessary.

OFFICE SPACE-SAVERS
1422 S. Patterson Street
Wichita, KS 67202

316-555-0255

Open Monday-Saturday, 10:00-6:00

- "Before and after illustrations" help bring your message to life. This humorous portrayal works perfectly on the two sides of the postcard.

SMILE. YOUR IN-HOUSE PHOTO ID NEEDS ARE UNDER CONTROL.

CUSTOM PHOTO I.D.
3312 Broadway
St. Paul, MN 55157

Suppliers to Minnesota business, industry, and government since 1975

U.S. POSTAGE
PAID
St. Paul, MN
Permit No. 000
ZIP CODE 55157

First, we'll review your current I.D. card program. Second, we'll help you design whatever changes are necessary. Third, we'll supply, set-up, and maintain all the equipment and supplies you'll need. And fourth, we'll train your people to operate this important in-house service.

Here's how we'll make you smile:

• Help you create the photo ID card system that fits your needs.

• Handle the installation and subsequent maintenance.

• Explain the variations in equipment and materials that are available to you, including laminators (desk top to industrial roll), photo cutters (electric, desk top or hand-held), badge clips and attachments, lettering systems and supplies, and everything else required for your operation.

• Show you how to use your existing personnel files to print data, barcode, and PC graphics.

Call us and we'll send you FREE samples of our quality photo ID cards, with electronic image counters, keyless entry and other features.

CALL 612-555-9494
for Sales, Information, Service

We service everything we sell. And we guarantee 48-hour repair service or you don't pay for the service!

SMILE

• A really good mailing can turn a negative into a positive by solving a difficult problem. This 7'" x 4" postcard offers solutions and instills confidence.

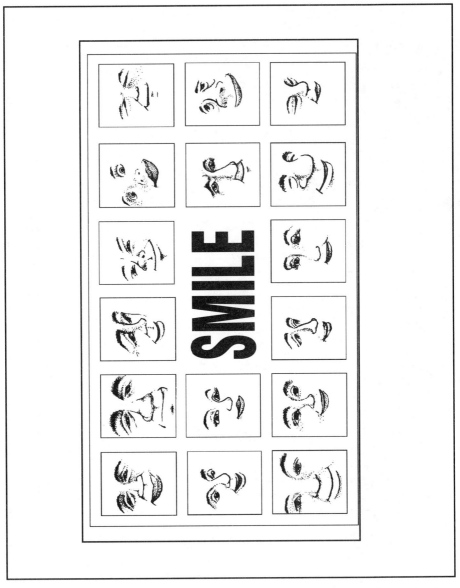

- The amusing and eye-catching graphic gets this mailing off on the right foot and makes the reader wonder what you're up to.

U.S. POSTAGE
PAID
St. Paul, MN
Permit No. 000
ZIP CODE 55157

CUSTOM
PHOTO I.D.
3312 Broadway
St. Paul, MN 55157

Suppliers to
Minnesota
business, industry,
and government
since 1975

SMILE. YOUR IN-HOUSE
PHOTO ID NEEDS ARE
UNDER CONTROL.

First, we'll review your current I.D. card program. Second, we'll help you design whatever changes are necessary. Third, we'll supply, set-up, and maintain all the equipment and supplies you'll need. And fourth, we'll train your people to operate this important in-house service.

Here's how we'll make you smile:

• Help you create the photo ID card system that fits your needs.

• Handle the installation and subsequent maintenance.

• Explain the variations in equipment and materials that are available to you, including laminators (desk top to industrial roll), photo cutters (electric, desk top or hand-held), badge clips and attachments, lettering systems and supplies, and everything else required for your operation.

• Show you how to use your existing personnel files to print data, barcode, and PC graphics.

Call us and we'll send you FREE samples of our quality photo ID cards, with electronic image counters, keyless entry and other features.

CALL 612-555-9494
for Sales, Information, Service

We service everything we sell. And we guarantee 48-hour repair service or you don't pay for the service!

• Follow through on the theme by explaining just what will cause the reader to feel happy. Here, the word "smile" is linked not only to photographs, but also to the way the reader will feel about your service.

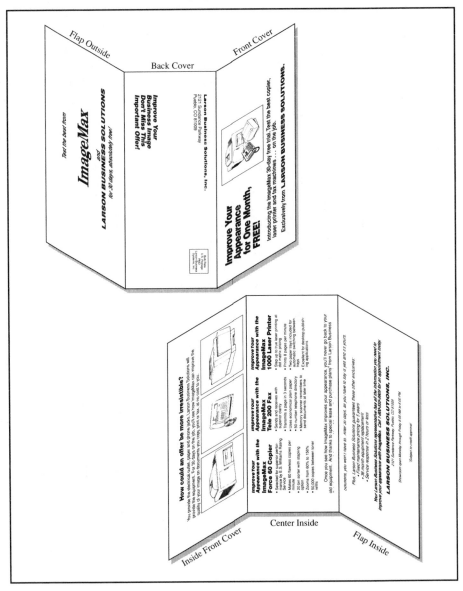

- A 6-panel brochure offers a good, relatively inexpensive compromise between a postcard and a traditional mailing (which would contain several components within an envelope). This brochure is created by folding a sheet of 8 1/2" x 11" paper or card stock into thirds.

Test the best from

ImageMax

and

LARSON BUSINESS SOLUTIONS

for 30 days, absolutely free!

Important Offer!
Don't Miss This
Business Image
Improve Your

2121 Sundance Parkway
Pueblo, CO 81009

Larson Business Solutions, Inc.

Bulk Rate
U.S. Postage
PAID
Larson Business
Systems, Inc.

Improve Your Appearance for One Month, FREE!

Introducing the ImageMax 30-day free trial. Test the best copier, laser printer and fax machines ... on the job.

Exclusively from **LARSON BUSINESS SOLUTIONS.**

- A clever play on words, such as "Improve Your Appearance" captures the reader's attention. Add the word "FREE" and you've got a very strong selling proposition.

How could an offer be more irresistible?

You provide the electrical outlet, paper and phone jacks. Larson Business Solutions will provide the equipment. For 30 days on the job, you'll see how ImageMax can improve the quality of your image on documents you copy, print or fax, at no cost to you.

ImproveYour Appearance with the ImageMax Force 60 Copier

- Selected for superior performance by E.S. Williams Rating Service
- Makes 60 flawless copies per minute
- 20 bin sorter with stapling option
- Zooms from 60% to 156%
- 50,000 copies between toner refills

ImproveYour Appearance with the ImageMax Tele 200 Fax

- Sends and receives with superior clarity
- Transmits a page in 3 seconds
- Uses economical plain paper
- 50-number telephone directory
- Memory scanner remembers to send documents at later time

ImproveYour Appearance with the ImageMax 1000 Laser Printer

- Step up to true laser printing at dot matrix pricing
- Prints 8 pages per minute
- Two paper trays included for automatic switching between trays
- Excellent for desktop publishing applications

Once you see how ImageMax improves your appearance, you'll never go back to your old equipment. And thanks to special lease and purchase plans* from Larson Business Solutions, you won't have to. After 30 days, all you have to say is yes and it's yours.

Plus, Larson Business Solutions guarantees these other exclusives:
- Fixed maintenance pricing for 5 years
- 36 month equipment replacement
- Service response in 2 hours or less

Your Larson Business Solutions representative has all the information you need to improve your appearance with ImageMax. Call 1-800-555-9909 for an appointment today.

LARSON BUSINESS SOLUTIONS, INC.

2121 Sundance Parkway, Pueblo, CO 81009

Showroom open Monday through Friday 8:00 AM to 6:00 PM.

*Subject to credit approval

- Be sure to mention any exclusive features you provide to enhance the appeal of your offer (for example "service response in 2 hours or less").

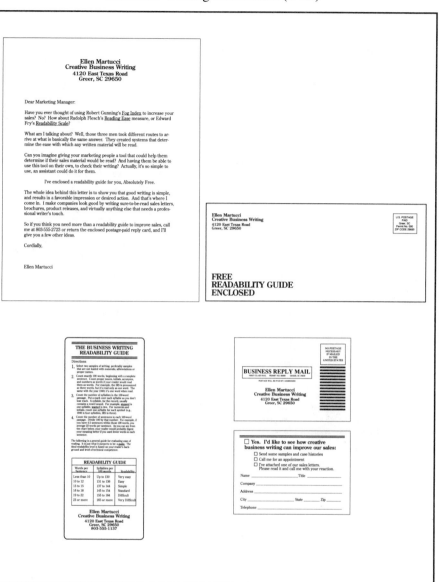

- A mailing's response can be improved by including a premium directly related to the product or service being offered. This package consists of a sales letter, a "readability guide" and a business reply card (BRC), inserted into a No. 10 envelope. The guide is 3 1/2" x 8 1/2", while the BRC is 5" x 3 1/2". With the sales letter folded in thirds, the elements easily fit into the No. 10 envelope, which measures 9 1/2" x 4 1/8".

Ellen Martucci
Creative Business Writing
4120 East Texas Road
Greer, SC 29650

Dear Marketing Manager:

Have you ever thought of using Robert Gunning's Fog Index to increase your sales? No? How about Rudolph Flesch's Reading Ease measure, or Edward Fry's Readability Scale?

What am I talking about? Well, those three men took different routes to arrive at what is basically the same answer. They created systems that determine the ease with which any written material will be read.

Can you imagine giving your marketing people a tool that could help them determine if their sales material would be read? And having them be able to use this tool on their own, to check their writing? Actually, it's so simple to use, an assistant could do it for them.

I've enclosed a readability guide for you, Absolutely Free.

The whole idea behind this letter is to show you that good writing is simple, and results in a favorable impression or desired action. And that's where I come in. I make companies look good by writing sure-to-be-read sales letters, brochures, product releases, and virtually anything else that needs a professional writer's touch.

So if you think you need more than a readability guide to improve sales, call me at 803-555-2723 or return the enclosed postage-paid reply card, and I'll give you a few other ideas.

Cordially,

Ellen Martucci

• This sales letter asks a lot of questions and raises a lot of issues, which only works when the subject matter is of particular interest to the reader. Any technique that makes the reader want to continue reading is worth using.

• Be sure to explain your premium in the sales letter—don't expect the reader to guess why it's been included in your mailing.

THE BUSINESS WRITING READABILITY GUIDE

Directions

1. Select two samples of writing, preferably samples that are not loaded with numerals, abbreviations or proper names.

2. Count exactly 100 words, beginning with a complete sentence. Count proper nouns, initials, acronyms, and numbers as words if your reader would read them as words. For example, the IRS is pronounced as three words, but it's read only as one word. The same with the year 1940; it's one word when read.

3. Count the number of syllables in the 100-word passage. Put a mark over each syllable so you don't lose track. A syllable, for the record, usually contains a vowel sound. For example, stopped is one syllable, wanted is two. For numerals and initials, count one syllable for each symbol (e.g., 1940 is four syllables, IRS is three).

4. Count the number of sentences in each 100-word passage. Divide 100 by that number. For example, if you have 4.5 sentences within those 100 words, you average 22 words per sentence. As you can see from the chart below, your reader would probably digest your meaning better if you used fewer words in each sentence.

The following is a general guide for evaluating ease of reading. It is just what it purports to be: a guide. The ideal readability level is based on your reader's background and level of technical competence.

READABILITY GUIDE

Words per Sentence	Syllables per 100 words	Readability
Less than 10	Up to 130	Very easy
10 to 12	131 to 136	Easy
13 to 15	137 to 144	Simple
16 to 18	145 to 154	Standard
19 to 22	155 to 164	Difficult
23 or more	165 or more	Very Difficult

Ellen Martucci
Creative Business Writing
4120 East Texas Road
Greer, SC 29650
803-555-1137

• The premium doesn't need to be expensive, but it should have value to the recipient and relate to the offer.

Ellen Martucci
Creative Business Writing
4120 East Texas Road
Greer, SC 29650

U.S. POSTAGE
PAID
Greer, SC
Permit No. 000
ZIP CODE 29650

**FREE
READABILITY GUIDE
ENCLOSED**

• The envelope prominently mentions the free premium, which will encourage the reader to open it.

NO POSTAGE
NECESSARY
IF MAILED
IN THE
UNITED STATES

BUSINESS REPLY MAIL

FIRST-CLASS MAIL   PERMIT NO. 00000   GREER, SC 29650

POSTAGE WILL BE PAID BY ADDRESSEE

Ellen Martucci
Creative Business Writing
4120 East Texas Road
Greer, SC 29650

☐ **Yes. I'd like to see how creative business writing can improve our sales:**

☐ Send some samples and case histories
☐ Call me for an appointment
☐ I've attached one of our sales letters.
   Please read it and call me with your reaction.

Name _____ Title _____

Company _____

Address _____

City _____ State _____ Zip _____

Telephone _____

- The business reply card provides a simple vehicle by which the customer can respond. (Asking the respondent to apply postage is a sure way to discourage response.)

- Check-off boxes give respondents choices—and make what might otherwise seem like a hard sell more "user friendly."

- Whether you're mailing to an existing customer base or targeting new prospects, your direct mail solicitation should tell your company's story as clearly and attractively as possible. This 6-panel brochure on 8 1/2" x 11" card stock is folded into thirds.

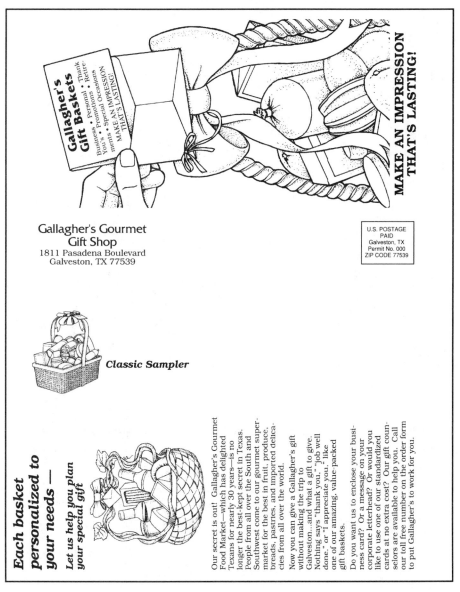

Gallagher's Gift Baskets
Business • Promotions • Personal • Thank
You's • Special Occasions • Retirements
MAKE AN IMPRESSION THAT'S LASTING!

MAKE AN IMPRESSION THAT'S LASTING!

**Gallagher's Gourmet
Gift Shop**
1811 Pasadena Boulevard
Galveston, TX 77539

U.S. POSTAGE
PAID
Galveston, TX
Permit No. 000
ZIP CODE 77539

Classic Sampler

Each basket personalized to your needs —

Let us help you plan your special gift

Our secret is out! Gallagher's Gourmet Food Market—which has delighted Texans for nearly 30 years—is no longer the best-kept secret in Texas. People from all over the South and Southwest come to our gourmet supermarket for the best in fruit, produce, breads, pastries, and imported delicacies from all over the world.

Now you can give a Gallagher's gift without making the trip to Galveston...and what a gift to give. Nothing says "thank you," "job well done," or "I appreciate you," like one of our amazing, value-packed gift baskets.

Do you want us to enclose your business card? Or a message on your corporate letterhead? Or would you like to use one of our standardized cards at no extra cost? Our gift counselors are available to help you. Call our toll free number on the order form to put Gallagher's to work for you.

• Retailers have discovered that direct mail can be a sales-builder. It can extend the reach of a store beyond driveable distance, and it can also generate more store traffic. Either way, it's a winner.

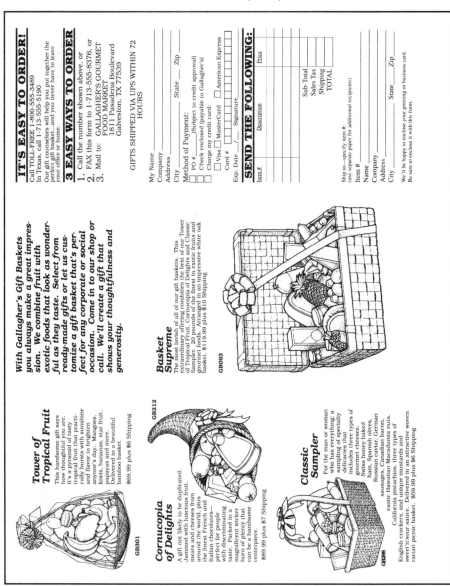

- Make sure the style of your graphics is in synch with your market. In this case, upscale gift baskets require the use of a somewhat refined art style.

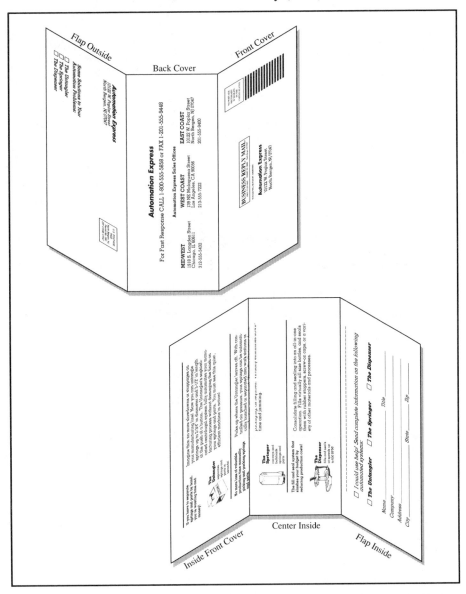

- Whatever your business, keep your mailings focused, clear and attractive, as in this 6-panel brochure which is printed on 8 1/2" x 11" card stock folded into thirds.

☐ **The Dispenser**
☐ **The Springer**
☐ **The Untangler**
Automation Problems:
Some Solutions to Your

U.S. POSTAGE
PAID
North Bergen, NJ
Permit No. 000
ZIP CODE 07047

North Bergen, NJ 07047
10122 W. Poplar Street
Automation Express

Automation Express

For Fast Response CALL 1-800-555-5858 or FAX 1-201-555-9448

Automation Express Sales Offices

MIDWEST	WEST COAST	EAST COAST
1918 S. Langden Street	139 NE Malaguena Street	10122 W. Poplar Street
Chicago, IL 60611	Los Angeles, CA 90056	North Bergen, NJ 07047
312-555-5432	213-555-7222	201-555-9400

NO POSTAGE
NECESSARY
IF MAILED
IN THE
UNITED STATES

BUSINESS REPLY MAIL
FIRST-CLASS MAIL   PERMIT NO. 00000   North Bergen, NJ 07047

POSTAGE WILL BE PAID BY ADDRESSEE

Automation Express
10122 W. Poplar Street
North Bergen, NJ 07047

• Be sure to utilize every inch of your mailing to best advantage. Your name, address, phone and fax numbers should be prominent, and are easy to find here on their own panel.

If you have to separate springs and parts by hand, you're wasting time and money!

The Untangler

separates springs and parts in seconds!

Imagine this: no more slowdowns or stoppages on your manufacturing line! Now you can untangle springs up to 2-3/4" in diameter and 3-1/2" in length at the push of a button. The Untangler's sophisticated centrifugal system fully automates your manufacturing process without damaging the finish on your springs and parts. You must see this quiet, efficient machine in action!

No more loss of valuable production time manually picking and packing springs and parts.

The Springer

conveys and bulkloads springs and parts.

Picks up where the Untangler leaves off. With controlled air pressure, your springs can be automatically bunched or separated into work stations or packaging, as required. Virtually eliminates downtime and jamming.

The fill and seal system that slashes your budget by reducing production costs!

The Dispenser

fills and seals at speeds up to 650 BPM!

Consolidate filling and sealing into an all-in-one operation. Fills virtually all size bottles, and seals them with rubber stoppers, screw-on caps, or a variety of other materials and processes.

☐ I could use help! Send complete information on the following automated systems:

☐ **The Untangler**   ☐ **The Springer**   ☐ **The Dispenser**

Name _____ Title _____

Company _____

Address _____

City _____ State _____ Zip _____

- Instead of sending expensive catalogs to untested mailing lists, first send mailings that will qualify a prospect's interest.

- Simple illustrations with captions tell the story quickly and keep your production costs low.

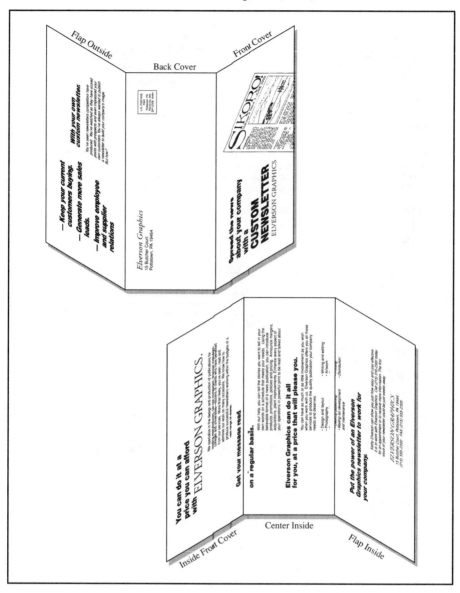

- If you're selling a design service, be extra careful to have your mailing reflect the quality of your work. Mail your offer to prospects or use it as a "take one" in your office or in locations that prospects might visit. This 6-panel brochure measures 8 1/2" x 11".

— Keep your current customers buying.
— Generate more sales leads.
— Improve employee and supplier relations

With your own custom newsletter.

You've seen newsletters competitors have produced. You've watched as they have scored points with prospects and even impressed your own customers. You've always wanted to publish a newsletter to build your company's image. But how?

Elverson Graphics
15 Butcher Court
Pottstown, PA 19464

U.S. POSTAGE
PAID
Pottstown, PA
Permit No. 000
ZIP CODE 19464

Spread the news about your company with a
CUSTOM NEWSLETTER
ELVERSON GRAPHICS

- Businesses are always looking for new ways to boost sales. Be sure to spell out the rationale for selecting your services.

- Illustrating the kind of work you do entices the reader.

You can do it at a price you can afford

with ELVERSON GRAPHICS.

We specialize in the design and production of publications for leading manufacturers, service companies, financial institutions, colleges and universities—dozens of clients who have benefited from our services. More than likely, you've seen, read and admired our work on many occasions. We know how to produce successful newsletters working within the budgets of a vast range of clients.

Get your message read on a regular basis.

With our help, you can tell the stories you want to tell in your own words on a schedule that meets your needs. Using the believable format of a news publication, you can introduce products, promotions, policies and pricing. Announce mergers, acquisitions, plant improvements. Enhance every aspect of your operations in powerful print to be read and talked about.

Elverson Graphics can do it all for you, at a price that will please you.

You can have as much or as little involvement as you wish when you work with us. Elverson Graphics offers you all these services to produce the quality publication your company needs and deserves:

- Design and layout
- Photography
- Desktop publishing
- Mailing list development and maintenance
- Writing and editing
- Artwork
- Printing
- Distribution

Put the power of an Elverson Graphics newsletter to work for your company.

Kathy Elverson can show you just how easy and cost effective it is to work with Elverson Graphics. Call (215) 555-2300 today for an appointment or to receive more information. The first issue of your newsletter could be just weeks away.

ELVERSON GRAPHICS
15 Butcher Court, Pottstown, PA 19464
(215) 555-2300   FAX (215) 555-2305

- Build your case through headlines and subheads which tell your overall story. Let supporting copy amplify your message.

- Don't wait for prospects to call you. Follow up by calling the people who have received your brochure.

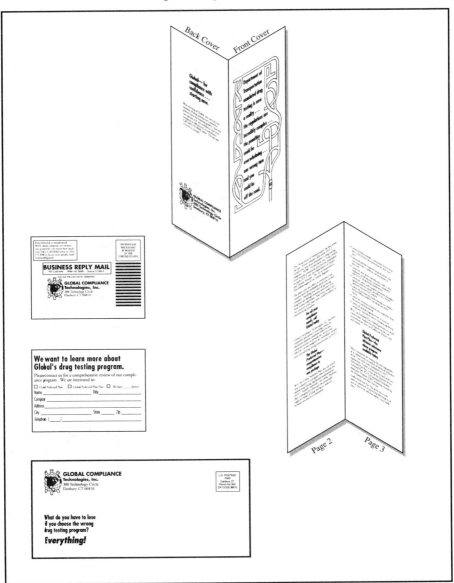

- Mailings that alert a targeted audience to new regulations will be sure to grab readers' attention if they combine strong graphics with critical information. This direct mail solicitation consists of a 4-panel brochure 8" x 8 1/2", folded in half, and a 5" x 3 1/2" business reply card, enclosed in a No. 10 envelope.

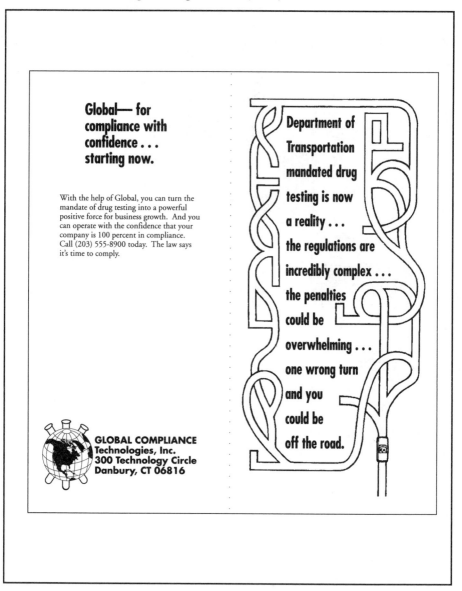

Global— for compliance with confidence . . . starting now.

With the help of Global, you can turn the mandate of drug testing into a powerful positive force for business growth. And you can operate with the confidence that your company is 100 percent in compliance. Call (203) 555-8900 today. The law says it's time to comply.

GLOBAL COMPLIANCE Technologies, Inc. 300 Technology Circle Danbury, CT 06816

Department of Transportation mandated drug testing is now a reality . . . the regulations are incredibly complex . . . the penalties could be overwhelming . . . one wrong turn and you could be off the road.

• Make sure your visual provides a clear, understandable connection to the message. In this case, the use of a maze is a literal interpretation of the possible problems faced by the reader in navigating through government regulations.

The Department of Transportation has laid down the law. If your company falls under D.O.T. jurisdiction, you must implement a drug testing program. NOW! Furthermore, you must comply with complex procedures and policies established by both D.O.T. and the Department of Health and Human Services. The list of requirements fills endless pages of the Federal Register.

The sheer time and effort of compliance can interfere with the profitable operations of your company. Handling your own drug testing program can damage relations with even your most trusted employees. And if you make just one innocent error, your firm could be subject to overwhelming penalties.

For all your compliance needs, call Global today

Global Compliance Technologies, Inc. has been created by specialists in trucking, medicine, laboratory analysis, employee relations and computer science to provide you with a cost-effective, turnkey program for immediate compliance with all drug testing requirements of D.O.T.

The Global Preferred Plan— comprehensive compliance in one package

With the Global Preferred Plan, you can enroll your company in a program which exceeds the federal drug testing regulations established by D.O.T. Equally important, the Global Preferred Plan is designed to eliminate the potentially negative impact of drug testing on relations between you and your employees.

- Global will help establish a customized, formal drug policy with written documentation for your company.
- Global will provide employee drug education, and train supervisors in policies and procedures in detection.
- Global will issue photo identification cards to your employees certifying your company's compliance with D.O.T. drug testing requirements.
- Global will collect and transport specimens through a rigorous chain-of-custody procedure to a NIDA-approved laboratory for analysis.
- Global will evaluate test results through our Medical Review Officers (MRO) and advise you of the results.
- Global will maintain records of your employees' drug education and drug testing.
- Global will provide ongoing review to maintain compliance required by new or changing regulations.

With the Preferred Plan, Global provides you with a worry-free, trouble-free program so you can concentrate on more profitable use of your time and money.

Global Preferred Plan Plus—the ultimate substance abuse program available today

Many companies are viewing the new regulations as an opportunity to combat all forms of substance abuse—not only those mandated by D.O.T. regulations. Global is meeting this need with our Preferred Plan Plus. It has all the features of our Preferred Plan, PLUS an expanded Employee Assistance Program (EAP) including counseling for employees and their families.

Global Preferred Plan Plus gives you a new, positive approach to protecting the integrity of one of your most precious assets—your work force.

- When offering a program that is mandated by the government, don't be afraid to focus on your prospects' fears. You're providing a legitimate service to keep them out of trouble.

- Offer reassurance that your service can handle all phases competently.

We want to learn more about Global's drug testing program.

Please contact us for a comprehensive review of our compliance program. We are interested in:

☐ Global Preferred Plan ☐ Global Preferred Plan Plus ☐ We have _____ drivers

Name _____ Title_____

Company _____

Address _____

City _____ State _____ Zip _____

Telephone (_____) _____

Don't be misled or misinformed! While certain companies are exempt, you may not be—no matter how small your firm is. Call Global today at (203) 555-8900 to discuss your specific needs without obligation!

NO POSTAGE
NECESSARY
IF MAILED
IN THE
UNITED STATES

BUSINESS REPLY MAIL
FIRST-CLASS MAIL   PERMIT NO. 00000   Danbury, CT 06810

POSTAGE WILL BE PAID BY ADDRESSEE

GLOBAL COMPLIANCE Technologies, Inc.
300 Technology Circle
Danbury, CT 06810

- Keep requests for information easy to fill out but ask for sufficient information so you can properly fulfill the request.

- Your sales message and company logo can be carried onto all parts of the direct mail package, including the business reply card.

- This envelope's urgent message will be hard for the recipient to ignore. They will almost certainly open the envelope if drug testing is done—or being considered—at their company.

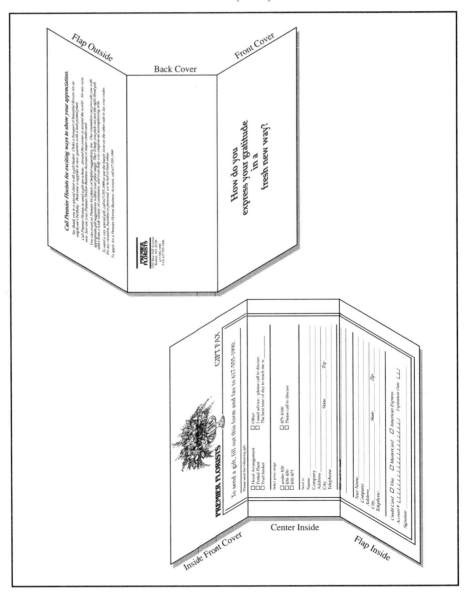

Flap Outside

Back Cover

Front Cover

Center Inside

Inside Front Cover

Flap Inside

- Direct mail can have many goals. This 8 1/2" x 11" self-mailer folded into thirds is designed to generate faxed orders. Key to its success is its easy-to-fill-out, yet comprehensive, order form.

Call Premier Florists for exciting ways to show your appreciation.

Say thank you to a special client with a gift basket. Order a bouquet of beautiful flowers for an employee's birthday. Welcome a supplier to new quarters with a lush potted plant.

Call Premier Florists to send a gift anywhere...around the corner or around the world...for any occasion. Just use your Premier Florists Business Account or major credit card.

You can count on Premier for plenty of helpful suggestions, too. Our counselors can provide you with appropriate gift suggestions within your price range. They'll help you pick out just the right floral gift, select from a wide variety of containers, and even help you compose an accompanying note.

To send a very special gift, call 617-555-1999 or use the handy form on the other side to fax your order. For any occasion, business or personal, we're full of fresh ideas.

To apply for a Premier Florists Business Account, call 617-555-1999

1232 Blue Hill Avenue
Boston, MA 02126
617-555-1999
FAX 617-555-1990

How do you express your gratitude in a fresh new way?

- Certain businesses, such as florists, are often called upon to help customers who don't really know how to select what they want. Offering to help resolve that uncertainty is a winning approach.

PREMIER FLORISTS   GIFT FAX

To send a gift, fill out this form and fax to 617-555-1990.

Please send the following gift:

☐ Floral Arrangement   ☐ Other
☐ Potted Plant   ☐ I need advice—please call to discuss.
☐ Fruit basket   The best time of day to reach me is _____

Select price range:

☐ under $30   ☐ $75–$100
☐ $30–$50   ☐ Please call to discuss
☐ $50–$75

Send to:
Name_____
Company _____
Address _____
City_____ State_____ Zip _____
Telephone _____

Gift card to read_____
_____

Your Name_____
Company _____
Address_____
City_____ State_____ Zip _____
Telephone _____

Credit Card ☐ Visa   ☐ MasterCard   ☐ American Express
Account # |_|_|_|_|_|_|_|_|_|_|_|_|_|_|_|_|_|_|_|_|_|_| Expiration Date |_|_|
Signature _____

- Everything the customer would communicate in person or on the phone is contained in this well executed order form. In addition, there is an option to have the florist call "to discuss."

- In the age of instant everything, customers will be pleased to use a convenient fax order form.

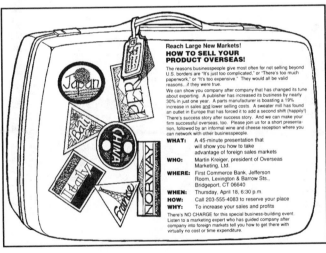

- An oversized postcard, such as this 7" x 5" piece, will get noticed—provided that it employs strong graphics and arresting copy.

• The front of this postcard allows ample space for a message and illustration.

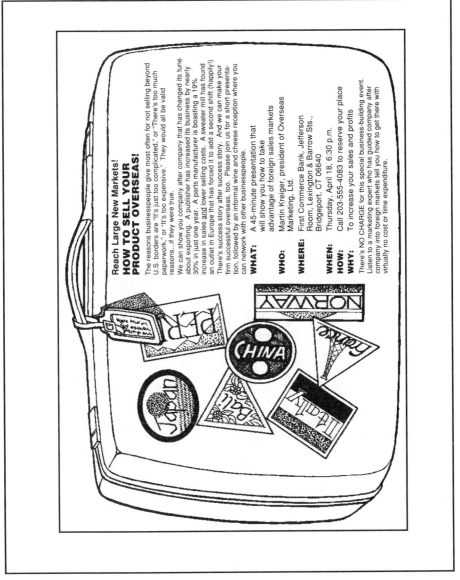

- Free public seminars can open doors that sales calls may not; they can attract large numbers of prospects who might not otherwise hear of your services.

- Include refreshments to increase attendance and demonstrate your eagerness to treat customers well.

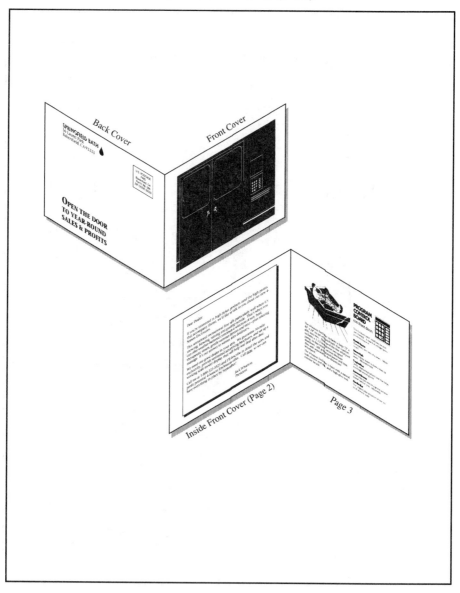

- Self-mailers don't always have to use conventional formats. This horizontal 5 1/2" x 4 1/4" mailer is well suited to dramatizing the product illustrations.

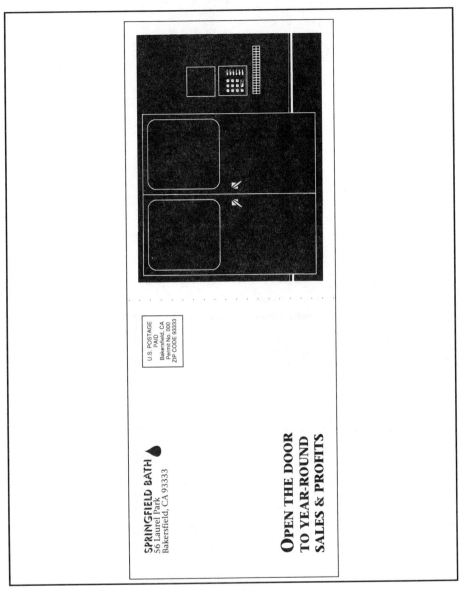

- The outside spread presents an intriguing message and mysterious doors, which generates irresistible curiosity.

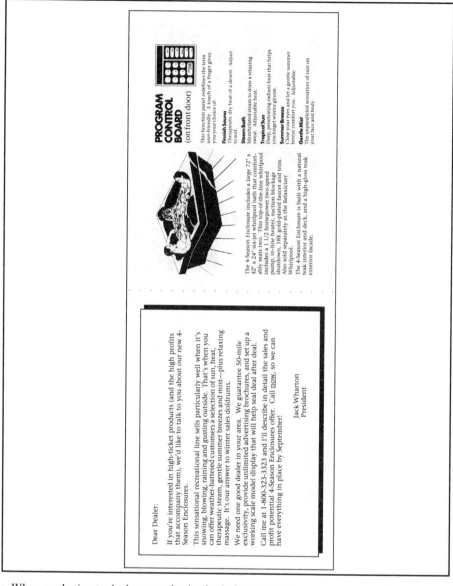

- When marketing to dealers, emphasize both the appeal of your products to the consumer and the opportunity to make substantial profits.

- Most product pictures have more sales appeal when humans are included.

Company Name
Address
City, State Zip

Date

There are two reasons
to notify you this early
about our October 1 price increase.

Dear Buyer:

Not much has changed in our nearly fifty years of providing you cost-effective cartons. Our boxes are still the best (conforming above government specifications) and our service is still the most dependable. And even though prices will show a modest increase in six months, you can turn that to your advantage:

Reason #1:   You have the opportunity to stock up on all your protective packaging needs at current pricing. (Save thousands of dollars by acting now!)

Reason #2:   You have plenty of time to budget for our modest price increase.

Our goal is to meet all your shipping needs at a reasonable cost, whether it's an inventory item or a custom-designed container. And we'll continue to do it—whether you need 10 boxes or 10,000—with our famous fast, personal service.

Thanks for your continued patronage.

Sincerely,

Edward Welles

P.S. Don't delay. Send the enclosed order form now (or call 1-800-555-2380) and earn super savings before next fall's price increases!

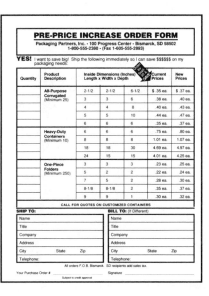

PRE-PRICE INCREASE ORDER FORM

Packaging Partners, Inc. • 100 Progress Center • Bismarck, SD 58502
1-800-555-2380 • (Fax 1-605-555-2893)

YES! I want to save big! Ship the following immediately so I can save $$$$$$ on my packaging needs:

Quantity	Product Description	Inside Dimensions (Inches) Length x Width x Depth			Current Prices	New Prices
	All-Purpose Corrugated (Minimum 25)	2-1/2	2-1/2	6-1/2	$ .35 ea.	$ .37 ea.
		3	3	6	.38 ea.	.40 ea.
		4	4	8	.40 ea.	.43 ea.
		5	5	10	.44 ea.	.47 ea.
		6	6	6	.35 ea.	.37 ea.
	Heavy-Duty Containers (Minimum 10)	6	6	6	.75 ea.	.80 ea.
		8	8	8	1.01 ea.	1.07 ea.
		18	18	30	4.69 ea.	4.97 ea.
		24	15	15	4.01 ea.	4.25 ea.
	One-Piece Folders (Minimum 250)	3	3	3	.23 ea.	.25 ea.
		5	2	2	.22 ea.	.24 ea.
		7	5	2	.28 ea.	.30 ea.
		8-1/8	8-1/8	2	.35 ea.	.37 ea.
		9	9	1	.30 ea.	.32 ea.

CALL FOR QUOTES ON CUSTOMIZED CONTAINERS

SHIP TO:			BILL TO: (If Different)		
Name			Name		
Title			Title		
Company			Company		
Address			Address		
City	State	Zip	City	State	Zip
Telephone:			Telephone:		

All orders F.O.B. Bismarck, SD recipients add sales tax.

Your Purchase Order # _____   Signature _____

Subject to credit approval

• Sometimes a direct mail package can be as simple in design as two sheets of letter-size paper that can be inserted into the company's regular business envelope. This package includes an announcement of a price increase, along with an order form allowing customers to order for a limited time at the old prices.

Company Name
Address
City, State Zip

Date

<u>There are two reasons</u>
<u>to notify you this early</u>
<u>about our October 1 price increase.</u>

Dear Buyer:

Not much has changed in our nearly fifty years of providing you cost-effective cartons. Our boxes are still the best (conforming <u>above</u> government specifications) and our service is still the most dependable. And even though prices will show a modest increase in six months, you can turn that to your advantage:

Reason #1:   You have the opportunity to stock up on all your protective packaging needs at current pricing. (<u>Save thousands of dollars</u> by acting now!)

Reason #2:   You have plenty of time to budget for our modest price increase.

Our goal is to meet all your shipping needs at a reasonable cost, whether it's an inventory item or a custom-designed container. And we'll continue to do it—whether you need 10 boxes or 10,000—with our famous fast, personal service.

Thanks for your continued patronage.

Sincerely,

Edward Welles

P.S. Don't delay. Send the enclosed order form now (or call 1-800-555-2380) and earn super savings before next fall's price increases!

• Don't apologize for price increases; they're part of doing business.

• Remember that every correspondence is an opportunity to sell a positive image. Reinforce your leadership role.

PRE-PRICE INCREASE ORDER FORM

Packaging Partners, Inc. • 100 Progress Center • Bismarck, SD 58502
1-800-555-2380 • (Fax 1-605-555-2893)

YES! I want to save big! Ship the following immediately so I can save $$$$$$ on my packaging needs:

Order by Sept. 30 & SAVE

Quantity	Product Description	Inside Dimensions (Inches) Length x Width x Depth			Current Prices	New Prices
	All-Purpose Corrugated (Minimum 25)	2-1/2	2-1/2	6-1/2	$ .35 ea.	$ .37 ea.
		3	3	6	.38 ea.	.40 ea.
		4	4	8	.40 ea.	.43 ea.
		5	5	10	.44 ea.	.47 ea.
		6	6	6	.35 ea.	.37 ea.
	Heavy-Duty Containers (Minimum 10)	6	6	6	.75 ea.	.80 ea.
		8	8	8	1.01 ea.	1.07 ea.
		18	18	30	4.69 ea.	4.97 ea.
		24	15	15	4.01 ea.	4.25 ea.
	One-Piece Folders (Minimum 250)	3	3	3	.23 ea.	.25 ea.
		5	2	2	.22 ea.	.24 ea.
		7	5	2	.28 ea.	.30 ea.
		8-1/8	8-1/8	2	.35 ea.	.37 ea.
		9	9	1	.30 ea.	.32 ea.

CALL FOR QUOTES ON CUSTOMIZED CONTAINERS

SHIP TO:

Name
Title
Company
Address
City   State   Zip
Telephone:

BILL TO: (If Different)

Name
Title
Company
Address
City   State   Zip
Telephone:

All orders F.O.B. Bismarck. SD recipients add sales tax.

Your Purchase Order # _____   Signature _____

Subject to credit approval

• Include an order form to encourage purchasing before prices go up.

• Be sure to indicate the "before and after" pricing clearly on the form.

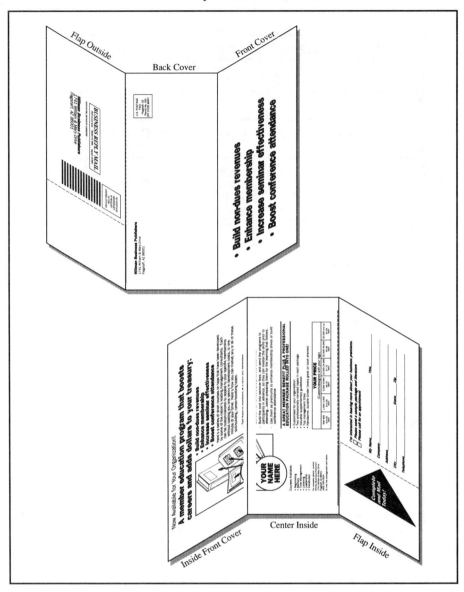

- Reply cards that give the recipient a way to request additional information are an essential element of any mailing designed to sell high-ticket items. The 8 1/2" x 11" format is sufficiently large to accommodate the reply card and still leave ample space for the specifics of the offer.

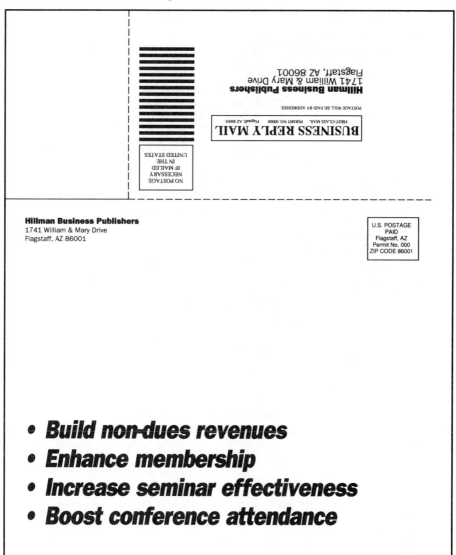

- Tailor your promotion to niche markets. For example, if you're trying to sell to non-profit organizations, you need to stress items such as "non-dues revenue." By speaking the language of the target audience you increase sales dramatically.

Now Available for Your Organization!
A member education program that boosts careers and adds dollars to your treasury:

YOUR NAME HERE

• Build non-dues revenues
• Enhance membership
• Increase seminar effectiveness
• Boost conference attendance

Here's a series of short courses on tape that have been developed by some of the nation's leading management consultants. Each can be custom-tailored to appeal to your specific membership without costing you one penny in development costs, or one minute of your time! Here's how you can market any or all of these skill-building, career-boosting tapes:

- Sell them to members at a price you determine.
- Build the cost into seminar fees, and send the programs to participants in advance, so they can master the skills prior to attending...better preparing them for the learning that follows.
- Use them as premiums to enhance membership drives or build conference attendance.

A GREAT MEMBER BENEFIT PLUS A PROFESSIONAL EDUCATION PACKAGE ROLLED INTO ONE!

• Customized for your organization
• Two professionally narrated tapes in each package
• Valuable supplementary guidebook
• Top management titles
• Handsome, durable binder (looks great on book shelves)

Courses Available:

• Negotiating
• Memory
• Time Management
• Listening
• Leadership
• Vocabulary

For complete details, contact
Hillman Business Publishers
1741 William & Mary Drive
Flagstaff, AZ 86001
(602) 555-3524
Or mail the postage-paid card below

YOUR PRICE
(Custom-designed with your logo)

500–999	1,000–4,999	5,000–9,999	10,000–24,999	25,000–49,999	50,000 and up
$14.60 each	$10.05 each	$8.70 each	$7.70 each	$5.95 each	$4.95 each

Complete and Mail Today!

I'm interested in hearing more about your business premiums.
☐ Please send a sample package and literature
☐ Please call for an appointment

My Name_____Title_____

Company_____

Address_____

City_____State_____Zip_____

Telephone_____

• Use a simple design to make your price schedule easy to understand at a glance.

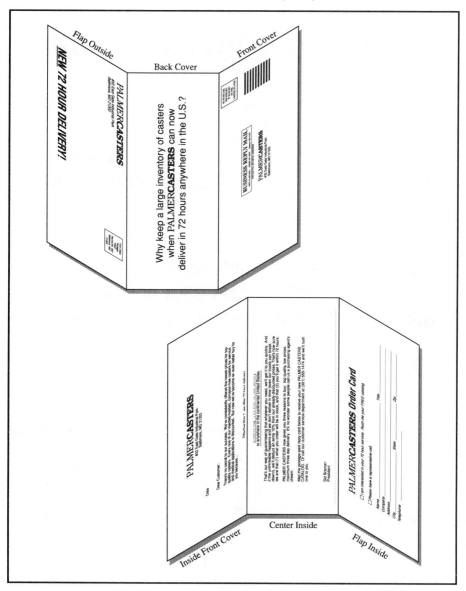

- Catalog offers, combined with announcements of new services, are a good way to keep in touch with existing customers—and prospect for new ones. This 8 1/2" x 11" self-mailer letter with tear-off business reply card is a format useful for a wide variety of products and services.

NEW 72 HOUR DELIVERY!

PALMER**CASTERS**

#32 East Gate Industrial Park
Baltimore, MD 21202

First Class
Postage
PAID
Permit No. 000
Baltimore, MD
21202

Why keep a large inventory of casters when PALMER**CASTERS** can now deliver in 72 hours anywhere in the U.S.?

NO POSTAGE
NECESSARY
IF MAILED
IN THE
UNITED STATES

BUSINESS REPLY MAIL

FIRST-CLASS MAIL   PERMIT NO. 99999   Baltimore, MD 21202

POSTAGE WILL BE PAID BY ADDRESSEE

PALMER**CASTERS**

#32 East Gate Industrial Park
Baltimore, MD 21202

• An announcement of an improvement in your service should be used as a means of generating new business.

PALMER**CASTERS**

#32 East Gate Industrial Park
Baltimore, MD 21202

Date

Dear Customer:

There's no secret to our success. We've consistently offered the lowest prices for top-quality casters. Every one of our injected-molded, corrosion-free casters for service and medical applications is discounted. But now we've become an even better buy for you because...

Effective May 1, we offer 72 hour delivery
to anywhere in the continental United States.

That's our way of guaranteeing that whatever you need, we'll get it to you quickly. And if the unthinkable happens and we don't deliver in time (even our trucks can break down!), we'll deduct an extra 10% from our already discounted prices. That's how sure we are that (1) what you order will be in stock, and that (2) you'll get it within 72 hours.

PALMER CASTERS now gives you three reasons to buy: top quality, low prices, maximum three day delivery. It's no wonder some people call us a purchasing agent's dream.

Mail the postage-paid reply card below to receive your new PALMER CASTERS CATALOG. Or call our customer service department at (301) 555-1474 and we'll rush one to you.

Sid Braman
President

PALMER**CASTERS** Order Card

☐ I am interested in your 72 hour service. Rush me your FREE catalog.

☐ Please have a representative call.

Name _____ Title _____
Company _____
Address _____
City_____ State _____ Zip_____
Telephone _____

• Affixing a top executive's name to an announcement signifies that the message is important.

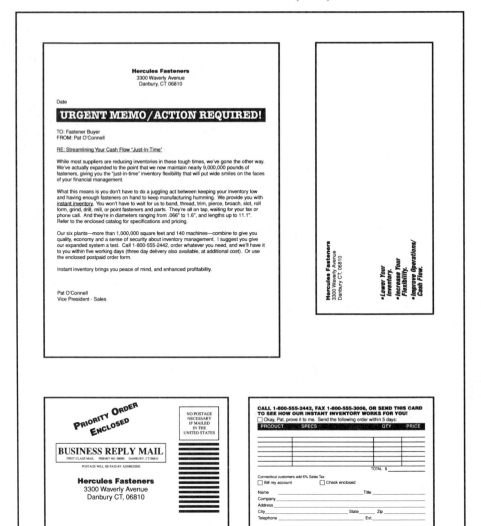

- Getting the order is frequently the name of the game. This mailing consisting of an 8 1/2" x 11" letter, order card, outer envelope and business reply envelope (along with a catalog, not illustrated) provides an effective method of producing orders.

Hercules Fasteners
3300 Waverly Avenue
Danbury, CT 06810

Date

URGENT MEMO/ACTION REQUIRED!

TO: Fastener Buyer
FROM: Pat O'Connell

RE: Streamlining Your Cash Flow "Just-In-Time"

While most suppliers are reducing inventories in these tough times, we've gone the other way. We've actually expanded to the point that we now maintain nearly 9,000,000 pounds of fasteners, giving you the "just-in-time" inventory flexibility that will put wide smiles on the faces of your financial management.

What this means is you don't have to do a juggling act between keeping your inventory low and having enough fasteners on hand to keep manufacturing humming. We provide you with instant inventory. You won't have to wait for us to band, thread, trim, pierce, broach, slot, roll form, grind, drill, mill, or point fasteners and parts. They're all on tap, waiting for your fax or phone call. And they're in diameters ranging from .066" to 1.6", and lengths up to 11.1". Refer to the enclosed catalog for specifications and pricing.

Our six plants—more than 1,000,000 square feet and 140 machines—combine to give you quality, economy and a sense of security about inventory management. I suggest you give our expanded system a test. Call 1-800-555-2442, order whatever you need, and we'll have it to you within five working days (three day delivery also available, at additional cost). Or use the enclosed postpaid order form.

Instant inventory brings you peace of mind, and enhanced profitability.

Pat O'Connell
Vice President - Sales

• Sometimes selling your service can be as compelling as selling your product, as in this case.

CALL 1-800-555-2442, FAX 1-800-555-3006, OR SEND THIS CARD TO SEE HOW OUR INSTANT INVENTORY WORKS FOR YOU!

☐ Okay, Pat, prove it to me. Send the following order within 5 days:

PRODUCT	SPECS	QTY	PRICE
		TOTAL $	

Connecticut customers add 6% Sales Tax

☐ Bill my account   ☐ Check enclosed

Name _____ Title _____

Company _____

Address _____

City _____ State _____ Zip _____

Telephone _____ Ext. _____

• This simple order form permits the customer to order in 3 ways: fax, phone and mail.

PRIORITY ORDER ENCLOSED

NO POSTAGE
NECESSARY
IF MAILED
IN THE
UNITED STATES

BUSINESS REPLY MAIL
FIRST-CLASS MAIL   PERMIT NO. 00000   DANBURY, CT 06810

POSTAGE WILL BE PAID BY ADDRESSEE

Hercules Fasteners
3300 Waverly Avenue
Danbury CT, 06810

- In addition to your company's name and address, adding a message such as "Priority order" will underscore how serious you are in turning around orders quickly.

Fasteners Manufacturer (5-40) *continued*

Hercules Fasteners
3300 Waverly Avenue
Danbury CT, 06810

•Lower Your Inventory.

•Increase Your Flexibility.

•Improve Operations/ Cash Flow.

- Short, punchy benefit statements listed as bullet items get the basic message across on the No. 10 envelope.

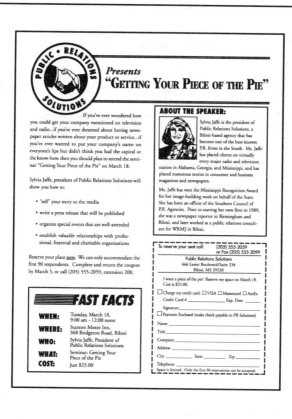

A newsletter format provides a sense of realism and immediacy, while the coupon in this 8 1/2" x 11" sheet offers a way to reserve a seat at the seminar.

Presents

"GETTING YOUR PIECE OF THE PIE"

If you've ever wondered how you could get your company mentioned on television and radio...if you've ever dreamed about having newspaper articles written about your product or service...if you've ever wanted to put your company's name on everyone's lips but didn't think you had the capital or the know-how, then you should plan to attend the seminar "Getting Your Piece of the Pie" on March 18.

Sylvia Jaffe, president of Public Relations Solutions will show you how to:

- "sell" your story to the media

- write a press release that will be published

- organize special events that are well-attended

- establish valuable relationships with professional, fraternal and charitable organizations

Reserve your place <u>now</u>. We can only accommodate the first 90 respondents. Complete and return the coupon by March 5, or call (205) 555-2059, extension 200.

ABOUT THE SPEAKER:

Sylvia Jaffe is the president of Public Relations Solutions, a Biloxi-based agency that has become one of the best-known P.R. firms in the South. Ms. Jaffe has placed clients on virtually every major radio and television station in Alabama, Georgia, and Mississippi, and has placed numerous stories in consumer and business magazines and newspapers.

Ms. Jaffe has won the Mississippi Recognition Award for her image-building work on behalf of the State. She has been an officer of the Southern Council of P.R. Agencies. Prior to starting her own firm in 1989, she was a newspaper reporter in Birmingham and Biloxi, and later worked as a public relations consultant for WKMJ in Biloxi.

To reserve your seat call: (205) 555-2059
or Fax (205) 555-2099

Public Relations Solutions
466 Lester Boulevard/Suite 234
Biloxi, MS 39530

I want a piece of the pie! Reserve my space on March 18. Cost is $25.00.

☐ Charge my credit card: ☐ VISA ☐ Mastercard ☐ AmEx

Credit Card # _____ Exp. Date _____

Signature_____

☐ Payment Enclosed (make check payable to PR Solutions)

Name _____

Title _____

Company_____

Address _____

City _____ State _____ Zip _____

Telephone _____

Space is limited. Only the first 90 reservations can be accepted.

▰▰▰▰▰FAST FACTS

WHEN:	Tuesday, March 18, 9:00 am - 12:00 noon
WHERE:	Stanton Motor Inn, 368 Bridgeton Road, Biloxi
WHO:	Sylvia Jaffe, President of Public Relations Solutions
WHAT:	Seminar: Getting Your Piece of the Pie
COST:	Just $25.00

- Seminars provide an excellent way to get new clients. Charging a nominal amount helps assure you'll get people who are genuinely interested in the subject.

PUBLIC RELATIONS SOLUTIONS
466 Lester Boulevard/Suite 234
Biloxi, MS 39530

**How would you
like to receive
thousands of
dollars in
FREE publicity?**

- Even though this type of promotion could be a self-mailer, response could increase if it were sent in an envelope with "teaser" copy on it. Mailing one version as a self-mailer to half your mailing list and the other in an envelope to the other half would give you a definitive answer. Be sure to ask the list owner to give you two equally representative samples of the list.

We are pleased to announce

THE CORLEY DISTRIBUTION COMPANY

has moved to spacious new headquarters:

242 Pacific Street
Stamford, CT 06901

TEL: 203-555-3111   FAX: 203-555-3133

THE CORLEY DISTRIBUTION COMPANY
242 Pacific Street
Stamford, CT 06901
TEL: 203-555-3111

*Please join us
for a cocktail party and reception
at our new facility
to help us officially open
our new executive and marketing offices*

Cocktails and hors d'oeuvres
4:00 p.m. - 7:00 p.m.

Wednesday, April 23
R.S.V.P. (Sandy Willis 203-555-3111)

• Announcing a move to a larger facility serves 2 purposes. The announcement card provides customers with the administrative details of a new address, phone and fax number. And it also says that your company is doing well and that it needs larger quarters. A second card provides information about a cocktail reception.

We are pleased to announce

THE CORLEY DISTRIBUTION COMPANY

has moved to spacious new headquarters:

242 Pacific Street
Stamford, CT 06901

TEL: 203-555-3111   FAX: 203-555-3133

- Paper quality counts. You can create a special image, for very little additional cost, by using thermography, which looks like engraving.

THE CORLEY DISTRIBUTION COMPANY

242 Pacific Street
Stamford, CT 06901
TEL: 203-555-3111

*Please join us
for a cocktail party and reception
at our new facility
to help us officially open
our new executive and marketing offices*

Cocktails and hors d'oeuvres
4:00 p.m. - 7:00 p.m.

Wednesday, April 23
R.S.V.P. (Sandy Willis 203-555-3111)

• Every customer and prospect receives the announcement card. Only selected people also receive the cocktail announcement.

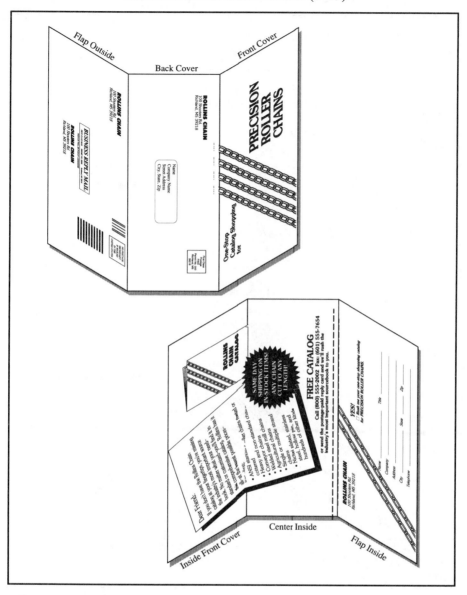

- Even rather utilitarian products can be marketed in a compelling way. This 8 1/2" x 11" self-mailer pulls out all the stops with: dramatic artwork, a free catalog offer and copy in the form of a friendly letter.

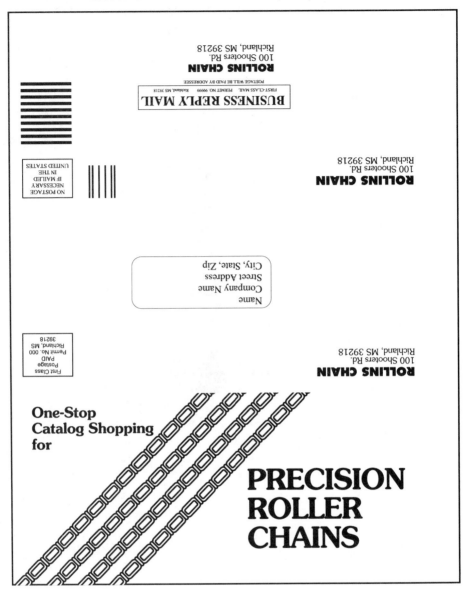

ROLLING CHAIN
100 Shooters Rd.
Richland, MS 39218

BUSINESS REPLY MAIL
FIRST-CLASS MAIL   PERMIT NO. 99999   Richland, MS 39218
POSTAGE WILL BE PAID BY ADDRESSEE

ROLLING CHAIN
100 Shooters Rd.
Richland, MS 39218

NO POSTAGE
NECESSARY
IF MAILED
IN THE
UNITED STATES

Name
Company Name
Street Address
City, State, Zip

First Class
Postage
PAID
Permit No. 000
Richland, MS
39218

ROLLING CHAIN
100 Shooters Rd.
Richland, MS 39218

**One-Stop
Catalog Shopping
for**

PRECISION
ROLLER
CHAINS

- Any aspect of your products or services that lends itself to a bold graphic theme, such as the chains in this brochure, will make your message all the more memorable.

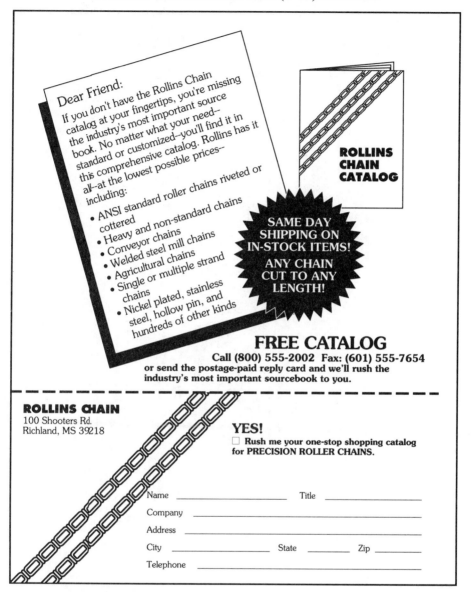

Dear Friend:

If you don't have the Rollins Chain catalog at your fingertips, you're missing the industry's most important source book. No matter what your need-- standard or customized--you'll find it in this comprehensive catalog. Rollins has it all--at the lowest possible prices-- including:

- ANSI standard roller chains riveted or cottered
- Heavy and non-standard chains
- Conveyor chains
- Welded steel mill chains
- Agricultural chains
- Single or multiple strand chains
- Nickel plated, stainless steel, hollow pin, and hundreds of other kinds

ROLLINS CHAIN CATALOG

SAME DAY SHIPPING ON IN-STOCK ITEMS!

ANY CHAIN CUT TO ANY LENGTH!

FREE CATALOG

Call (800) 555-2002 Fax: (601) 555-7654
or send the postage-paid reply card and we'll rush the industry's most important sourcebook to you.

ROLLINS CHAIN
100 Shooters Rd.
Richland, MS 39218

YES!
☐ **Rush me your one-stop shopping catalog for PRECISION ROLLER CHAINS.**

Name _____ Title _____

Company _____

Address _____

City _____ State _____ Zip _____

Telephone _____

- Don't assume buyers know about all your products or services. List the items that have the broadest appeal.

- Highlight key services (for example, same day shipping).

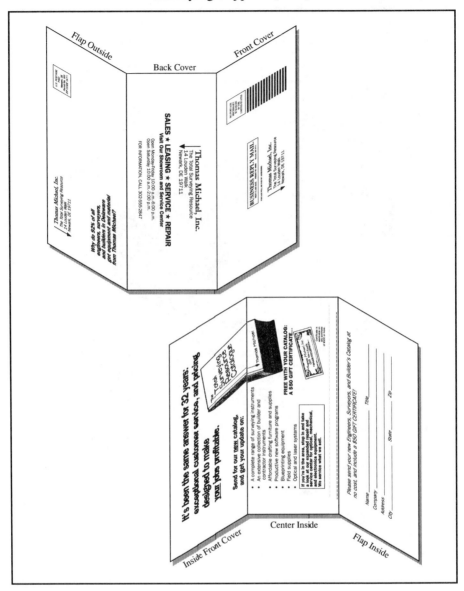

- The combination of a free catalog and a $50 gift certificate make this 8 1/2" x 11" self-mailer all but irresistible for its target market.

Thomas Michael, Inc.
The Total Surveying Resource
14 Louden Walk
Newark, DE 19711

U.S. POSTAGE
PAID
Newark, DE
Permit No. 000
ZIP CODE 19711

**Why do 92% of all
engineers, surveyors,
and builders in Delaware
get equipment and material
from Thomas Michael?**

FOR INFORMATION, CALL 302-555-2847

Open Monday-Friday 10:00 a.m.-6:00 p.m.
Open Saturday 10:00 a.m.-2:00 p.m.

Visit Our Showroom and Service Center

SALES ★ LEASING ★ SERVICE ★ REPAIR

Thomas Michael, Inc.
The Total Surveying Resource
14 Louden Walk
Newark, DE 19711

NO POSTAGE
NECESSARY
IF MAILED
IN THE
UNITED STATES

BUSINESS REPLY MAIL
FIRST-CLASS MAIL   PERMIT NO. 00000   Newark, DE 19711

POSTAGE WILL BE PAID BY ADDRESSEE

Thomas Michael, Inc.
The Total Surveying Resource
14 Louden Walk
Newark, DE 19711

- When a company controls a large share of the market, highlighting that fact tends to make prospects feel that they might be missing something if they don't "get on the bandwagon."

It's been the same answer for 32 years: exceptional customer service, and pricing designed to make your jobs profitable.

Send for our <u>new</u> catalog, and get your update on:

- A complete range of surveying instruments
- An extensive collection of builder and contractor instruments
- Affordable drafting furniture and supplies
- Productive new software programs
- Blueprinting equipment
- Field supplies
- Optical and laser systems

If you're in the area, stop in and take a look at our expanded repair and service center for optical, mechanical, and electronics equipment. We service what we sell.

FREE WITH YOUR CATALOG: A $50 GIFT CERTIFICATE...

Certificate is applicable on any purchase of $500 or more.

Please send your new Engineers, Surveyors, and Builder's Catalog at no cost, and include a $50 GIFT CERTIFICATE!

Name _____ Title_____

Company _____

Address _____

City _____ State _____ Zip _____

- Asking people to request a catalog helps you build a list of interested prospects (as opposed to simply sending the catalog to everyone on a rented list).

- You can reinforce your company's position as a price leader by offering an incentive for people to use your catalog, as in this case with a $50 certificate applicable to any purchase over $500.

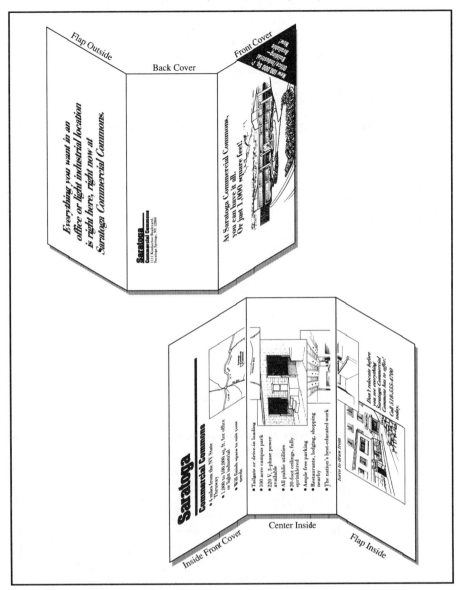

- Direct mail can be a powerful medium for reaching commercial real estate prospects because it provides the opportunity to show property or buildings in the best light. This 8 1/2" x 11" self-mailer provides ample space to show the real estate and even a map of the locale.

Everything you want in an office or light industrial location is right here, right now at Saratoga Commercial Commons.

Saratoga
Commercial Commons
1111 Kimberton Boulevard,
Saratoga Springs, NY 12866

At Saratoga Commercial Commons, you can have it all.
Or just 1,000 square feet!

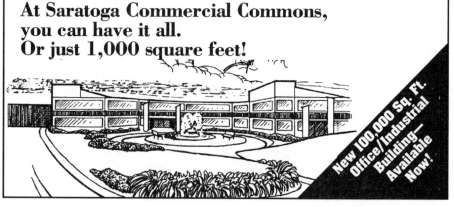

- Hire a professional photographer or artist to depict the real estate—don't short circuit your sale by using blurry photos from a point-and-shoot camera.

Saratoga

Commercial Commons

- 4 miles from the NY State Thruway

- 1,000 to 100,000 sq. ft. for office or light industrial

- Will finish space to suit your needs

- Tailgate or drive-in loading

- 100 acre campus park

- 220 V, 3-phase power available

- All public utilities

- 20-foot ceilings, fully sprinklered

- Ample free parking

- Restaurants, lodging, shopping nearby

- The nation's best-educated work force to draw from

Don't relocate before you see everything Saratoga Commercial Commons has to offer!

Call 518-555-4700 today.

• Bulleted copy highlights the property's features and photographs support the bulleted items.

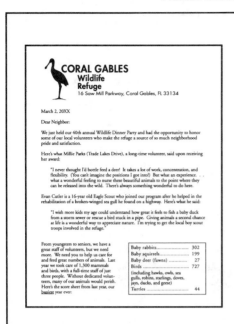

CORAL GABLES Wildlife Refuge
16 Saw Mill Parkway, Coral Gables, FL 33134

March 2, 20XX

Dear Neighbor:

We just held our 40th annual Wildlife Dinner Party and had the opportunity to honor some of our local volunteers who make the refuge a source of so much neighborhood pride and satisfaction.

Here's what Millie Parks (Trade Lakes Drive), a long-time volunteer, said upon receiving her award:

"I never thought I'd bottle feed a deer! It takes a lot of work, concentration, and flexibility. (You can't imagine the positions I got into!) But what an experience. . . what a wonderful feeling to nurse these beautiful animals to the point where they can be released into the wild. There's always something wonderful to do here.

Evan Cutler is a 16-year old Eagle Scout who joined our program after he helped in the rehabilitation of a broken-winged sea gull he found on a highway. Here's what he said:

"I wish more kids my age could understand how great it feels to fish a baby duck from a storm sewer or rescue a bird stuck in a pipe. Giving animals a second chance at life is a wonderful way to appreciate nature. I'm trying to get the local boy scout troops involved in the refuge."

From youngsters to seniors, we have a great staff of volunteers, but we need more. We need you to help us care for and feed great numbers of animals. Last year we took care of 1,300 mammals and birds, with a full-time staff of just three people. Without dedicated volunteers, many of our animals would perish. Here's the score sheet from last year, our busiest year ever:

Baby rabbits	302
Baby squirrels	199
Baby deer (fawns)	27
Birds	727
(including hawks, owls, sea gulls, robins, starlings, doves, jays, ducks, and geese)	
Turtles	44

WHAT CAN YOU DO TO HELP?

While we need plenty of volunteers to help with the care and feeding of our animals, we also have an urgent need for people who can round up donations of basic items we never have enough of.

We're looking for paper toweling, tissues, disposable gloves, bleach, soap, food for the animals, caging, aquariums, flashlights, power tools...and we're starting a drive for a new pick-up truck. Baling wire and chewing gum have kept the current one going for 140,000 miles!

Send the enclosed card and we'll mail you a list of the specific items we need. Or better yet, stop at the refuge and pick one up; that will give us a chance to talk about the animals and how much they add to our lives.

MEET THE STAFF

Carole Robinson started as a volunteer seven years ago and now, because of her dedication and devotion to animals, she's our rehabilitation manager. She's not bad with people, either. When you visit the refuge, ask to speak with Carole and you'll receive an education about how the Coral Gables Wildlife Refuge protects its animals.

Ed Williamson handles the front desk and is the gregarious fellow who puts our best face forward to the public. He's been entertaining our guests for nearly 16 years and helping them figure out where they're going, what they want to see, matching parents with lost children (and vice versa), and doing just about anything else that has to be done.

Melanie Czestowa is a certified refuge manager, and came to us three years ago from Hawk Mountain Refuge in southeastern Pennsylvania. She's a Floridian by birth, but earned her degrees at Penn State University. She decided, much to our delight, to return to Florida. Melanie's made a major impact on the refuge, and has been instrumental in helping us gain some much-needed government grants.

PLEASE SEND THE ENCLOSED CARD

Coral Gables Wildlife Refuge is a source of great pride to our neighborhood and, for that matter, the entire State. You can play a major role by working with us as a volunteer or a contributor. Please help us...and do something that makes you feel good while you're at it!

Pam Wonderman
President

CORAL GABLES Wildlife Refuge
16 Saw Mill Parkway, Coral Gables, FL 33134

I'd like to get involved! Please contact me with full details on the following:

☐ Wildlife Rehabilitation Volunteer
☐ Visitor Guide
☐ I would like to contribute:
  ☐ $10 Personal Gift   ☐ $25 One-Year Member
  ☐ $100 Family Membership   ☐ $1,000 Lifetime Membership
  ☐ (other amount) $_____
☐ I have enclosed a check
Charge to my ___AmEx ___Visa ___MC
Card #_____
Exp. date ___/___ Signature_____

Name_____
Address_____
City_____
State_____
ZIP_____
Telephone_____

Membership packages include free admissions, a newsletter, and free discounts on special events

CORAL GABLES Wildlife Refuge
16 Saw Mill, Coral Gables, FL 33134

Nonprofit Organization
U.S. POSTAGE
PAID
Coral Gables, FL
PERMIT NO. 000

"I never thought I'd bottle feed a deer. . ."

Yes, I want to help save the wildlife!

NO POSTAGE NECESSARY IF MAILED IN THE UNITED STATES

BUSINESS REPLY MAIL
FIRST-CLASS MAIL   PERMIT NO. 000   CORAL GABLES, FL 33134

POSTAGE WILL BE PAID BY ADDRESSEE

CORAL GABLES Wildlife Refuge
16 Saw Mill Parkway
Coral Gables, FL 33134

- Non-profit solicitations needn't (and shouldn't) be dull. This mailing features a No. 10 outer envelope with interesting "teaser" copy, a compelling sales letter, a well designed reply card, and a business reply envelope.

CORAL GABLES
Wildlife
Refuge

16 Saw Mill Parkway, Coral Gables, FL 33134

March 2, 20XX

Dear Neighbor:

We just held our 40th annual Wildlife Dinner Party and had the opportunity to honor some of our local volunteers who make the refuge a source of so much neighborhood pride and satisfaction.

Here's what Millie Parks (Trade Lakes Drive), a long-time volunteer, said upon receiving her award:

> "I never thought I'd bottle feed a deer! It takes a lot of work, concentration, and flexibility. (You can't imagine the positions I got into!) But what an experience. . . what a wonderful feeling to nurse these beautiful animals to the point where they can be released into the wild. There's always something wonderful to do here.

Evan Cutler is a 16-year old Eagle Scout who joined our program after he helped in the rehabilitation of a broken-winged sea gull he found on a highway. Here's what he said:

> "I wish more kids my age could understand how great it feels to fish a baby duck from a storm sewer or rescue a bird stuck in a pipe. Giving animals a second chance at life is a wonderful way to appreciate nature. I'm trying to get the local boy scout troops involved in the refuge."

From youngsters to seniors, we have a great staff of volunteers, but we need more. We need you to help us care for and feed great numbers of animals. Last year we took care of 1,300 mammals and birds, with a full-time staff of just three people. Without dedicated volunteers, many of our animals would perish. Here's the score sheet from last year, our busiest year ever:

Baby rabbits......................	302
Baby squirrels.....................	199
Baby deer (fawns)	27
Birds	727
(including hawks, owls, sea gulls, robins, starlings, doves, jays, ducks, and geese)	
Turtles	44

• This sales letter humanizes the activities of the organization by using testimonials from volunteers that prospects can identify with.

WHAT CAN YOU DO TO HELP?

While we need plenty of volunteers to help with the care and feeding of our animals, we also have an urgent need for people who can round up donations of basic items we never have enough of.

We're looking for paper toweling, tissues, disposable gloves, bleach, soap, food for the animals, caging, aquariums, flashlights, power tools...and we're starting a drive for a new pick-up truck. Baling wire and chewing gum have kept the current one going for 140,000 miles!

Send the enclosed card and we'll mail you a list of the specific items we need. Or better yet, stop at the refuge and pick one up; that will give us a chance to talk about the animals and how much they add to our lives.

MEET THE STAFF

Carole Robinson started as a volunteer seven years ago and now, because of her dedication and devotion to animals, she's our rehabilitation manager. She's not bad with people, either. When you visit the refuge, ask to speak with Carole and you'll receive an education about how the Coral Gables Wildlife Refuge protects its animals.

Ed Williamson handles the front desk and is the gregarious fellow who puts our best face forward to the public. He's been entertaining our guests for nearly 16 years and helping them figure out where they're going, what they want to see, matching parents with lost children (and vice versa), and doing just about anything else that has to be done.

Melanie Czestowa is a certified refuge manager, and came to us three years ago from Hawk Mountain Refuge in southeastern Pennsylvania. She's a Floridian by birth, but earned her degrees at Penn State University. She decided, much to our delight, to return to Florida. Melanie's made a major impact on the refuge, and has been instrumental in helping us gain some much-needed government grants.

PLEASE SEND THE ENCLOSED CARD

Coral Gables Wildlife Refuge is a source of great pride to our neighborhood and, for that matter, the entire State. You can play a major role by working with us as a volunteer or a contributor. Please help us...and do something that makes you feel good while you're at it!

Pam Wonderman
President

- This package includes all the information the reader needs to decide if they want to volunteer—presented in such a compelling way that it's hard to say no to the appeal.

CORAL GABLES
Wildlife
Refuge
16 Saw Mill Parkway, Coral Gables, FL 33134

I'd like to get involved! Please contact me with full details on the following:

☐ Wildlife Rehabilitation Volunteer
☐ Visitor Guide
☐ I would like to contribute:
  ☐ $10 Personal Gift   ☐ $25 One-Year Member
  ☐ $100 Family Membership   ☐ $1,000 Lifetime Membership
  ☐ (other amount) $_____
☐ I have enclosed a check
Charge to my___AmEx ___Visa ___MC
Card #_____
Exp. date___/____ Signature_____

Name _____
Address_____
City _____
State _____
ZIP_____
Telephone_____

Membership packages include free admissions, a newsletter, and free discounts on special events

- Most non-profit organizations need volunteer help and money in nearly equal proportions. This response card solicits both.

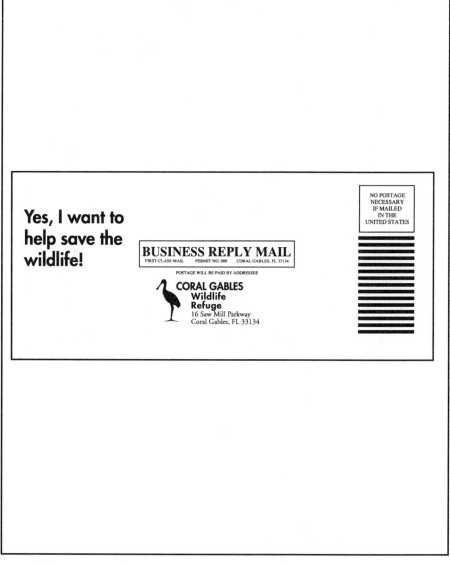

- Placing a message on the business reply envelope which echoes the feelings expressed in the mailing, encourages the recipient to participate.

- Using your logo on all your advertising material including the business reply envelope presents a unified look to your literature and contributes to the image of your organization.

CORAL GABLES
Wildlife
Refuge
16 Saw Mill Parkway, Coral Gables, FL 33134

Nonprofit Organization
U.S. POSTAGE
PAID
Coral Gables, FL
PERMIT NO. 000

"I never thought
I'd bottle feed
a deer. . ."

- "Teaser" copy on the envelope helps get the reader to open it—one of the biggest challenges of a direct mail package.

- Dramatic graphics and enticing copy ensure that your mailing will get looked at. This 8 1/2" x 11" sheet folded in half employs a strong illustration and simple but powerful headlines to announce the unusual nature of the promotion.

FIRST PRIZE*

Two weeks in a lavishly-decorated riverside mansion, surrounded by millions of dollars of original oil paintings, one-of-a-kind oriental rugs and screens, Elizabethan furniture and period pieces, German cut crystal chandeliers, never-before-seen Austrian wood carvings, Italian inlaid marble floors, luxurious, museum-quality accessories, Louis XIV bedrooms...

Participating Designers in the

8th ANNUAL DESIGNER SHOW HOUSE
(The Spiegel Mansion)

Sponsored by the Yaeger Health Foundation to benefit the physical therapy division of West Wilmington Hospital, and the diagnostic and education programs of the Women's Center of Schuylkill Hospital.

John Gary Interior Design • McCaffery and Prince • Barton Interiors • Grace Li Accessories • Garber Associates • Betsy Clark Interiors • Dorothy Horner Furniture • Canhers Limited • Wilton Fabrics • Arlene Rosenberg, ASID • William Lempke Interiors • Art and Artists • Sarah Drescher • Trinicum Antiques and Reproductions • Marsh Designs • Carthen Williams & Hardy • Marjory Soltoff Grand Creations • Alben Woosner, Designer • Anton Hall Interiors • Slade Wilson • Asher Custom Decor • Larry Devon Design House • Main Line Interiors • Parker Antiques • Showcase Galleries • Golden Ward Accents • Aaron's Crafts • Schoonmaker and Ross • Brad Elgar, ASID • Suzy Ross Williams' Outlook Design • Wellesley Price • Alexander Interior Landscaping

Open House Sunday, September 6 through Saturday, September 19
Monday through Friday 10:00 a.m. - 4:00 p.m.
Saturday and Sunday 12:00 noon - 4:00 p.m.
Evening on Tuesday and Thursday 6:00 p.m. - 9:00 p.m.

First Class
Postage
PAID
Permit #000
Wilmington, DE

YAEGER HEALTH FOUNDATION
8th ANNUAL
DESIGNER SHOW HOUSE
c/o West Wilmington Hospital
322 Broad Street
Wilmington, DE 19876

• While it may be enough for some people to "give" without getting anything concrete in return, the extra incentive of a possible prize for participation can't hurt your response.

* When asking for volunteers, remember that many people who won't volunteer may become paying attendees. So be sure to promote the event, not just the volunteer aspect.

Fliers 6

A flier is generally defined as a single piece of paper printed on one side. For centuries, fliers and handbills have performed as the simplest, most direct and most commonly used advertising medium for small businesses and individuals wishing to reach the masses. Effective use of fliers can inspire people to act. Consider the results of Thomas Paine's famous political handbill, *Common Sense*, urging his fellow colonists to resist British taxation. It proves that a well-conceived flier delivered to the right audience can be extremely effective.

Now, with access to high quality copiers, computers, and fax machines, it's easier than ever to create and distribute powerful advertising and promotions directly to your prospects. Working with a small budget, you can make fliers a mainstay of your advertising program and enjoy substantial results. As with all advertising, you need to break through the clutter creatively to stand out in the crowd.

Content. Make your message bold and highly visible. Graphics can "shout" in this medium. Use fliers to make special offers or announce new services. Keep the copy short and to the point. And be sure to include your company or organization's name, address and phone number so prospects know how to reach you.

Production. The selection of commercial papers available is an inspiration in itself. You can also choose from an incredible range of papers specially manufactured for desktop publishing that feature printed backgrounds. Imagine a special offer for a window cleaning service printed over a blue sky, or a men's clothing store special sale on gray flannel! Also, consider using unusual ink colors.

No matter what paper and ink you choose, be sensible about the size of your flier. In most cases, your flier will be handed to someone—keep the size small enough that they can carry it home, yet large enough to tell your story. The fliers in this chapter are 8 1/2" x 11".

Distribution. The methods for getting your fliers into the hands of prospects are virtually limitless. Hand your fliers to likely prospects on the street. Slip them into their shopping bags after they make a purchase. Place them under windshield wipers at shopping centers, malls and parking lots. Pass them out at trade shows. Deliver them door-to-door (but don't put them in mailboxes—it's against the law). Combine them with a cover letter and mail them to prospects and customers. If you're a retailer, place them on your counter for customers to pick up. And don't forget to ask other friendly businesses if you may leave a supply for distribution to their customers.

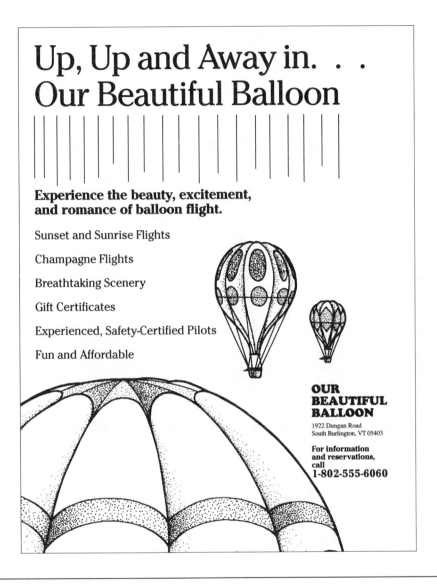

Up, Up and Away in. . . Our Beautiful Balloon

Experience the beauty, excitement, and romance of balloon flight.

Sunset and Sunrise Flights

Champagne Flights

Breathtaking Scenery

Gift Certificates

Experienced, Safety-Certified Pilots

Fun and Affordable

OUR BEAUTIFUL BALLOON

1922 Dungan Road
South Burlington, VT 05403

For information and reservations, call
1-802-555-6060

- Flier copy and graphics should be instantly readable—since they are likely to be quickly discarded.

- Make the graphics very strong to grab reader attention.

One topping *free* with each scoop!

Pick your favorite ice cream or frozen yogurt in a cone or cup. With each scoop you choose, select one topping free!

Order as many scoops as you wish. Hurry—offer expires June 15th!

The Silver SCOOP

Homemade ice cream, fresh daily

510 Community Drive
Manhasset, NY 11030

PARTIES WELCOME—
Call for details: 516-555-5468
Open 7 days a week: 11:00 AM to 11:00 PM

ICE CREAM
Vanilla
Chocolate
Strawberry
Banana
Fudge Swirl
Butter Pecan
Cherry Vanilla
Peach
Pistachio
Maple Walnut

FROZEN YOGURT
Vanilla
Strawberry
Chocolate

FREE TOPPINGS
Hot Fudge
Chocolate Sauce
Walnuts
Peanuts
Butterscotch
Nonpareils
Coconut
Jimmies
Sprinkles
M & M's
Reese's Pieces

- Offering a free item with the purchase of another is almost as good as offering something entirely free. Try tying in the free item in a creative way to make the offer exciting.

- Even though your ad will focus on a special offer, don't forget to include information about your basic business, such as "Homemade ice cream, fresh daily."

The Roswell Merchants Association

Joyfully Invites You
to Get into the Christmas Spirit

Candlelight Shopping & Caroling
Every Friday Night (6:00-10:00 p.m.)
From November 19 through December 17

A new Christmas theme each week:

* Elizabethan Christmas (November 19)

* Turn-of-the Century Christmas (November 26)

* Christmas of the Future (December 3)

* Christmas Around the World (December 10)

* Sugar Plum Christmas (December 17)

Games and goodies for the kids.
Join us at the Kiosk on Main Street
and kick off the holiday season.

sponsored by:
Roswell Merchants Association
342 E. Main Street
Roswell, NM 88201
For info call: 505-555-0864

- A flier such as this can serve more than one function. It can be designed for use as a hand-out by each participating merchant; it can be blown up, poster-size, for display in store-fronts and other key areas, or it can be mailed to residents in surrounding communities.

- Keep the graphics and message simple for maximum impact.

If you purchase a comparable computer with stereo CD-ROM from any other discount computer store, it should cost you about $2,500. But that doesn't include training. . . and without proper training you can lose valuable days trying to get up to speed. What's your time worth to you?

If you purchase the same unit from us, you'll pay a little less for the hardware but, more importantly, you'll receive FREE TRAINING . . . and you'll also receive, absolutely FREE, a CD-ROM library that includes software worth over $2,000. And wait 'til you hear the sound quality from our ASAKI Stereo CD-ROM! Music sounds like you're in a concert hall. . . and games really come alive!

Get all this PLUS FREE TRAINING and the spectacular CD-ROM LIBRARY. . . FREE!

For complete details, visit our showroom and talk to one of our computer experts. You'll get a full demonstration of the new KIMI 1000X. . . and you can select your FREE training sessions.

- KIMI 1000X Desktop or mini tower
- 1 gig of RAM
- 200 gig Hard Disk
- 2 1/2" CDX drive
- KIMI Ultra TXA Monitor
- ASAKI Stereo CD-ROM
- CD-ROM Library (worth over $2,000)
- 6 256-Bit Expansion Slots
- Windows 2100
- KIMI Keyboard and mouse
- FREE TRAINING: Select one of our 48 certified courses

> ## WAREHOUSE PRICES
> ## WITH ★★★★ SERVICE!

COMPUTER COLOSSUS

Hardware ★ Software ★ Training ★ Consulting
336 E. Norriton Street
Harahan, LA 70123
504-555-6006

OPEN DAILY
Monday-Saturday 9:30 a.m.-6:00 p.m.

Ask about our easy credit terms.

- In many product categories, there's very little variation in pricing from store to store, or mailer to mailer. The key to gaining an edge is having the most attractive add-ons and service.

- Free training for technical products is a major inducement to buy, particularly if you're searching for first-time buyers.

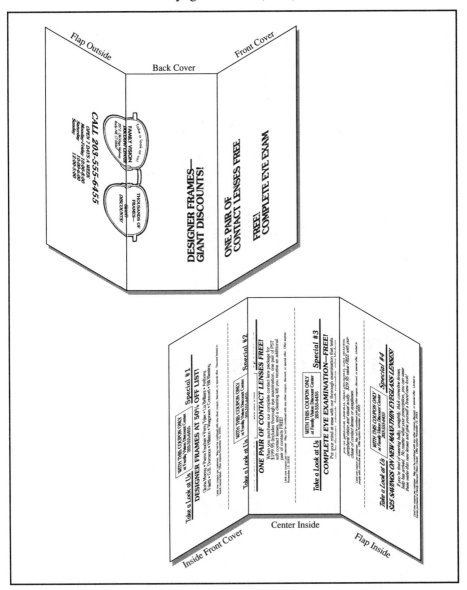

- This six-panel flier on 8 1/2" x 11" paper or card stock is folded into thirds. The top illustration, above, shows the outside "spread" of three panels (including the front and back "covers"). The bottom illustration shows the inside "spread" of three panels. See the following two pages for larger views of the inside and outside panels.

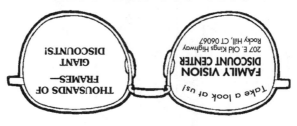

CALL 203-555-6455

OPEN 7 DAYS A WEEK

Monday-Friday 10:00-8:00
Saturday 10:00-6:00
Sunday 12:00-5:00

FAMILY VISION
DISCOUNT CENTER
207 E. Old Kings Highway
Rocky Hill, CT 06067

Take a look at us!

THOUSANDS OF
—FRAMES—
GIANT
DISCOUNTS!

DESIGNER FRAMES—
GIANT DISCOUNTS!

ONE PAIR OF
CONTACT LENSES FREE

FREE!
COMPLETE EYE EXAM

- This flier is folded intentionally to put one part of the eyeglasses on the center panel and the other on an end panel. This produces a nearly irresistible urge to open the flier.

Take a Look at Us

WITH THIS COUPON ONLY
at Family Vision Discount Center
203-555-6455

Special #1

DESIGNER FRAMES AT 50% OFF LIST!

Gloria Murray • Pierre Faucher • Perry Tyler • Liz Brilliant • Anthony
Faletti • G.B. Dorrance • Hillston • Wagoneer • Concord • Bill Blessing

Limit one coupon per customer. May not be combined with any other coupon, discount, or special offer. Discount limited to brand names listed. Offer expires November 15, 20XX.

Take a Look at Us

WITH THIS COUPON ONLY
at Family Vision Discount Center
203-555-6455

Special #2

ONE PAIR OF CONTACT LENSES FREE!

When you purchase our complete contact lens package for
$199.95 (includes thorough eye examination, one pair of PST
soft contact lenses, and a cleaning kit) you receive an additional
pair of contacts FREE!

Limit one coupon per customer. May not be combined with any other coupon, discount, or special offer. Offer expires November 15, 20XX.

Take a Look at Us

WITH THIS COUPON ONLY
at Family Vision Discount Center
203-555-6455

Special #3

COMPLETE EYE EXAMINATION—FREE!

Put your mind at ease with our thorough examination that tests
you for glaucoma, cataracts, depth perception, color blindness,
peripheral vision and visual acuity. $29.95 value FREE with pur-
chase of contact lenses or eyeglasses.

Limit one coupon per customer. May not be combined with any other coupon, discount, or special offer. Limited to people with corrective lenses. Offer expires November 15, 20XX.

Take a Look at Us

WITH THIS COUPON ONLY
at Family Vision Discount Center
203-555-6455

Special #4

$25 SAVINGS ON NEW MAXI-THIN EYEGLASS LENSES!

If you're tired of wearing bulky, unsightly, thick corrective lenses,
help has arrived. No matter what your prescription, you can wear
these wafer-thin new lenses and give yourself a brand-new look!

Limit one coupon per customer. May not be combined with any other coupon, discount, or special offer. Limited to frames purchased at Family Discount Vision Center. Offer expires November 15, 20XX.

• A sheet of coupons makes an effective flier.

• If the coupons can stand on their own (i.e., if people understand them and their value), there's no need to clutter the promotion with extra copy.

Can You Imagine The Results of Smoking 4 Packs of Cigarettes Every Day?

Radon Gas Can Cause the Same Harmful Effect. . . Except You and Your Family Won't Know It — Until It's Too Late.

Concentrations of deadly radon gas in parts of New Jersey have been found to be well above the national average. Your neighborhood has been identified by the New Jersey Department of Environmental Protection and Energy (NJDPE) as a potential trouble spot. Here's why you should have your home tested immediately:

1. Radon is odorless, tasteless and invisible.
2. According to the U.S. Environmental Protection Agency and the Center for Disease Control, radon ranks second only to smoking as a leading cause of lung cancer.
3. NJDEPE estimates that approximately 30% of all homes in northern New Jersey contain radon levels *above* what is considered safe.
4. The adjacent chart will give you an idea of the risk. 4 pCi/l is the maximum acceptable level. Although not shown on the chart, some areas have reached levels of 1,000 pCi/l.
5. The good news is that Radon can be controlled. You can remove the risk to your family. Simply call us at the number shown below for a low-cost radon test.

Potentially High Concentrations of Radon Gas*

RADON RISK EVALUATION CHART*

COMPARABLE EXPOSURE LEVEL	PCI/L	COMPARABLE RISK
100 TIMES AVERAGE OUTDOOR LEVEL	◄ 200	MORE THAN 60 TIMES NON-SMOKER RISK
100 TIMES AVERAGE INDOOR LEVEL	◄100	4 PACK-A-DAY SMOKER
	◄ 40	
100 TIMES AVERAGE OUTDOOR LEVEL	◄ 20	1 PACK-A-DAY SMOKER
EPA GUIDELINE FOR CONTINUOUS EXPOSURE	◄ 4	
AVERAGE INDOOR LEVEL	◄ 1	NON-SMOKER RISK OF DYING OF LUNG CANCER
AVERAGE OUTDOOR LEVEL	◄ 0.2	20 CHEST X-RAYS PER YEAR

PROTECT YOURSELF AND YOUR FAMILY!
CALL 1- 201- 555- 1776
Schedule a Radon Test Today!

SAFEGARD SERVICES, INC.
Radon Testing and Mitigation
1418 Downing Street
Patterson, NJ 07540

NJ RADON LIC.# 00392

* NJ Dept. of Environmental Protection & Energy

- Fliers are ideal for targeting specific geographic areas. Blanket parking lots, malls, churches and homes.

- Government documents, brochures, etc., are rich sources of charts and statistics. Since they are taxpayer supported, their use is free.

4 Ways to Save on

FAMILY FOTO

finishing!

After you've put all that care and attention into your family's special moments, bring your film to Family Foto. We're the people who process every roll of film as if it were our own. Even when you ask for one hour processing.

Depend on Family Foto for all your photography and video needs including:

Cameras and accessories • Repairs • Video camcorders and accessories • Film and processing • Darkroom supplies • Film to video transfers • Video tapes • Passport photos • Photo restoration

Clip and save with these special offers!

FAMILY FOTO

1204 Broadway
Pitman, NJ 08071
609-555-1881

FREE Second Set of Prints

with any color film processing
One coupon per roll
Expires 12/31/20XX

FREE Film

with any color film processing
One coupon per roll
Expires 12/31/20XX

Save $3.00 on Quality Film Processing

with Aurora Paper
One coupon per roll
Expires 12/31/20XX

Save $2.00 on Poster Size Prints

from your color negative or slide
Choose 12" x 18" or 20" x 30"
Expires 12/31/20XX

- Emphasize the value of your promotion with a number in your headline such as "4 Ways to save..." Reinforce the message with bold, graphic typography in your coupons.

- Mention other products and services in your flier, even if they are not offered at special savings during this particular promotion.

Exclusive Listing
FRANKLIN PLACE
The hottest commercial growth area in Philadelphia!

For Sale or Lease
The Sadler Building
101,000 square feet
on a 2-1/2 acre site

Artist Rendering
Future Commercial Development
American Street and
Penn Avenue

Situated at the southern gateway to FRANKLIN PLACE, the newest commercial section in revitalized downtown Philadelphia, this highly visible property has 350 feet fronting a new six lane highway, and is well positioned for a wide range of commercial uses.

The steady growth that has characterized the old waterfront and warehouse section on Penn Avenue has turned into a full-blown explosion. Now under construction are a 12-screen multiplex theatre and an office supply superstore, complimenting a new, successful 16-store strip mall (that includes two thriving magnet restaurants).

This large property is prominently positioned to serve new and existing consumer traffic from downtown Philadelphia, as well as International Airport (10 minute drive), the sports complex (5 minute drive), and communities from southern New Jersey (Perry Bridge is 5 minutes away).

Access from Interstate 95 (on/off ramp is one block away), Cross-Town Expressway and Interstate 76. This landmark site is positioned to draw customers from a broad geographic area.

HERE'S YOUR OPPORTUNITY TO ANCHOR THE SOUTHERN GATEWAY TO FRANKLIN PLACE!

FRANKLIN PLACE

TO I-76

NORTH

INTERSTATE 95

1   Office Building
2   Nightclub
3   Health Spa
4   Hotel
5   Waterfront Recreation Plaza
6   Restaurant
7   Mall (including 2 restaurants)
8   Office Superstore
9   Multiplex cinema
10 Sadler Building

For an on-site inspection, please contact Stacy Robinson at 215-555-6621.
This is an exclusive listing of Wayne & Stavros Commercial Realty, 722 Birch Street, Philadelphia, PA 19123.

- Graphics (in this case a rendering and a map) will double the impact of your words.

- In addition to being used as a mailing, this versatile flier can be given out to business groups and faxed to prospective clients.

HERE'S ANOTHER GREAT REASON TO SHOP AT CARMEN'S

UNADVERTISED SPECIAL!

BRAS AVAILABLE IN SIZES 32-38 A-C
BIKINI PANTIES AVAILABLE IN SIZES S,M,L

Hurry . . . Offer is good only on Thursday, May 15, from 10:00 a.m. to 8:00 p.m.

BUY TWO. . . GET ONE *FREE!*

STOCK UP. . . WHILE THEY LAST!

- Buy 2 Carlysle glamour bras at our low, low price of $19.95 each and get a third bra ABSOLUTELY *FREE!*

- Buy 2 Carlysle matching bikini panties at our regular low price of $4.95 each and get a third pair ABSOLUTELY *FREE!*

ARK ROAD AT ROUTE 516
FAYETTEVILLE, AR 72702
501-555-2870

Carmen's

THE MORE YOU SHOP, THE MORE YOU SAVE

- Regular use of fliers/handouts can help build store traffic.

- Fliers can be distributed in-store and in lobbies of nearby businesses (with their permission) to attract lunchtime shoppers.

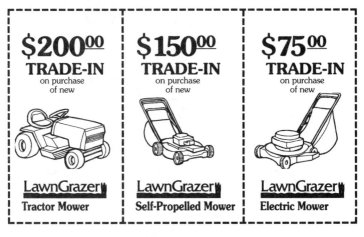

- If you have a well-known brand to advertise, maximize its sales appeal by including its name and logo in your headline.

- Consider using artwork provided by the manufacturer in your flier to illustrate the products offered. Line art often reproduces better than photographs on quick-printed or photocopied fliers and in newspapers.

SALE NOTICE!

NF NORWEGIAN FURNITURE

EVERYTHING MUST GO!

All Furniture! All Bedding! All Accessories!

STORE HOURS DURING THE SALE
Daily from 9:00 a.m.-9:00 p.m.
Sunday 9:00 a.m.-6:00 p.m.
July 16-July 22

SPECIAL STORE DISCOUNT
Bring this notice with you and take an additional
20% off
every single item!

We have to SACRIFICE TO SURVIVE
Top brands - All styles

All sales CASH & CARRY—
All sales final

Dear Customer:

We've hit a financial wall and we'll do whatever we have to to survive. And that means putting a sale tag on every piece of furniture and bedding, and even accessories.

Starting Monday July 16 and continuing through Sunday July 22, you're invited to examine the area's largest furniture collection...and get the items you've always dreamed about at the prices you've always hoped for.

We're not holding anything back. We need an infusion of cash to be able to continue to serve you...and we need it now. And the only way we know how to get it is to give you the deals of the decade. Tables, chairs, sofas, love seats, dining room sets, lamps, beds, bedding, paintings, prints, screens, and accessories...all priced to move!

When you come to this private customer sale, you can take a whopping 20% off our already heavily discounted prices, just by bringing this notice with you. Come in as early as you can and choose from the biggest selection. Many of the items are one-of-a-kind, and we can't hold any of them. You've got to see this sale to believe it.

You benefit. We survive. Everybody wins!

Enthusiastically,

Karl Vogel

Karl Vogel
Owner

Four Great Locations for Your Convenience

EAGLE PLAZA	MILITIAMAN PLAZA
23 Spring House Road	22 Grays Ferry Road
Stamford, CT 06925	Old Lyme, CT 06371
203-555-5588	203-555-8765
BARTON RUN MALL	**OLDE CITY CENTER**
Highway #38	4872 Sweet Briar Road
Milford, CT 06460	Hartford, CT 06175
203-555-0904	203-555-6042

BRING THIS COUPON FOR AN ADDITIONAL 20% OFF OUR ALREADY LOW, LOW, PRICES

- Sometimes graphics are more important than words. Feature key points in boxes (in this case, label tags) to get your main message across.

- Sale events are often best presented in a crowded, promotional format, which gives a sense of excitement.

CALENDAR OF SAVINGS EVENTS

OCTOBER 20XX

SUNDAY	MONDAY	TUESDAY	WEDNESDAY	THURSDAY	FRIDAY	SATURDAY
				$5 OFF Stokes Drills — 1	One floodlight **FREE** when you purchase three — 2	**CLEARANCE SALE!** Up to **$100 OFF** every gas grill — 3
$10 OFF every electric edger — 4	5	**$50 OFF** Parnell leaf mulcher — 6	**$150 OFF** Rhymer 5 hp snow blower — 7	**$25.00 OFF** JayCo porcelain toilets — 8	One gallon anti-freeze **FREE** when you purchase three — 9	**10% OFF** all fencing — 10
$5 OFF every aluminum trash can — 11	12	**$35 OFF** storage sheds — 13	**10% OFF** all wood window shutters — 14	**15% OFF** all storm doors — 15	One gallon Allen's Interior Paint **FREE** when you purchase three — 16	**$3 OFF** Jensen's burglar-proof dead bolts. — 17
$1 OFF every Wacommo tool — 18	19	**$3 OFF** all 30' extension cords — 20	**$15 OFF** every electric saw — 21	**15% OFF** any custom mini-blind — 22	One box fireplace matches **FREE** when you purchase three — 23	PAPER DRIVE — Bring 5 pounds or more of newspaper and take **5% OFF** any store item. — 24
$35 OFF any Sampson's work/tool table — 25	26	**$10 OFF** Herrold's 64-tool kit — 27	**$5 OFF** every sledge hammer — 28	**$5 OFF** every Acme rake — 29	One box assorted nails **FREE** when you purchase 3 — 30	**$25 GIFT CERTIFICATE** to best Halloween Costume — 31

Thousands of dollars in discounts!*

Happy's Hardware

The Neighborhood Meeting Place

18 S. LaSalle Street
Casper, WY 82601

Call
307-555-1331

* Discounts based on availability. If it's not in inventory, it's not available for sale. No rain checks. First-come, first-served. Sales are confined to listed dates.

- This kind of flier has many tie-in opportunities. It can be repeated as an ad in the local newspaper, or blown up as a window poster.

- Good customer relations depend on your listing all selling conditions.

Full service, just like the old days... at no extra charge

You get more for your money at Watson's Petrolux.

- We pump the gas for you—for about the same price as a self-serve station.
- We check your oil, even your tire pressure, if you like.
- We wash your windshield til it sparkles.

You don't pay any more for all this service at Watson's Petrolux either.
We figure you'll like it so much you'll come back for all your car servicing needs. Like hundreds of other folks do.

OIL CHANGE	TIRES ROTATED	RADIATOR DRAIN & FLUSH
15 minutes or less	while you wait	
$14.95	**$12.95**	**$29.95**
Includes 4 quarts of oil and filter	Balancing, $2.50 per wheel	Anti-freeze included

ELECTRONIC TUNE-UP	AIR CONDITIONER RECHARGE
$59.95	**$39.95**
6-cylinder engines	We recycle the refrigerant, too.

Watson's Petrolux™

We're more than a gas station, we're a *service* station

Corner of Shawnee & Waring Streets, Stroudsburg, PA 18360

717-555-1603

Petrolux and major credit cards accepted.

- If you're promoting good old-fashioned service, keep your language warm and friendly. Also, make sure you tell people everything your service includes to make it special.

- Use coupons in your flier to promote seasonal services.

- Illustrate what will be on display.

- Make your free admission offer stand out.

Take a Coffee Break With Us!

Here's a great new reason to stop in and see our amazing collection of kitchen necessities, gadgets and exotic foods from all over the world: savor a complimentary cup of gourmet coffee from the far corners of the globe.

SCHEDULE OF TASTINGS

MONDAY • Colombian Excellente

TUESDAY • Swiss Chocolat

WEDNESDAY • Israeli Almond

THURSDAY • French Vanilla Bean

FRIDAY • Irish Cream (non-alcoholic)

SATURDAY • Swedish Ambrosia

SUNDAY • Italian Cappuccino

Coffee Break Special . . .

and if you like what you taste, take 25% OFF any purchase of these superb new flavors.
(Offer limited to one purchase)
Expires 6/30/XX

For the gourmet explorer . . .

Kitchen Adventures

Allendale Shopping Center
1200 Cleveland Boulevard
Portland, ME 04102
207-555-9020

• With fliers, the reader's immediate understanding is the critical issue. Use a recognizable image from your business (in this case, a coffee mug) to convey your primary message.

• Create promotional excitement with "events."

- Be specific about quantities to avoid confusion and misunderstanding.

- Print plenty of extra copies of the flier to distribute in-store.

Spiritwood Band Annual Car Wash

We'll march for you...
we'll play for you...
best of all, we'll wash your car
until you can see your
reflection in it. It's the most
entertaining car wash ever,
and all proceeds support the
Spiritwood Band Booster Club's
drive for new uniforms.

*Come on out. And if your car's
not dirty, drive through a
puddle. We'll make it shine like
a brass sax.*

Car Wash & Dry—$5.00 (Vans—$6.00)

Saturday & Sunday
April 23 & 24—9 AM to 5 PM
Rain dates April 30 & May 1

Spiritwood High School Parking Lot
Main and Prairie
Spiritwood, ND 58481
701-555-1144

- To draw the largest response and to attract volunteers, convey enthusiasm and fun throughout your flier.

- Include a rain date for outdoor events.

Order your holiday candies now and support the Trinity Sunday School Charities!

If these candies weren't for a good cause, they'd almost be sinful. That's how delicious every selection is. Order now for delivery before the holidays and a portion of each dollar collected will help purchase the new van for the Trinity Sunday School.

Don't forget—these wonderful candies make excellent gifts. With any luck you'll not only give them to others—you'll receive some too.

ALL SELECTIONS 6 OZ., $4.00 EACH

SELECTION	QTY	SUBTOTAL
Chocolate Caramels	x $4.00=	
Chocolate Covered Cherries	x $4.00=	
Chocolate Covered Peanut Clusters	x $4.00=	
Chocolate Covered Mints	x $4.00=	
Chocolate Covered Coconut Patties	x $4.00=	
Chocolate Butter Creams	x $4.00=	
Chocolate Cashew Clusters	x $4.00=	
TOTAL ORDER		$

Name		
Address		
City	State	Zip
Telephone		

Please bring or send this form with your check (do not send cash) to the address below.
Make check payable to: Trinity Lutheran Church.
Thank you for your contribution!

Trinity Lutheran Church
Sunday School

615 Wheatsheaf Road
Battle Creek, MI 49016
616-555-1231

- When soliciting an order, be sure the order form provides all necessary information, including where the order is to be sent.

- This form can be adapted for house-to-house solicitation by removing the mailing address at the bottom and adding the name of the order taker.

Let's make beautiful music together.
JOIN THE
SOMERVILLE SYMPHONY SUPPORTERS
and save on every breathtaking performance.

Subscribe now to the Somerville Symphony and enjoy a season of magnificent music. You'll feel good knowing you're supporting one of the areas great cultural assets. You'll hear the world's most beautiful music, performed by outstanding musicians. Plus you'll save money off the regular ticket price as a Somerville Symphony Supporter.

Subscribe by phone, or send in the order form below with your check or money order today.

Somerville Symphony
Saturday Performances at
Somerville Community Center

OCTOBER 22	Handel Concerto Grosso, Op. 6 No. 5 Ravel Boléro
NOVEMBER 5	Beethoven Piano Concerto No. 2 Haydn Symphony No. 82
DECEMBER 3	Tchaikovsky Symphony No. 6, "Pathétique" Beethoven Violin Concerto
JANUARY 7	Schubert Symphony No. 8, "Unfinished" Ravel Piano Concerto in G Major Bartok Concerto for Orchestra
FEBRUARY 4	Mozart Overture to "Don Giovanni" Mozart "Eine Kleine Nachtmusik" Mozart Violin Concerto No. 5
APRIL 15	Tchaikovsky Symphony No. 3, "Polish" Prokofiev, Piano Concerto No. 3

Volunteers welcome to help with all phases of production—backstage, box office and ushers.

ORDER FORM

Membership Categories:

☐ Individual – $300
$50.00 per performance
(Regular price , $75.00)

☐ Pair – $540
(2 seats), $90.00 per performance
(Regular price, $150.00)

☐ Student/Senior – $240
$40.00 per performance
(Regular price, $45.00)

☐ Check or money order enclosed* (Payable to Somerville Symphony Supporters)
☐ Charge my credit card:

☐ Visa   ☐ MasterCard   ☐ American Express

Card # _____ Exp. Date _____

Signature _____

Name _____

Address _____

City _____ State _____ Zip _____

Telephone (_____) _____

MAIL TO: Somerville Symphony Supporters
P.O. Box 1420
Somerville, NJ 08876
To subscribe by phone: 908-555-0600, Monday through Friday, 9 AM to 5 PM

*Payment by check or money order saves the symphony the cost of the credit card surcharge.

- To entice new subscribers and subscription renewals, offer a savings off the regular ticket price and indicate the savings.

- If you have a preference for method of payment, such as check or money order, say so.

Image 7
Builders

What image have you built for your company? That question goes far beyond the products or services you offer; it goes to the heart of how you conduct every aspect of your business.

Image is a composite of the way you are viewed by your customers or clients. In addition to providing the finest products, the best prices, and excellent service, you should use image enhancing advertising to improve how you are perceived. (Public Relations is another tool to achieve a positive image. Refer to the Press Releases chapter for examples.)

Image building is something that needs to be done every day of the week to be effective. Here are a few examples:

- Send a hand-written postcard to a buyer that says, "Thank you. I appreciate your business."
- Mail a letter to a company expressing appreciation for the opportunity to bid (even though you lost the job).
- Send reprints of favorable newspaper articles to clients with a cover letter.
- Prepare a tasteful announcement of a business milestone (an anniversary, award, sales achievement, charitable contribution, or scientific breakthrough).

Pay the same attention to image advertising as you do to any of your marketing programs. Employ high standards for the appearance of your image material, mail it on a timely basis, and always keep the recipient in mind.

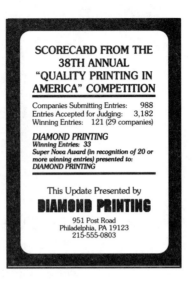

SCORECARD FROM THE
38TH ANNUAL
"QUALITY PRINTING IN
AMERICA" COMPETITION

Companies Submitting Entries: 988
Entries Accepted for Judging: 3,182
Winning Entries: 121 (29 companies)

DIAMOND PRINTING
Winning Entries: 33
Super Nova Award (in recognition of 20 or
more winning entries) presented to:
DIAMOND PRINTING

This Update Presented by

DIAMOND PRINTING

951 Post Road
Philadelphia, PA 19123
215-555-0803

DIAMOND PRINTING
951 Post Road
Philadelphia, PA 19123

U.S. POSTAGE
PAID
Philadelphia, PA
Permit No. 000
ZIP CODE 19123

**In case you
missed it . . .**

- Postcard mailings are an inexpensive yet effective way to boost your image.

- You needn't be modest about your accomplishments when you're in a field that's crowded with competitors.

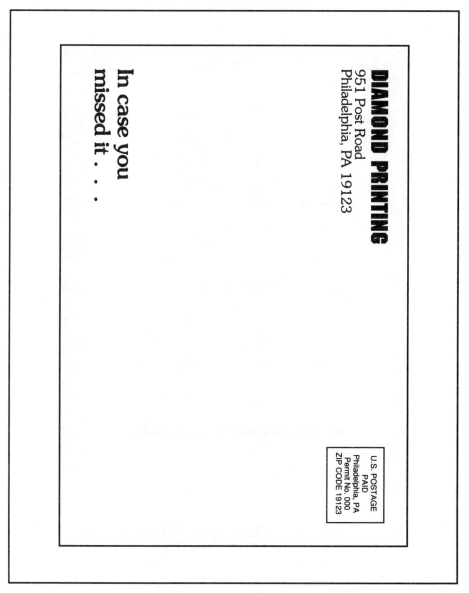

- Among the simplest ways to get the reader to turn the card over is to use the ellipsis (three spaced periods) to show that something more is coming.

SCORECARD FROM THE 38TH ANNUAL "QUALITY PRINTING IN AMERICA" COMPETITION

Companies Submitting Entries: 988
Entries Accepted for Judging: 3,182
Winning Entries: 121 (29 companies)

DIAMOND PRINTING
Winning Entries: 33
Super Nova Award (in recognition of 20 or more winning entries) presented to:
DIAMOND PRINTING

This Update Presented by

DIAMOND PRINTING

951 Post Road
Philadelphia, PA 19123
215-555-0803

- Awards impress potential clients. Boost your image by notifying clients and prospects of any prestigious honors. Don't depend on their seeing it in the trade press or local news.

- Mentioning the number of entrants is an impressive way to highlight the significance of the award.

*In appreciation
of the dedication and devotion
of the men and women
who teach us to read and think*

BRAVO BOOK STORES

offers every teacher in Indiana

a 10% discount on every book in stock...
every day, every week, every month, every year.

Thank You!

Paul Bravermann
President

BRAVO BOOK STORES:

175 Tyson Avenue
Bloomington, IN 47401
812-555-9000

1900 W. Golf Road
Fort Wayne, IN 46809
219-555-3313

2500 Lincoln Boulevard
South Bend, IN 46628
219-555-0504

1812 SW Drive
Indianapolis, IN 46256
317-555-4845

• By showing support of a particular group, you will attract patrons who share that support, as well as members of the group you're supporting.

• Discounts are always traffic builders. And a discount that's always available builds a loyal following.

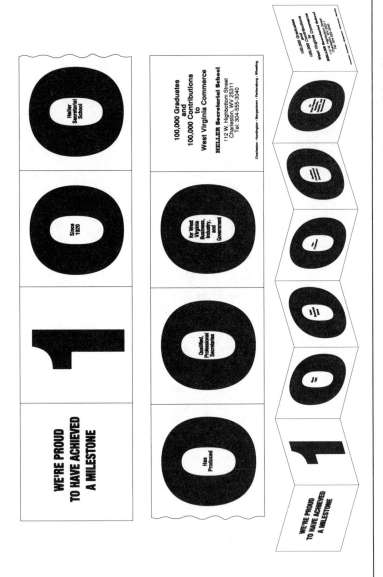

- The format lends itself to the image; the <u>unfolding</u> of the piece is what delivers a sense of the size of the achievement.

- Keeping words to a bare minimum lends focus to the event.

JANESVILLE CORP.
2200 N. Circle Drive
Bellingham, WA 98226

TO: All our Customers and Friends
FROM: Alvin Robertson, President

Reprinted from
The BELLINGHAM EXPRESS

JANESVILLE CORP. ESTABLISHES HIGHEST PER CAPITA DONATIONS TO THE UNITED FUND

Bellingham—The Janesville Corporation, a manufacturer of metal parts for the defense and automobile industries, led the way in Bellingham's United Fund campaign last year. In addition to making its art and in-house printing departments available for posters, flyers and mailers, Janesville employees have contributed the highest per capita amount to the United Fund of any corporation in the metropolitan area.

Janesville president Alvin Robertson said, "Our employees are all from the community and they're fiercely proud of this wonderful city. Their voluntary contributions, which exceeded our projections, will go a long way towards helping the community upgrade its youth services and facilities, and continue to provide much-needed support for senior citizens."

With the help of Janesville's record contribution, the Bellingham United Fund exceeded its goal by nearly 10%. Sarah Wattley, Chairperson for the local effort, extended "thanks to all contributors, with a special tip of the hat to Janesville." The awards dinner, set for Saturday night, August 10, will feature a special ceremony honoring Janesville and other major corporate contributors.

We're proud to be a part of this wonderful community and we pledge to continue our partnership

Alvin

• Good will is an asset. And so is public relations that helps build it. Promote your special activities.

• Your promotion can serve many purposes: the same piece can be used as a newspaper ad, a mailer, a flyer that goes out with all correspondence, etc.

Q: What do you call a tiny, out-of-the-way advertising agency that wins a Chicago Art Director's Award of Excellence?

A: **Matthews & Gerlick Creative Solutions**
Small-town prices with big-time results

For a copy of the award-winning brochure, write or call:

Matthews & Gerlick Creative Solutions
521A Marietta Centre Road
Gulfport, MS 39505
601-555-3050

- Winning awards only helps you get new business if you tell others about it. Newspaper ads will reach your local business community.

- When appropriate, try to give people a reason to contact you (more info, samples, etc.).

- One of the best ways to enhance your image is to say "Thank You." A simple postcard that arrives after the sale is a strong reminder to your customer of how much you value their business.

- Use a real stamp. It's far more personal than metered postage. The Post Office sells postcard-rate stamps.

Newspaper Ads 8

To reach large numbers of prospects for your business, consider newspapers. In your area you'll probably find dozens of options to consider. You can choose from daily, weekly or even monthly...urban, rural or suburban...papers for special interest groups, religions or nationalities. Within individual newspapers, special sections help target your message to an even narrower group of readers. You could advertise a fitness center to the sports minded, a gourmet food store to cooking enthusiasts, a business consultancy to readers of the business news. Decide whom you want to reach, where you want to reach them, and create your ad to target that market.

Scheduling. To achieve the greatest impact on newspaper readers, buy the largest ad your budget will permit and run it as frequently as possible. Tailor your media schedule to meet specific objectives. For a special event, sale or other occasion, schedule the ads to give your readers adequate time to react. If your advertising is meant to create long term awareness of your company, spread the ads over a greater period of time. Large national advertisers concentrate their campaigns in "flights" of 8 to 12 weeks to build awareness, with sustaining levels in between.

Content. Familiarity builds sales, so develop a consistent look to your advertising and maintain it. Choose a particular typeface to use in every ad. Keep your name and logo in a consistent position. People will start to recognize your ads and "shop" them.

Use strong graphics to make your ad stand out in the clutter of the many ads in newspapers—a powerful piece of art or a photo that directly relates to what you are offering. Make sure that whatever you use is simple enough in design that the coarseness of newspaper printing won't make it look muddy.

Remember to include as much information as the reader will need to reach a buying decision. Depending on your business or profession, you may wish to include hours of operation, days of the week you're open, address, phone, fax, credit cards accepted, and brand names carried. Always include a clear call to action so your customers will know what you want them to do. Use words that are short, direct and to the point like: buy, try, see, order, call.

Variety. Consider developing a campaign of ads to market all aspects of your products and services. Prepare at least one ad that focuses on your overall business, then develop individual ads for separate aspects of what you do. By running a variety of interesting ads, you'll make a much wider presentation of your capabilities and invite people with specific needs to respond.

IT'S OUR BIRTHDAY BUT YOU TAKE THE CAKE!

Join the party! Test drive the brand new Cheetah, experience the sports car drive of a lifetime, and receive a FREE birthday cake to help us celebrate our 5th year of great deals and customer satisfaction!

5 Years of Savings & Satisfaction

BLOW OUT SALE

FREE CAR PHONE WITH LEASE OR PURCHASE

Giant Birthday Discounts on Every Car in Stock

The Cheetah Convertible

$199 per month 36-month lease

36 month equal-payment closed-end lease. 1st month's payment of $199, $450 cash/trade down, $450 acquisition fee. Residual value of $6,582.60. Total payments $199 x 36=$7164. Tax, title & reg. additional. 36,000 mile lease. Excess mileage $0.15 per mile. M.S.R.P. $13,145.

GUSTO XE	ROAD RIDER	TRENDSETTER	SETTLER PICK-UP
MSRP $19,299 $249 mo.	MSRP $29,900 $349 mo.	MSRP $21,109. $279 mo.	MSRP $12,945. $179 mo.

CARSON CITY AUTO

OPEN WEEKDAYS 9 AM - 10 PM
OPEN SATURDAY 9 AM - 5 PM

806 ROUTE 22 • CALL 715-555-1818
SHEBOYGAN WI (ACROSS FROM TYLER MALL)

- Special events lend a sense of excitement, but they need to be coordinated with on-premises activities. A birthday or anniversary sale advertisement, for example, should tie in with point-of-purchase displays and appropriate premiums/incentives. Otherwise, the sense of excitement that drew the customer is lost.

- Use a well known landmark (in this case, the mall) to advise new customers where you're located.

$AVE

COLD CASH BEFORE IT GETS HOT

Now, while it's freezing outside, cash in on pre-season savings on Blizzard Central Air Conditioning Systems. Save up to 30% on state-of-the-art whole-house cooling from Blizzard, expertly installed by Murray Brothers.

You can enjoy unmatched comfort in every room this summer with an efficient Blizzard Central Air Conditioning System. Call now and we'll tell you how.

Blizzard Central Air Conditioning Pre-Season Sale

Save up to 30% now through March 31st—financing available

Complete Systems from $2,000 Installed!

Free Survey & Estimate Call (516) 555-7100

Murray Brothers

14 Engineers Drive, Farmingdale, NY 11735

Heating & Air Conditioning Specialists Since 1951

Residential • Commercial • Industrial

Also Available for Emergency Heating & Air Conditioning Service
24 Hours A Day • All Major Credit Cards Accepted

- Use a pre-season sale to boost business during slow periods.

- Include a cut-off date to stimulate action.

- List other services prospects may need.

It's a miracle.

If your business is going places, take your office along with DAC Commander.

It's the briefcase that packs a fully featured DAC cellular phone, powerful DAC notebook computer and notebook printer with laser-like output. Keeps you in command wherever you are.

We'll prove the power of the DAC Commander to you in person. Stop by our booth for a hands-on demonstration at the Tri-State Office Expo in the Coliseum next weekend and get a FREE Commander pocket guide to cellular computing.

(It's also a cellular phone, a notebook computer and printer all in one briefcase!)

DAC Commander®
You're Always in Command

FREE DEMONSTRATION at Tri-State Office Expo—Booth 413
Friday and Saturday-November 16 & 17, 9 AM to 6 PM
Sunday-November 18, Noon to 5 PM

SPECIAL SHOW DISCOUNT
10% Off DAC Commander with this ad

- To draw crowds to your trade show booth, advertise a free demonstration of a new or improved product.

- Offer extra savings at the show only, but don't advertise the price if you think it might scare prospects away. Let the demonstration do the convincing for you.

Who has time for holiday gift baking?

We do!

(314) 555-0393

Open Monday through Saturday 8:00 AM to 6:00 PM. Sundays 9:00 AM to 1:00 PM

If your schedule is too demanding to leave time for baking, Himmelfarb's has fresh ideas for the holidays—mouthwatering gifts from our ovens to give to all your special friends and relatives . . . and to surprise and delight your family. Order now and your specially baked cakes, cookies, breads, rolls and other treats will be ready when you want a spectacular presentation. To place your orders, call today. Even better, come in to make (and taste!) your selections in person.

SPECIAL ORDERS
accepted until December 22nd. Shipping and gift wrapping available for slight additional charge.

Ḧimmelfarb's Bakery
1422 Clements Street Jefferson City, MO 65102

- Sell your services as a convenience to those who would rather do it themselves but don't have the time. Most people today understand that situation all too well and are receptive to such a message.

- If there are special ordering requirements, such as deadlines, be sure to mention them.

- Postcards can be effective sales generators. But work with the format by keeping copy short and tightly focused on your product or service.

- Use graphics that "telegraph" your product or service.

A Fresh Way to Show Your Appreciation.

Say thank you to a special client with a flower arrangement. Order a bouquet of fresh flowers for an employee's birthday. Welcome a supplier to new quarters with a lush potted plant.

Call Premier Florists to send a gift anywhere...around the corner or around the world...for any occasion...with one phone call. Just use your Premier Florists Business Account or major credit card.

You can count on Premier for plenty of helpful suggestions, too. Our staff can provide you with appropriate gift suggestions within your price range. They'll help you select from a wide variety of containers, pick out a ribbon, even help you compose an accompanying note.

To send a gift or apply for a Premier Florists Business Account today, call 617-555-1999. For any occasion, business or personal, we're full of fresh ideas.

PREMIER FLORISTS
Since 1975

1232 Blue Hill Avenue,
Boston, MA 02126
617-555-1999
FAX 617-555-1990

- If you're selling to business people, offer the option of opening a business account for those who would rather not use a personal credit card.

- Personal service is a strong benefit for any business, but particularly for one in which creativity is important.

Prices fall on Summer Fashions!

Trim up to an extra 25% off already reduced summer merchandise with these valuable coupons. Select from sportswear, casual wear, business wear, formal dresses and more. Some items already reduced as much as 50%. It's your last chance to save big on the best of summer from Valerie's Closet.

VALERIE'S CLOSET

Bald Eagle Village on Mountain Parkway
Colorado Springs, CO 80901

719-555-0400

Open Monday-Saturday: 10 AM to 6 PM

All sales final

EXTRA 25% OFF
any purchase of $300 or more

Present this coupon for an extra 25% off any single item—summer clearance merchandise only. Coupon good Thursday, Sept. 8 through Monday, Sept. 12 only.
Only one coupon can be applied to a purchase

EXTRA 20% OFF
any purchase of $200 or more

Present this coupon for an extra 20% off any single item—summer clearance merchandise only. Coupon good Thursday, Sept. 8 through Monday, Sept. 12 only.
Only one coupon can be applied to a purchase

EXTRA 15% OFF
any purchase of $100 or more

Present this coupon for an extra 20% off any single item—summer clearance merchandise only. Coupon good Thursday, Sept. 8 through Monday, Sept. 12 only.

Only one coupon can be applied to a purchase

EXTRA 10% OFF
any purchase of $50 or more

Present this coupon for an extra 10% off any single item—summer clearance merchandise only. Coupon good Thursday, Sept. 8 through Monday, Sept. 12 only.

Only one coupon can be applied to a purchase

- Use multiple coupons and structure discounts to promote the sale of higher priced merchandise. Be absolutely clear about what merchandise each coupon applies to.

- Specify any restrictions in the coupons to avoid annoyed customers—and possible lawsuits.

Back-to-School Sneaker Trade-in

$5.00 credit towards the purchase of any pair of sneakers

Take off your old sneaks and bring them to us (regardless of condition) and we'll take $5.00 off the purchase of any new pair! And that's in addition to our already discounted everyday prices. Regardless of condition, your old sneakers are worth a fast $5.00 towards a new pair of Pro-Stars, Ramblers, Hooplas or any of our terrific athletic shoes. This offer ends August 28th, so get a jump on Fall and bring in your old sneaks today.

704-555-1565

The SNEAK ATTACK

2107 Blue Ridge Plaza, Charlotte, NC
Monday through Saturday 10 AM to 9 PM
Sunday 11 AM to 6 PM

Major credit cards accepted

LIMIT: ONE $5.00 trade-in per person

- Trade-in allowances give you an exciting new way of presenting a special discount.

- Be sure to mention that all products qualify, regardless of condition.

- Keep your message simple and emphasize it throughout your ad (in this case, "soup to nuts" selection and quality).

- If you sell top brands, feature them in your ad to draw knowledgeable customers. Co-op advertising funds may also be available from the manufacturers.

Logan Bath Designers Showroom Warehouse

Save 50% to 60% with wholesale-to-you prices

Until now, you could only come to our showroom with a designer. You had to have an appointment just to look. You had to pay costly commissions. Now, everything's changed and you can come in any time and save big every time!

JUST CHECK OUT THE SAVINGS:

	Was	Now
Peerless Victorian Pedestal Sink	$199.99	$ 99.99
Marbella Low Profile Toilet	$329.99	$169.99
Niagara Waterfall Bath Faucet	$459.99	$249.99
Roman Whirlpool Spa	$1,299.99	$799.99
Naturelle Counter Tops		50% Off

120 NW Fifth Street,
Oklahoma City, OK
73102

405-555-8385

Monday thru Friday
8 AM to 6 PM
Saturday
9 AM to 5 PM

LOGAN
Bath Designers Showroom
"The best in bathrooms
now costs less"

- Comparing old (or regular) prices to new (or sale) prices is a dramatic way to drive home to the customer how much he or she will save.

- One of the most powerful words (with Free being the most powerful) is Save. Use it as often as you can.

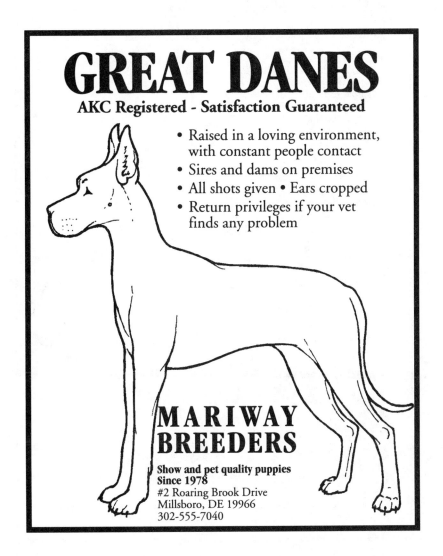

- Simple ads can be very effective. Keeping copy short and to the point lets you focus on a strong illustration.

- Longevity is critical in certain kinds of businesses. If you've been around a long time, be sure to say so.

SALE— Factory Direct Savings on Quality Papers

For over 75 years, Aspen Mills has supplied the printing and publishing industries with the finest in paper and board products. Now we open our doors to you, offering a full line of text and cover papers, envelopes and more for desktop publishing and office reproduction papers. Choose from a vast array of colors and finishes in stock.

All prices cash and carry. No charge cards accepted. Corporate accounts welcome.

Copier paper, 20-lb. white .... Ream: $2.79
Copier paper, 20-lb. colors .... Ream: $3.99
Letterhead paper, 24-lb. white ...... Ream: $6.79
Letterhead paper, 20-lb. white ...... Ream: $7.79
Letterhead paper, 20-lb. colors ..... Ream: $9.79
Letterhead paper, 24-lb. colors ... Ream: $10.79
Matching #10 Envelopes .... Box of 500: $6.29

This is just a partial listing— thousands of items in stock. Delivery available within 25 mile radius of store for only $5.00 per order.

ASPEN MILLS PAPER OUTLET

Building 1A — Redmond Industrial Park, 2100 154th Avenue, Redmond, WA 98052 206-555-PAPER Open Mon. thru Sat. 8:30 AM to 5:30 PM

• If your prices are really competitive, putting them in your ad is a great selling tool.

• When delivery is an additional cost, be sure to mention it.

Santa's helpers know what every woman really wants for Christmas.

Pamper the woman in your life with a gift of sheer indulgence... lavish lingerie she'd love to wear but would never buy herself. This Christmas, one of our Santa's Helpers can make it easy for you to choose the perfect gift. Come in for a private consultation. Give us an idea about her personality and tastes. Then we'll show you a wealth of choices she's dreaming of!

For an appointment with a Lacy Nights Santa's Helper, call 817-555-5223 today.

LACY○NIGHTS
Nightwear & Intimate Apparel
1555 Mesquite Highway West, Denton TX 76201
Open: Monday through Saturday 9 til 9 thru Christmas Eve

- Broaden your thinking in terms of who your market is. In this case, target men as purchasers of gifts for women.

- Assistance in shopping for a gift can put someone at ease, especially when they have no experience in choosing your particular merchandise. Offer a private consultation to make the customer feel more comfortable.

- Use pictures of your store, decorated for the grand opening. It captures the enthusiasm and reality of the event and also acts as a landmark for consumers.

- Consider a prize drawing to boost traffic. If you're scheduling special events or personal appearances during your opening, list the days and times in your ad.

Introducing
Evershine 2000
the hardwood floor with the permanent shine.

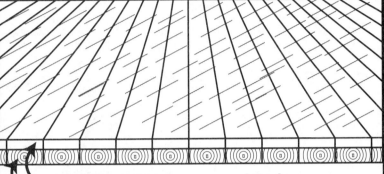

Evershine 2000 never wax shine layer

Solid oak

Imagine the beauty of solid oak hardwood floors in your home, with the ease and convenience of a shine that never needs waxing. Evershine 2000 from AmeriFlor is here. Made of native oak in a variety of hardwood stains, Evershine 2000 is finished with a patented space age surface that keeps its shine through years of wear. It's the perfect choice for new construction and remodeling...a stunning idea for kitchen or family room. See the possibilities for yourself at one of the AmeriFlor dealers listed below!

Evershine 2000
**and other fine products
from AmeriFlor are available
at these quality New Jersey
dealers:**
Morristown–Allan Flooring (201) 555-6800
Passaic–Benjamin Brothers (201) 555-2400
Hackettstown–Floors Unlimited (201) 555-3202
Orange–Techniques for Tomorrow (201) 555-1001

For other dealers or
more information, call:
800-555-FLOR

★≡≡ **AmeriFlor**

P.O. Box 2000
Rockville, MD 20850

• To explain a product feature, use a photograph or artwork with a caption.

• For easy selection, list dealers with their town or city location first, rather than by name. Also include your telephone number and address to answer questions or provide additional information.

June Dads & Grads Sale

We have the perfect gifts for Father's Day and graduations. For example, the top rated Worthington speakers. Shimamatsu XL CD players with full featured remote. Famous Nakahama CDT amp/speaker systems. And more! And all at unbelievable prices that will make you glad while shopping for that Dad or Grad.

The perfect gift at the perfect price:
Merrill Earspeakers

The music experience you keep all to yourself. Merrill fits every home audio system, and every taste, with an amazing selection of handsome, comfortable lightweight earphones. No matter how noisy your household, you can escape into your private world of personal audio. From $149.00.

30% OFF UNTIL JUNE 30!
PERFECT FOR DAD

Hobbes Loudspeakers

Find out why these British speakers are considered among the best in the world... despite their low, low price. They're compact, and can be used in the smallest room or the largest studio. Available in a variety of finishes, at only $199.95.

25% OFF UNTIL JUNE 30!
GREAT GRADUATION GIFT

Savings of 25-50%. Build the home audio/theater system you've dreamed about.

Monday, Tuesday, Thursday, Saturday, Sunday 9:30 - 6:00
Wednesday and Friday 9:30 - 8:00
All major credit cards accepted.
Financing available for home theaters.

HOME AUDIO

22-801 LaSalle Street, Palm Desert, CA 92260
Phone: 619-555-9292

- Create a sense of urgency about the sale. Cut-off dates will increase store traffic.

- Help focus shoppers by suggesting gift items.

A BRIGHT IDEA!
Buy Wholesale and Save 50% or More on All Your Lighting Needs

For big savings on all your lighting needs, Pearlman Wholesale Lighting is now selling to the public at wholesale prices. Come in for super savings of 50% to 70% on everything from light bulbs to chandeliers, all at prices never before possible.

- **2,500 table and floor lamps**
- **Outdoor lighting**
- **Track systems**
- **Recessed fixtures**
- **Ceiling fans**
- **All major brands**
- **Cash or check only (at these prices we can't accept credit cards)**

Now Open to the Public
Showroom Hours:
Daily and Saturday
8:00 to 5:30

PEARLMAN WHOLESALE LIGHTING

Allegheny Industrial Commons
400 Forbes Avenue,
Pittsburgh, PA 15205
412-555-1420

- A strong graphic brings readers into your ad.

- State your payment terms clearly. If you don't accept credit cards, for example, let potential customers know in advance.

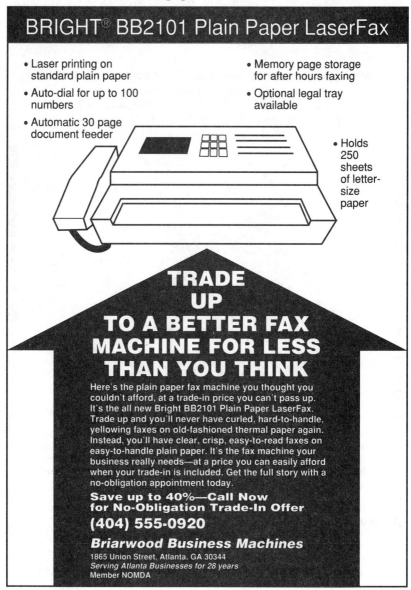

- Offering trade-ins is an excellent way to present discounts without diminishing the value of what you're selling.

- Place important selling points next to the illustration to help the reader "shop" without having to read long copy.

Spring Air Conditioner Tune-Up Sale*

The heating season is over...the cooling season hasn't started. Now's the time to have your window air conditioning system tuned to peak performance at substantial savings. For just $59.95 (regularly $79.95), here's what we'll do:

- ☑ **Clean and lubricate compressor and fan**
- ☑ **Clean and lubricate all moving parts**
- ☑ **Recharge refrigerant**
- ☑ **Clean and tighten all electrical connections**
- ☑ **Replace filter**
- ☑ **Adjust thermostat**

You'll breeze into summer with your air conditioner tuned up for maximum efficiency and comfort. Plus you'll save $20.00 over the regular in-season price. This offer is only good through April 30th so don't delay—call now to set up an appointment.

For an appointment, call now:

915-555-1425

Service plans available—ask for details.

Spring Tune-Up Sale

Any Brand— Just $59.95

Save $20!

Residential systems only
Offer expires April 30

*Window unit only

Odessa

HEATING & COOLING

421 Petroleum Way,
Odessa, TX 79760

- Spell out the savings in big, bold type for maximum impact.

- For easy reading, create a checklist to emphasize all the services you provide.

SEE YOU LATER

SEE YOU LATER

SEE YOU LATER

SEE YOU LATER

SEE YOU LATER

SEE YOU LATER

SEE YOU LATER

SEE YOU LATER

You asked for later hours and now we have them. So effective immediately, *come in until midnight* Monday through Friday for all your copying needs.

We'll see you later.

NOW OPEN:

MONDAY through FRIDAY 7:00 AM to MIDNIGHT SATURDAY AND SUNDAY 8:00 AM to 6:00 PM

**COPYING
FOLDING
TRIMMING
BINDING**

THE

CCCOPY SHOP

1500 Columbus Road,
Quincy, IL 62328

618-555-6644

- Extending your hours will please your customers. Here's a friendly way to tell them — and give them credit for making it possible.

- As with any good ad, the graphics tell the story. Use strong visuals that convey the message instantly.

GRAND OPENING PARTY All this Week!

Center City Cellular, the area's newest and largest source for cellular telephones and accessories, is now open to serve you. There's no better facility for selecting, demonstrating, installing or servicing your cellular phone.

Come in and see for yourself during our Grand Opening. You could win a $299 value CarFone System plus a year of cellular service free!

- All Major Brands of Cellular Phone Systems in Stock...and on Display
- One-hour Installation Available
- Complete Line of Accessories including Mobile Fax & Answering Machines
- Authorized Service Center for All Major Brands

CITY CELLULAR

MetroCall Master Dealer

111 Pine Street
San Francisco, CA 94111
(415) 555-2424

FREE DOOR PRIZES AND REFRESHMENTS

WIN
a $299 Value CarFone System Plus a Year of Cellular Service
FREE!
(no purchase necessary)

Open Weekdays & Saturday 9 AM to 5 PM
Open Wednesday Till 9 PM
All Major Credit Cards Accepted

- Offer enticements such as refreshments, free gifts and prizes at your grand opening to encourage attendance.

- Make your ad visually dynamic to convey the excitement of the event.

- Use reprints of your ad as flyers to hand out and mail before the opening.

Go ahead. Pamper yourself.

For an unforgettable day at Spa Francais, simply call one of our consultants to arrange an appointment. It's more pampering than you can imagine in six luxurious hours which include: eastern and western full body massage, aromatherapy facial, spa luncheon, manicure, pedicure, haircut and/or styling and makeup. It's a day every woman should experience at least once.

For an appointment or to arrange a gift certificate, Call 216-555-0930.

pa francais

29001 Detroit Road,
Westlake, OH 44145

Major credit cards accepted

• Keep art simple for best reproduction in a newspaper ad.

• Offering gift certificates is an easy way to increase sales.

The Perfect Gift For Any Woman.

Give the woman in your life a day with us and she'll talk about it for years to come. At Desert Spa, every moment will focus on her enjoyment.

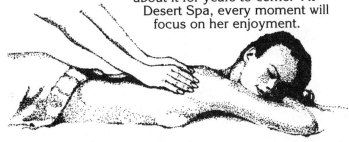

FULL BODY MASSAGE • MUD PACK • STEAM BATH • FACIAL • AROMA THERAPY • HAIR CUT, COLOR AND STYLING • MANICURE AND PEDICURE • MAKE UP CONSULTATION • THREE-COURSE SPA LUNCHEON

It's the ultimate, intimate gift that pampers beyond description. For more information, or to arrange a reservation,

Call Now: 602-555-0303.

Desert Spa

227 Mesa Boulevard Scottsdale, AZ

- List all your services to entice the greatest number of customers.

- Use bullets to separate items for easy reading.

Introducing

NORDIC® kitchens
from
Swensen Designs!

Praised by chefs, architects and interior designers around the world, Nordic kitchen cabinets are now available from Swensen Designs.

Visit our showroom now and examine the incomparable Nordic styling and craftsmanship combined with the latest ideas in Eurostyle kitchen systems. Discuss your personal kitchen needs with a Swensen Designs planner without obligation. Discover the difference Nordic and Swensen can make in your home and your style of living!

Introductory Offer —
Free Scrubmaster Dishwasher
with any full kitchen
Retail value $425.00
Offer expires May 31. Prior sales excluded

S W E N S E N • D E S I G N S
kitchen and bath design and installation

100 New Road, Colby, WI 54421 414-555-9372   Open Monday thru Saturday 10 AM to 6 PM, Thursday 10 AM to 9 PM

- Feature a photograph or artwork provided by the manufacturer or take a photo of your own in-store display to showcase the beauty of your product line.
- To increase traffic and build sales, include a limited time bonus offer with purchase. Be sure to mention the retail value of the bonus.

Give

MOM

Our Best

We've prepared a special menu for Mother's Day
on Sunday, May 10th. Call today to reserve a table for
a feast Mom will never forget.

Choice of Lobster Bisque or Pietro's Salad Vinaigrette

ENTREES

Chicken Breast Diablo
Grilled Sirloin
Spinach Fettucine Alfredo
Grilled Lemon Sole
Veal Marsala

DESSERT

(featuring Mom's apple pie)
Coffee or tea from our bottomless pot

Mother's Day special—
complete dinner for only $14.95

Sunday only, 2 PM to 8 PM – Reservations required

❀Pietro's❀

11 Providence Place, Cranston, RI 02920
401-555-2920

Advertise early to promote an occasion before your prospects make other plans.

Add something special (in this case, the price) to strengthen the promotion.

Full Service Nail Salon Opens

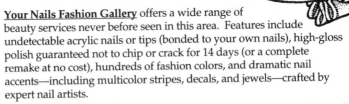

The first full service nail salon serving southern New Mexico and northwest Texas has opened in the Barclay Shopping Center near Interstate 70.

<u>Your Nails Fashion Gallery</u> offers a wide range of beauty services never before seen in this area. Features include undetectable acrylic nails or tips (bonded to your own nails), high-gloss polish guaranteed not to chip or crack for 14 days (or a complete remake at no cost), hundreds of fashion colors, and dramatic nail accents—including multicolor stripes, decals, and jewels—crafted by expert nail artists.

According to Lola, the owner of <u>Your Nails Fashion Gallery</u> and one of the four nail artists on premises, "Outstanding nails are a fashion and beauty statement. They mark you as someone with a commitment to fine grooming." Lola offers award winning nail painting and decorating, wraps, and gels, along with a full range of manicuring services.

<u>Your Nails Fashion Gallery</u> is conveniently located at Pavilion 122 in the Barclay Shopping Center, just East of the State Road Exit on Interstate 70. Hours are 9:30am-6:00pm Monday, Tuesday, Friday, and Saturday, and 9:30am-8:00pm Wednesday and Thursday. Special appointments also available. Call 505-555-1595.

- Using quotes gives this ad a news style which lends credibility.

- Mention all your services to interest the greatest number of readers.

10% OFF LANDSCAPING
Design services
Installation
Mulching
Sodding & seeding
Expires 11/1/XX

FALL LANDSCAPING SPECIALS

Use these valuable coupons to save on seasonal landscaping services from BENSON BROTHERS

25% OFF FALL CLEAN-UP
Lawn raked, mowed, trimmed and edged. Leaves blown and vacuumed
$100.00 minimum
Expires 11/30/XX

FREE SOIL ANALYSIS
with purchase of lawn fertilization
Expires 10/31/XX

- *Call for free estimates*
- *Fully insured and bonded*

10% OFF TREE PRUNING AND REMOVAL
Expires 10/15/XX

SHRUBS— BUY 2, GET 1 FREE
Rhododendrons, Azaleas, Hollies
Installation included
Expires 10/1/XX

BENSON BROTHERS LANDSCAPING CO.
3229 Beverly Drive,
Beverly, NJ 08010
609-555-2595

• Increase the immediacy of seasonal offers with the use of coupons with expiration dates.

• Offering a variety of services with different expiration dates spreads out your workload and stimulates more business.

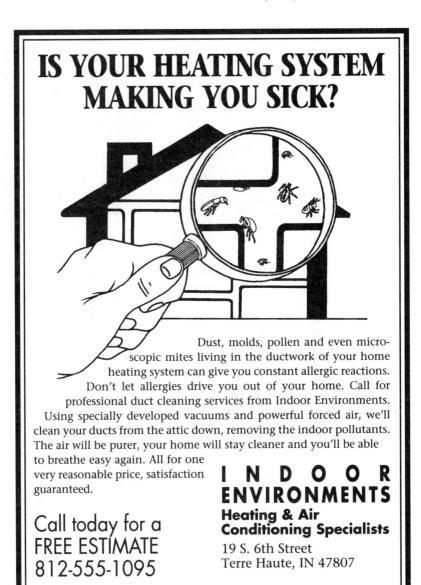

IS YOUR HEATING SYSTEM MAKING YOU SICK?

Dust, molds, pollen and even microscopic mites living in the ductwork of your home heating system can give you constant allergic reactions. Don't let allergies drive you out of your home. Call for professional duct cleaning services from Indoor Environments. Using specially developed vacuums and powerful forced air, we'll clean your ducts from the attic down, removing the indoor pollutants. The air will be purer, your home will stay cleaner and you'll be able to breathe easy again. All for one very reasonable price, satisfaction guaranteed.

Call today for a
FREE ESTIMATE
812-555-1095

**I N D O O R
ENVIRONMENTS**
**Heating & Air
Conditioning Specialists**
19 S. 6th Street
Terre Haute, IN 47807

- Using a question in your headline permits you to present a problem and introduce your solution as the expert.

- Explain how you solve the problem without getting so detailed you overwhelm—or bore—the reader.

THE PRINT SHOPPE

Whether you need 50 copies of a resume or 10,000 full color brochures, come to the Print Shoppe. We'll turn your job around fast, give you quality work and save you money. And just to prove it, here's a coupon good for 10% off your order.

Photocopies • Offset Printing • Color Copies Typesetting • Desktop Publishing • Trimming • Folding • Binding

Major Credit Cards Accepted

FREE Pick-Up
FREE Delivery
FREE Quotes
FREE Advice

10% OFF
ANY SERVICE
THE PRINT SHOPPE
21 Polar Boulevard, Kodiak, AK 99615
555-2653 • Fax 555-2659
Monday Through Saturday,
8:30 am To 6:00 pm
One coupon per customer. Expires 9/30/20XX.
Present this coupon when placing order. Not to
be combined with any other offer.

- Ads with discount coupons are a good way to introduce a new company or service, or to stimulate sales. But don't discount too frequently, or your regular prices will lose credibility.

- Put all important information in your coupon: name, address, phone, fax, hours—everything you want the prospect to know when they're ready to use it.

- List any limitations, such as a cut-off date.

We introduced the brushless car wash to Biloxi and you loved it. You kept coming back again and again because Premium Wash made your car cleaner and brighter than even hand-washing! Thanks to your loyalty, we've grown to five locations.

We want to express our appreciation during our 15th Anniversary with this special Savings Coupon. Come in, celebrate with us and save!

5 convenient locations:

1420 Popps Ferry Road, Biloxi, MS

1111 W. Beach Boulevard, Biloxi, MS

541 Tombigbee, Biloxi, MS

2219 E. Woodrow Wilson, Biloxi, MS

1710 N. State, Biloxi, MS

Hours:
Monday thru Saturday 8 AM to 6 PM
Sunday 9 AM to Noon

All Major Credit Cards Welcome

PREMIUM WASH
The Softest Touch Around

PREMIUM WASH

15th Anniversary Coupon

Good for

20% off
ANY WASH

Not to be combined with any other discount offer.

Expires May 31, 20XX.

- Any milestone in your business presents an opportunity to celebrate, thank customers and increase traffic and sales. Don't let an opportunity pass.

- Include a bold, dashed border around your coupon to encourage clipping, and an expiration date to increase response.

GRAND OPENING!

FIRST NATIONAL HAS ANNVILLE'S BEST INTERESTS AT HEART

That's why we're opening a new branch, right here. First National, the good neighbor bankers, are opening our new branch this Monday. Come in for the Grand Opening celebration and get to know us.

Find out about our higher interest rates on savings… lower rates on loans…plus all the other full service banking programs from First National.

Come by for the party. We're offering refreshments, free gifts and the chance to win a $2,000 home entertainment center or one of 99 other exciting prizes!

GRAND OPENING
of our new Annville branch
Monday, May 7th • 9 am to 8 pm

First National Bancorp. Now serving the valley with over 40 offices. Annville Court—110 Main Street, Annville, PA 17003 • (717) 555-9753
Monday thru Thursday 9:00AM to 4:00PM, Friday 9:00AM to 8:00PM

No deposit necessary
Member FDIC

- A grand opening celebration generates the traffic to get a new business off to a flying start.

- Give potential customers more than one reason to visit: serve refreshments, hand out free gifts, hold a prize drawing.

- Don't rely on newspaper ads alone to get maximum attendance …also use radio, flyers, direct mail.

TELEPHONE ANSWERING—FIRST MONTH FREE!

If you've been missing phone calls, we have the answer. It's us—
ANSWER-4-U Answering Service.

Sign up with us and you'll never miss another call. We'll answer your phones promptly and professionally. We'll hold your messages or, if you prefer, signal you through a pager. Your customers will be pleased to have their messages received by a real person, not voice mail or an answering machine. And you'll be pleased that your calls are being handled courteously and accurately!

Best of all, for a limited time, get our special offer: **Sign up for a year and the first month is free!** Satisfaction guaranteed. Offer limited to new customers only. Telephone charges not included.

- 24-Hour Answering Service
- Weekend Monitoring
- Call Forwarding
- Fax Receiving
- Paging Service
- Wake-up Calls
- Mail Services Available

ANSWER-4-U—We get the message
2001 Bach Street, Burbank, CA 91508   (818) 555-4444

- The most powerful word in advertising is "Free." If you have a free offer, tell the world.

- If your offer is for a specific group (for example, "new customers only") say so in your ad and to prevent misunderstandings. And spell out any special conditions ("Telephone charges not included.")

- List other services—they could be the ones that get someone to select you over a competitor.

What Every Accountant Needs To Know About Accounting Software. FREE!

This is the day you can't afford to miss. In four intensive hours, learn from the industry's leading experts on accounting software. Charles Franks, the creator of ACC-WARE, and Lance Farnsworth of Micro Solutions, Ltd., have joined forces to offer a powerful FREE seminar for accountants and their clients. These are just a few of the issues that will be addressed.

- 10 steps to making the right decision in selecting accounting software

- How to be sure your software will grow with your business

- Training— the biggest cost in installing a management information system

- How to match your software needs with the hardware you have

- The importance of joining a user group dedicated to the software you choose

- What to look for in a service and support consultant

INCLUDES ONE-HOUR INTRODUCTION TO ACCOUNTING SOFTWARE BASICS

General Ledger	Inventory Control
Accounts Payable	Order Entry
Accounts Receivable	Retail Invoicing
Job Costing	Sales Analysis

Accounting Software for Accounting Professionals

GOLDEN STATE CENTER
Tuesday, March 7
1:00 PM to 5:00 PM
(Refreshments served)
Free Admission by
Reservation Only

MICRO
Solutions, Ltd.
Software Consultants
to the Accounting
Profession

2440 Sepulveda Blvd.
Van Nuys, CA 91411
Phone: 818/555-7800 • Fax: 818/555-7878

- Expand the appeal of your seminar by enlisting the help of a supplier, as in this example, a software company demonstrating its software. But beware, don't turn the demonstration into an outright sales pitch, or you'll lose your credibility.

- Free admission will generate the largest attendance. Offering refreshments will also boost response.

Reward your employees with the Caribbean... Hawaii... or Europe

Nothing motivates employees like the chance to win a vacation at company expense. That's why, even in slow times, our clients see sales go up consistently when they offer a custom incentive travel program from Passport.

Call Darlene Simmonds today for a detailed presentation of the proven performance you can expect from Passport's Incentive Travel Programs.

PASSPORT TRAVEL

Mon.–Sat. 9am–6pm
1528 Yankee St.
Bangor, ME 04401
207-555-4040

- Include the name of a contact at your company to call as a follow-up.

- Using art in a dynamic way enhances readership of your ad.

With Longcore Design, you'll discover the difference quality can make in the look and impact of your communications materials. Whether you need a simple letterhead, a corporate identity system, a brochure or a comprehensive catalog, our designers will give your work the same creative flair and attention to detail that's won awards for our clients again and again. And more importantly, has produced results that keep them coming back for more.

To see how quality can pay for itself, call Miles Longcore today at 404-555-1980 for a free consultation.

LONGCOR E ◆ DESIGN

20 Marietta NW, Atlanta, GA 30303 • 404-555-1980 • FAX 404-555-1985

- Assure prospects that no matter how large or small their own company may be, they will receive first class work.

- An all-type ad can be highly effective, provided that the copy and design work well together.

Your words
+ our designs
= cost effective
professional brochures

Bring us your brochure copy and we'll turn it into a powerful selling tool. Using our talent, desktop design tools and professional quality output equipment, we can transform your words into a brochure or mailing piece that stops prospects in their tracks. And we'll do it all for a fee that any company can afford.

For an appointment during or after business hours, call Marilyn Saunders today.

SAUNDERS DESIGN STUDIO
Advertising & Graphic Design Services

1 East 1st Street, Reno, NV 89501

702-555-5315
FAX 702-555-5318
MODEM 702-555-5319

- Emphasizing the affordability of your product or service is very effective when your prospects are not sure how expensive it will be.

- Many start-up companies may be too busy to meet with you during regular business hours. Include an offer to meet after hours.

Continental Graphics and United Printing are combining forces.

NOW THERE'S ONE SOURCE FOR ALL YOUR PRINTING NEEDS

We're pooling our talents and resources to serve you even better. Count on United Continental for all your printing requirements including short or long runs, single sheets or multi-page catalogs, one to six colors. Now, one source does it all. Quality prepress services and bindery operations under one roof to give you total control of any project for maximum efficiency and economy.

Call or write today for our new brochure describing all of our combined resources.

UNITED CONTINENTAL GRAPHICS SERVICES

7200 Northwest Boulevard
Davenport, IA 52806

NOW ONE SOURCE FOR ALL YOUR PRINTING NEEDS
319-555-1200
FAX 319-555-1250

A merger presents an exciting marketing opportunity. Use it to offer more services to existing customers, and attract new customers with your increased resources.

Be sure to produce a sales brochure which details your combined services, then offer it as a response-generating vehicle in your advertising.

PURCHASING PROPERTY?

An Environmental Audit Can Avoid Costly Problems

If you are about to purchase property—either an existing building or land—you could be in for unpleasant environmental surprises. Hazardous wastes, underground storage tanks and asbestos are just a few of the potential problems that can have a devastating effect on your business.

Before you go through with the purchase, do what leading real estate developers and financial institutions do. Have Schaefer Environmental Consultants perform a comprehensive site audit. We'll provide you with a thorough site assessment using the latest technology. If we find problems, we can recommend solutions to help you keep the project viable.

Don't make a purchase you'll regret for years. Get to the bottom of environmental concerns with Schaefer Environmental Consultants.

SCHAEFER
Environmental Consultants
518 Thompson Street
Saginaw, MI 48607
517-555-3475 • FAX 517-555-3478

- Fear of losing money triggers response—but be sure the case is stated in a credible manner.

- Don't just offer to find problems. Let readers know that you also can recommend solutions.

Providing Unmatched Service to Hazelwood's Finest Companies for

OVER 40 YEARS

In 1949, we started out with little more than a pickup truck, a few cleaning tools and the determination to provide our clients with superior maintenance services. Thanks to loyal customers throughout the area, Charles Interior Maintenance Service has grown and expanded. Today we offer the most complete range of services available to property owners and managers, realtors and contractors in and around Hazelwood.

Janitorial services • Carpet cleaning • Building maintenance • Duct cleaning • Snow removal • Landscape maintenance • Window cleaning • Trash removal • Construction cleaning

CHARLES INTERIOR MAINTENANCE SERVICE

Put our experience to work for you—call 314-555-0900

50 Center Street, Hazelwood, MO 63042

Bonded, Licensed & Fully Insured

• In any business, particularly a service business, longevity is an indication of success. Don't be shy—state it in your headline.

• Make it easy for your readers to imagine how they could use your services. List your services and make it clear what kinds of businesses you serve.

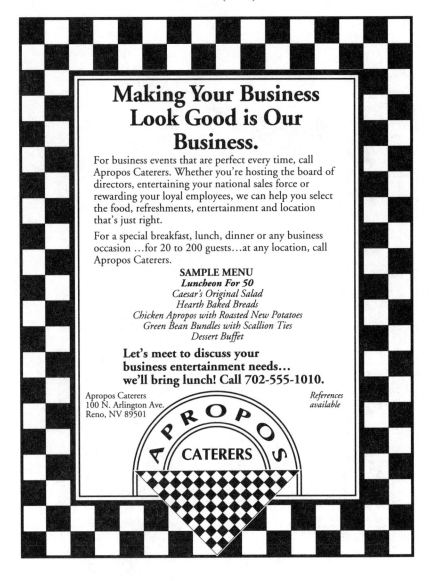

- Distinguish your business from the competition by describing the range of services and stating specific examples where appropriate (the sample menu, in this case).

- Try to offer a "free sample" (such as lunch in this ad) to get your foot in the door.

IF YOU'RE READY TO START YOUR OWN BUSINESS WE'RE READY TO HELP YOU SUCCEED

If you are seriously considering starting your own business, we can help you start it right. From helping to prepare your business plan to finding quality employees, our comprehensive range of services will help you hit the ground running—headed for success.

The Hausman Group has over 25 years of experience assisting new companies. We can also help you:

- Secure capital
- Establish credit with suppliers
- Locate office space and negotiate a lease
- Set up accounting and information management systems
- Many other services available

Call now for a free consultation
301-555-2666

Jay Hausman, President

THE HAUSMAN GROUP
Management Consultants
3 Tower Center, Bethesda, MD 20815

- The headline should address your specific market.

- Stating the length of time in business, or the amount of experience of the principals or key employees, builds confidence in your company.

- If you can, offer a free consultation. It allows prospects to size you up—and allows you to sell your company's abilities.

FULL-SERVICE BOOKKEEPING on a PART-TIME BASIS.

Now you can keep your bookkeeping costs low and your quality high with part time services from Peterson. For a morning, a day or whatever time you require, you can have the quality services of a Peterson's bookkeeper conveniently at your location. We can work with your existing books, or set up a new, highly efficient system to suit your needs—manual or computerized. For more information, or to arrange an appointment without obligation, call today.

- Accounts Payable
- Accounts Receivable
- Bank Reconciliation
- Payroll
- Federal, State & Local Taxes
- Data Entry
- Profit & Loss Statements

Plus More

(402) 555-3765
PETERSON'S BOOKKEEPING SERVICES
2002 Yolande Avenue, Lincoln, NE 68521   References available

---

- Use the headline to clearly target prospects (here, implicitly, small businesses).

- Itemize the services you provide to reinforce what full service is all about.

- Providing references reassures readers and legitimizes your claims.

Bank (8-43)

This is the perfect ad to run on the business page of your daily newspaper or a business weekly.

State your lending range to attract businesses with appropriate needs.

Include the name of a loan officer and a direct telephone line to increase response.

ELECTRONIC TESTING EQUIPMENT

BUY DIRECT AND SAVE

No middlemen...no distributors...no salespeople taking up your valuable time...and no extra cost for commissions! Order the electronic testing equipment you need direct from TestTek, recognized worldwide for quality and performance. Call for our free catalog of TestTek equipment. All items are in stock and ready for delivery.

Call toll-free 1-800-555-TEST

for our new catalog of controllers, multimeters, oscilloscopes and recorders!

TestTek Testing Equipment Co.

1428 Briley Parkway, Nashville, TN 37217
1-800-555-TEST   (1-800-555-8378)

- The advantages of buying direct from the manufacturer include convenience, no sales pressure, and savings. Play up all of these factors in your ad.

- Offer free sales literature tied to an 800 phone number.

When announcing a new specialty or treatment, target the type of patient you're trying to attract.

Have reprints made of your ad and send them to your current patients.

We are pleased to welcome
our newest associate

Lawrence W. Thornton, M.D.
specializing in vitreo-retinal surgery.

SHREVEPORT OPHTHALMIC ASSOCIATES

Frances M. Newham, M.D., F.A.C.S.	Charles M. Hitchens, M.D.	Richard S. Davies, M.D., F.A.A.O.
Cataract surgery, intra-ocular lenses, corneal transplantation, oculo-plastic and lacrimal surgery	Pediatric ophthalmology, neuro-ophthalmology, adult strabismus	Refractive disorders, contact lenses including keratoconus and specialty lenses, low vision aids, aniseikonia

SHREVEPORT OPHTHALMIC ASSOCIATES
1800 Warrington Place, Shreveport, LA 71101
318-555-5000

- Welcome your new associate in the headline of your ad, listing his or her qualifications or specialty.

- If space permits, list all associates and their specialties.

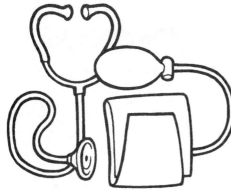

To Your Health!

19th Annual Peachtree Medical Center Health Fair

Dalton Mall – Highway 71
Thursday through Saturday
September 12 to 14
10:00 AM to 5:00 PM daily

The physicians and health professionals at Peachtree Medical Center care about you and your family. We're dedicated to your well-being. That's why we're hosting our health fair for the 19th consecutive year.

Join us at the largest health fair in Georgia. Take advantage of free health screenings and consultations with our physicians. Find out all you need to know to start living a healthier and happier life.

Peachtree Medical Center
1400 Whitfield Avenue, Dalton, GA 30720
404-555-1000

HEALTH SCREENING BOOTHS

1 Blood pressure screening
2 Cholesterol screening
3 Vision screening
4 Height/weight evaluation
5 Skin cancer screening
6 Diabetes screening
7 Substance abuse, mental health information
8 EEG demonstrations
9 Cosmetic surgery consultations
10 Breast self-exam instruction
11 Circulatory disorder consultations
12 Physician referral services

FREE LITERATURE AVAILABLE

• Be sure to display the location prominently.

• To maximize attendance, list all the screening programs and consultations you will have available.

Lewisburg Family Clinic

14 Spring Lake Road
Lewisburg, TN 37091
615-555-1525

Your family medical group

Serving Lewisburg since 1962

Treating the needs of the entire family. Specialties in pediatrics, internal medicine and geriatrics.

MELVIN GORVAN, M.D.
MILLICENT BARTELL, M.D.
GRANT WOJOWSKI, M.D.

All major insurance plans accepted.
Medicare assignments accepted.

Monday thru Friday — 9 AM to 8 PM,
Saturdays to 1 PM
By appointment or walk-in

- Your office hours are important to prospective patients. Feature them prominently.

- Keep the tone of your ad serious, befitting a professional practice.

At Physicians University Hospital, we know what makes a good doctor. We've been a leader in training physicians for over 90 years.

We have hundreds of doctors in primary care and dozens of specialties available to see you in neighborhoods throughout the Richmond area. Each one is supported by the full resources of our major teaching institution. For more information or to arrange an appointment, call our Physician Referral Service at **804-555-1999**.

When it comes to finding good doctors, we always have the right prescription for you.

213 S. Jefferson Street, Richmond, VA 24011

PHYSICIANS UNIVERSITY HOSPITAL

- A play on words in the headline grabs attention. But be careful not to obscure your message.

- If you offer information via telephone, make sure the phone is answered promptly and courteously by people who can provide the necessary information.

The Women's Lawyers

Arlene Comstock and Candace Berman

For legal services from a woman's point of view, trust the experience of Arlene Comstock and Candace Berman. For more than 25 years, they've specialized in making the legal system work for women. For an appointment to discuss your legal questions, without obligation, call now.

- **Domestic law including divorce, support and custody issues**

- **Sexual discrimination**

- **Sexual harassment**

- **Alternative lifestyles**

COMSTOCK & BERMAN, P.C.

(Across from Family Court)
1201 Market Street, Providence, RI 02903
401-555-8564

- Feature photos or illustrations of the principals in the firm.

- If you're in a familiar location or near a landmark, mention it near your address.

When You Need a Lawyer for

Personal Matters

For personal legal problems, you need a personal lawyer you can depend on. Not a business lawyer, but a specialist in law affecting individuals like you. Call the law firm of Brian E. Williams for assistance in all forms of law for individuals and families including:

- **Accidents, personal injury and wrongful death**
- **Workers compensation**
- **Wills, trust, estate planning and probate**
- **Divorce and family law**
- **Real estate transactions**
- **Medical negligence and malpractice**
- **D.U.I. and criminal law**

Free initial consultation
319-555-6300

Evening and weekend appointments available

Brian E. Williams, Esq.
Specializing in personal and family law

2740 1st Avenue N.E. • Cedar Rapids, IA 52401

- Target the headline to your specific market—and be sure the copy addresses the needs of your prospects.

- If you offer special hours, mention them in the ad.

Avoid probate with a living trust

As specialists in estate planning for individuals with a net worth of $1 million and more, we will help you set up a living trust and avoid costly probate. We will provide you with the combined expertise of seasoned tax attorneys and certified public accountants to set up your estate advantageously. Free consultation with you, your attorney or your financial adviser.

Ask about our seminar program for organizations.

HOUSER, FRITZ & JOSEPHS
Attorneys at law

Estate planning & probate law
Wills & trusts
3201 Providence Drive, Bloomington, IL 61704
309-555-4350

- This ad also can be run in an upscale cultural or business magazine.

- Use the offer of a seminar to stimulate speaking engagements—and additional business.

If you have <u>debts</u>, we'll help take the pressure off.

Talk to the leading bankruptcy attorneys in Lorain for help with your business and personal financial problems.

We can assist you with:

- negotiating payment arrangements with your creditors
- stopping foreclosure or repossession
- preventing creditor harassment
- filing for bankruptcy, if deemed necessary

Free consultation: 216-555-0710

Evening and weekend appointments available

DAVIDSON & HILTON, P.C.

Bankruptcy Attorneys Since 1961
200 Sheffield Street, Lorain, OH 44052
(216) 555-7010

- Don't beat around the bush—put problem words such as "debt" in your headline.

- Consider using the same ad as a classified listing in a newspaper or business magazine.

**FREE—
the 1/2 hour
that could
save you
thousands.**

If you think you need legal assistance, call us for a consultation. The first half-hour is free. We'll discuss your situation and recommend a course of action. Over the years, Cunningham, Stein & Walsh has saved clients thousands of dollars with our expertise and experience. Many of these cases started with a simple phone call and a free consultation. So don't lose another second, call now.

• Divorce & Family Matters
• Bankruptcy
• Wills & Probate
• Personal Injury
• Medical Malpractice
• Workers' Compensation

Evening and Saturday appointments available

914-555-8147

Cunningham, Stein & Walsh, P.C.
Attorneys at Law
640 White Plains Road
Scarsdale, NY 10583

• A strong headline grabs your readers' attention and gets them into your ad. Check with your professional association to be sure you are in compliance with their advertising regulations.

• List your areas of specialization or expertise separate from the copy to make them easy to find.

Lawrence, McCarey & Coleman
is pleased to announce that

Stephen M. Schmidt

has joined the firm as a
partner in the litigation department.

❧ ❧

Lawrence, McCarey & Coleman, P.C.
1600 Medford Plaza, Medford, NJ 08055
(609) 555-1400 • Fax (609) 555-1410

• This style of ad is called a tombstone because of its shape, centered typography and serious tone. It is especially effective in making a straightforward announcement while conveying a professional image.

• For best results, keep the entire ad in one typeface to maintain simplicity.

W. J. Smith & Co.
Personalized Service for All Your Insurance Needs

At W. J. Smith & Co. you'll receive quality personalized service from our experienced insurance experts. And with over 20 companies to draw from, we can provide you with creative solutions for your every insurance need. We'll tailor a program to fit your lifestyle, your future plans *and* your budget. For a private consultation in our offices or at your home, call Bill Smith today at 404-555-8648.

LIFE • HEALTH • HOMEOWNERS • AUTO • FIRE • BOAT INSURANCE • SPECIALIZING IN SENIOR CITIZEN HEALTH CARE & LONG TERM NURSING HOME CARE POLICIES

Call for competitive quotes!
404-555-8648

W. J. Smith & Co. Insurance
14 Buford Parkway, Gainesville, GA 30501

• Stress personal attention, experience and a wide range of services to gain the competitive edge.

• Assign someone to answer your phone who is knowledgeable about your business and good with people, to make that important first impression.

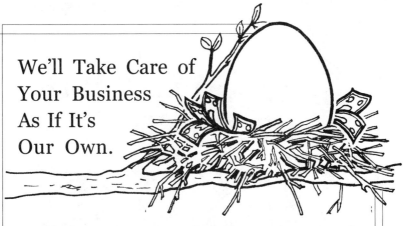

We'll Take Care of Your Business As If It's Our Own.

(We've been doing just that for over 40 years.)

Ask any of our clients—they'll tell you there's no substitute for the personal attention they get from the Tilton Agency. We built our business insurance brokerage through personal service and long-term relationships. Several of our very first clients are still with us today—forty years later!

As your business insurance broker, we'll learn the unique aspects of your business. We'll seek out the most effective and economical solutions to your insurance requirements. We'll give you the benefit of our experience in writing superior business insurance policies for a broad range of businesses.

If you're looking for a business insurance broker that's totally committed to your company, call the Tilton Agency. We'll be there for you.

THE TILTON AGENCY

Serving the insurance needs of Scranton businesses since 1952

436 Spruce Street, Scranton, PA 19603
717-555-8585

- Regardless of the business you're in, stressing personal service is a strong appeal. If you can couple that with experience (long time in business, principals with a great deal of experience), you've got a winning combination.

- With this kind of "philosophy" ad, discuss general concepts instead of specifics.

Make April 15th Less

Taxing

Make it easy on yourself this year. We'll do all the work for you. Just make an appointment, bring in your records, and we'll do the rest.

Our tax experts will dig deep to find every deduction you're entitled to. We'll reduce your tax liabilities to the legal minimum. We'll prepare your return by computer. And if you're entitled to a refund, we'll file your return electronically to get your money back in two to three weeks!

Call Now to Get Your Refund Quickly!

C. MacIntosh & Associates, CPA

Experts in federal and state income tax for over 25 years
Member AICPA

8501 Central Avenue, Sea Isle, NJ 08243

(609) 555-1234

Monday through Friday 9 to 9, Saturday 9 to 6

- Put strong benefits in your headline.

- Use a statement that prompts action ("Call now . . .").

- Remember, experience counts. List your years in business.

• Saving time and money gets everyone's attention.

• Credit cards are an important selling point no matter what business you're in. Remember to list those you accept.

Is Your Company Getting Everything It Needs from Your CPA?

Questions:

Which accounting and business services are most important for the health and growth of a small company?

What more should you be looking for?

Answers:

Consider these services the Grayson Group offers to help your firm grow and prosper:

- Direct personal attention from our principals at all times
- Development and implementation of streamlined accounting systems
- Training for your employees to handle bookkeeping in-house
- Tax planning 12 months of the year to minimize your liabilities
- Assistance with purchases, leases, contracts and other commitments
- Controlling costs of wages and benefits programs
- Financial planning to maximize the value of your company
- Preparation of tax returns for proprietorships, partnerships, corporations and individuals

The Grayson Group offers you over 20 years of experience in serving the needs of small business. You can count on us for the hands-on attention you need to continue your growth and success.

Call the Grayson Group for your no-obligation free consultation. To set up an appointment, call (215) 555-7070 today.

THE GRAYSON GROUP

Accounting Services for Small Business
Thirteen Grenox Commons, Wynnewood, PA 19096

(215) 555-7070 • Fax (215) 555-7075   AICPA

- Target the ad to your audience—in this case, small companies.

- Questions entice the prospect to read your ad to learn the answers.

- Offering a free consultation provides an effective way to generate response—and sell your services.

EXACTLY HOW WILL THE NEW

TAX LAWS

AFFECT YOU?

Find out at this <u>FREE</u> Seminar

Forget the old tax laws and throw away your current strategies. It's time to take a fresh look at your investment programs in light of the new tax laws going into effect this year. You need to listen to the advice of an accountant who understands the new laws. Better still, hear what an expert tax lawyer and CPA who knows investing has to say. Best of all, this seminar is absolutely FREE!

Beverly Simon-Knox, C.P.A., J.D. is a tax attorney with over 15 years' experience, and an accountant with 7 years experience at the country's largest accounting firms. You're invited to receive the full benefit of her understanding of the new tax laws at a two-hour seminar. Her graphic examples of key tax problems and solutions will show you new concepts for keeping more of what you make and making it grow faster.

Seating for this FREE seminar is limited. For reservations, call now: 1-714-555-4333

Monday, Nov. 16 7:00 PM
Torrance Lodge
20771 Madron Ave.
Torrance, CA 90509

Sponsored by
SK Tax Consultants Ltd.
1401 Madison St.,
Torrance, CA 90509

Beverly Simon-Knox, C.P.A., J.D.
Founder and President of
SK Tax Consultants Ltd.

- To attract the greatest number of prospects, the general rule is *not* to charge for business-producing seminars.

- Promoting your seminar is crucial. In addition to newspaper space, upscale local magazines, radio commercials and press releases are all important in getting the word out.

Where are you going financially? Will the money be there when you need it?

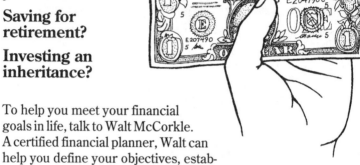

Funding college tuition for your kids?

Saving for retirement?

Investing an inheritance?

To help you meet your financial goals in life, talk to Walt McCorkle. A certified financial planner, Walt can help you define your objectives, establish a realistic plan and set up the programs you need to succeed. Make sure that when you need the money, it will be there.

FREE PERSONAL FINANCIAL REVIEW CALL 407-555-7680

McCorkle & Associates
Certified Financial Planners

Financial & Investment Planning • Stocks & Bonds • Mutual Funds • IRA & SEP Retirement Plans • Insurance

600 E. Rollins Avenue, Orlando, FL 32803 • 407-555-7680

- Asking questions in a headline involves the reader—and makes them think about the subject you're presenting.

- Free offers (as in this case, a free financial review) increase response.

HOW TO CREATE WEALTH AND KEEP IT.

FREE: Villanueva Pension Planners presents a wealth-building seminar on investment and retirement planning.

Thursday, September 28, 7:30 PM
Minuteman Room, Concord Manor,
Concord, MA

Anthony Villanueva, Certified Financial Planner, will tell you how, even in uncertain economic times, you can invest wisely for short and long term growth. In just two hours you'll learn Mr. Villanueva's nationally renowned techniques for using stocks, bonds, mutual funds and other investment vehicles to build and secure your personal portfolio. It's an evening with benefits that can pay off for generations.

ANTHONY VILLANUEVA
Certified
Financial
Planner

Seating is limited. Reserve now for this FREE seminar
Call 617-555-1900

Villanueva Pension Planners
1775 Lexington Parkway
Concord, MA 01742

• If the location of your seminar is different from your regular address, make the seminar address more prominent.

• Make the word "free" stand out with capital letters, bold type, underlining or italics.

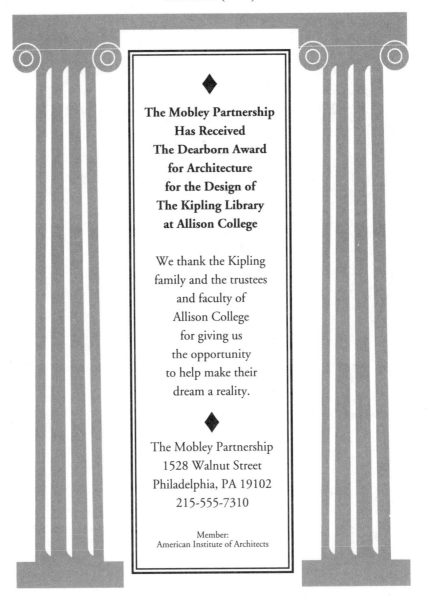

The Mobley Partnership
Has Received
The Dearborn Award
for Architecture
for the Design of
The Kipling Library
at Allison College

We thank the Kipling
family and the trustees
and faculty of
Allison College
for giving us
the opportunity
to help make their
dream a reality.

The Mobley Partnership
1528 Walnut Street
Philadelphia, PA 19102
215-555-7310

Member:
American Institute of Architects

- An announcement of a professional award should be quiet and dignified.

- Remember to thank those who made the award possible—the clients.

ALL THIS AND THE FIRST MONTH IS

FREE

The ideal combination of luxury and location, overlooking the river on Chestnut Street. Newly renovated 1 and 2 bedroom apartments with many extras, starting at $795 a month. And the first month's rent is free!

- Unique floor plans
- Designer baths
- Gourmet kitchens with microwaves
- Cable TV
- Security system

- Wall-to-wall carpeting
- Health club
- Off street parking
- Individual washers and dryers
- Free shuttle bus to city center

Leasing Office Open 7 Days A Week—Call 215-555-2600

S♦C♦H♦U♦Y♦L♦K♦I♦L♦L
LANDING
2601 Chestnut Street
Philadelphia, PA 19102

- A month's free rent is an almost irresistible offer. It works for apartments, office suites, storage spaces…practically anything that requires a monthly rental agreement.

- For maximum sales appeal, combine your offer with the primary selling benefits—in this case, location, view, amenities.

Find your dream with Avalon Real Estate.

Condos, townhomes and singles homes. Homes for newlyweds, homes for big families, homes for empty nesters, too. To find the home you've been dreaming of, just look for our sign!

PENN VALLEY-Mulberry Hill Estates, $125,000+
2 & 3 BR condos on rolling park-like lawns. Pool, tennis, clubhouse. Financing available. Dir: Rt. 23 East. L on Valley, L on Clover. Follow signs.

RADNOR HUNT, 15 Thornbury Rd., $179,000
Sophisticated townhome on lovely cul-de-sac. Private front and rear yards, den w/fp, lg. closets, 3 BR., 2-1/2 baths. Dir: From Rt. 3, S. on Rt. 926 to Thornbury, turn R.

MERION, 210 Ardmore Ave., $229,000
Fresh, young colonial seeks caring family. Lovely grounds and large deck. Gourmet kitchen, large LR w/fp, 4 BRs, 2-1/2 baths. Walk to schools. Dir: Rt. 1 South, Left on Old Lancaster, Left on Ardmore.

For more listings, see our ad every Sunday in the classified section.

FOR SALE
AVALON
REAL ESTATE
215-555-4900

1900 Montgomery Avenue, Ardmore, PA 19003

Open Monday thru Saturday
9 am to 5 pm
Sunday 11 am to 4 pm

Equal Housing Opportunity

- To build impact, run your open house ad in the more expensive display advertising section and steer buyers to look for the rest of your listings in the classified section.

- It's okay to keep descriptions brief, but include copy that sells the properties. If you use abbreviations, make sure they are easily understood.

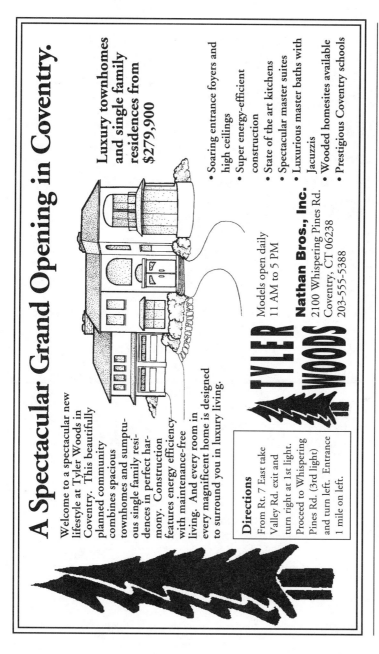

A Spectacular Grand Opening in Coventry.

Luxury townhomes and single family residences from $279,900

Welcome to a spectacular new lifestyle at Tyler Woods in Coventry. This beautifully planned community combines spacious townhomes and sumptuous single family residences in perfect harmony. Construction features energy efficiency with maintenance-free living. And every room in every magnificent home is designed to surround you in luxury living.

Directions

From Rt. 7 East take Valley Rd. exit and turn right at 1st light. Proceed to Whispering Pines Rd. (3rd light) and turn left. Entrance 1 mile on left.

- Soaring entrance foyers and high ceilings
- Super energy-efficient construction
- State of the art kitchens
- Spectacular master suites
- Luxurious master baths with Jacuzzis
- Wooded homesites available
- Prestigious Coventry schools

TYLER WOODS

Models open daily 11 AM to 5 PM

Nathan Bros., Inc.
2100 Whispering Pines Rd.
Coventry, CT 06238
203-555-5388

- For a real estate grand opening, include as much descriptive information as possible to entice your prospects, including a typical model design.

- If directions aren't simple, show a map.

Picture Your Company in this Choice Location

- 4 miles from the NY State Thruway
- 1,000 to 100,000 sq. ft.
- Perfect for office or light industrial
- Tailgate or drive-in loading
- 100 acre campus park
- 220 V, 3-phase power available
- All public utilities
- 20-foot ceilings
- Ample free parking
- The nation's best-educated work force to draw from

Don't relocate before you see everything Saratoga Commercial Commons has to offer! Call **518-555-4700** *today.*

1111 Kimberton Boulevard,
Saratoga Springs, NY 12866

BROKER PARTICIPATION INVITED • WILL BUILD TO SUIT

- When you have strong benefits to offer, build your ad around them.

- Use language your market understands (for example, "tailgate or drive-in loading").

CORPORATE HQ FACILITY FOR SALE OR LEASE

Eagle Oak
Industrial
Park,
Champaign,
Illinois

**THINK
LOCATION!**

Handsome two-story 28,000 sq. ft. building with newly renovated lobby, corridors and bathrooms. State-of-the-art security system. Ample parking. College town ambiance with big city amenities. 10 minutes from shopping, restaurants, banks, library, university, and prestigious Souderton Golf Club. Public bus stop at front door.

OWNER WILL DEAL!

Contact Morris Amsterdam, Hergenreder Properties, 1401 E. 24th St., Champaign, IL 61820

Phone 217-555-1188.

- While the facility is important, so is the area and ease of access. It's worth an extra line or two of copy to describe the proximity of life-enhancing qualities.

- Presenting contrasting benefits ("college town ambiance and big city amenities") paints a powerful picture of the best situation possible.

Our brightest star—
Caitlin Reynolds.

Miller Real Estate salutes the unprecedented sales performance of Caitlin Reynolds from our Redwood City office. In less than ten months this year, Caitlin sold residential properties in excess of $10 million.

INCREDIBLE!

We also salute these other stars of the Miller Real Estate team for their successes this year.

J.T. Whalen, Belmont office—$8 million
Harold Baker, San Carlos office—$5 million
Constance Lopez-Miller, San Carlos office—$2 million

Miller Real Estate
Premier properties are our specialty

2000 El Camino Real, Redwood City, CA 94065
404-555-6161

- If individual performance is worthy of an "INCREDIBLE," don't hold back. Showing enthusiasm for your employees and their achievements will result in improved motivation, increased productivity and higher sales.

- Everyone admires success. This theme can be used with any significant award an employee wins.

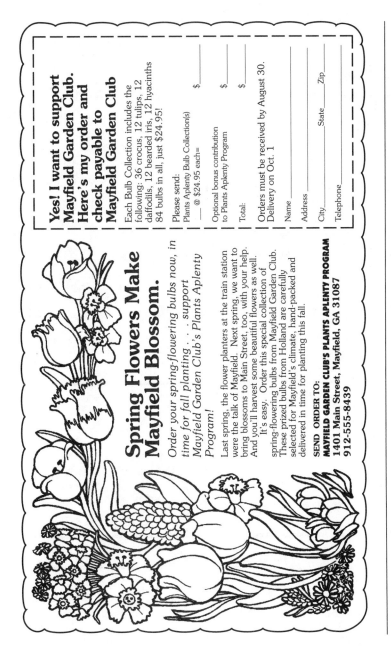

Spring Flowers Make Mayfield Blossom.

Order your spring-flowering bulbs now, in time for fall planting . . . support Mayfield Garden Club's Plants Aplenty Program!

Last spring, the flower planters at the train station were the talk of Mayfield. Next spring, we want to bring blossoms to Main Street, too, with your help. And you'll harvest some beautiful flowers as well.

It's easy. Order this special collection of spring-flowering bulbs from Mayfield Garden Club. These prized bulbs from Holland are carefully selected for Mayfield's climate, hand-packed and delivered in time for planting this fall.

SEND ORDER TO:
MAYFIELD GARDEN CLUB'S PLANTS APLENTY PROGRAM
1401 Main Street, Mayfield, GA 31087
912-555-8439

Yes! I want to support Mayfield Garden Club. Here's my order and check payable to Mayfield Garden Club

Each Bulb Collection includes the following: 36 crocus, 12 tulips, 12 daffodils, 12 bearded iris, 12 hyacinths 84 bulbs in all, just $24.95!

Please send:

Plants Aplenty Bulb Collection(s)
_____ @ $24.95 each= $ _____

Optional bonus contribution
to Plants Aplenty Program $ _____

Total: $ _____

Orders must be received by August 30.
Delivery on Oct. 1

Name _____

Address _____

City _____ State ___ Zip ___

Telephone _____

- Make the line "Yes! I want to support..." boldface in your order form to act as a rallying cry for your fundraising program.

- Include an extra space for contributors to use to donate extra money.

You called on us over

2,000 Times

last year.
Now we're calling on you.

Last year, Danvers volunteers responded to your calls for emergency assistance 2,048 times including:

- 992 traffic accidents
- 257 fires
- 628 household emergencies
- 114 school incidents
- 57 swimming and boating rescues

Whenever lives are on the line in Danvers Township, your all-volunteer rescue crew is there. Serving with care and compassion. Delivering life-saving assistance with highly trained skills. Every second of every day, your support and donations make our service possible. Thank you for helping us help our community.

Now we need your help again. Please contribute generously so we can continue to serve you in the future as we have in the past.

Danvers Volunteer Emergency Corps
P.O. Box 19
Danvers, MA 01923
(508) 555-4200

Thank You, Danvers Volunteers

Enclosed is my tax deductible donation in the amount of:

☐ $25.00   ☐ $100.00
☐ $50.00   ☐ Other $_____

Make check payable to:
Danvers Volunteer Emergency Corps

I would like to volunteer my services. Please contact me regarding:

☐ Rescue service
☐ Fund raising
☐ Telephone answering

Name _____

Address _____

City/State/Zip _____

Telephone _____

- Performance counts—it lets people know that their donations are producing results. Try to include statistics in your ad.

- Use a coupon to stimulate action. Don't limit your requests to money—ask for volunteers to donate their time, too.

7th ANNUAL FLEA MARKET—BUYERS & SELLERS WANTED

If you want to get rid of it, this is the place to sell it. If you're looking for it, this is the place to buy it. Household goods, clothing, toys, dolls, antiques, bric-a-brac, antiques, junque...it's all here at the event you've been waiting for!

Over 100 Tables—Rain Or Shine
9 am to 6 pm—Saturday & Sunday, Oct. 17 & 18

First Presbyterian Church
Corner 2nd & Elm Street, Ames, IA 50010
Information: (319) 555-4659

- If your event has been going on for a number of years, tell people. It lets them know it's established and worthwhile.

- For a one day or one weekend event, there's no second chance to draw crowds. Feature your dates, days and hours clearly.

Help us feed battered women and rebuild their lives.

Beans, stewed tomatoes, chicken soup—we'll take it all during our annual food drive. Please donate as much as you can to help us feed and care for battered women and their children. Give them the strength to build a new and better life.

Donations of canned goods and dried foods are now being accepted at:

**St. Mary's Church,
200 University Ave.**

**First Baptist Church,
2004 Randolph St.**

**Congregation Beth Hillel,
301 Pleasant St.**

**Twin Cities Women's League,
444 Cedar Lane**

**Please give as much as you can, as often as you can.
Food Drive ends November 7th.**

ST. PAUL WOMEN'S SHELTER FOOD DRIVE

Cash donations and volunteers also welcome—call 612-555-9982

- The same rules apply for fund-raising as for a commerical ad. For example, a strong illustration and headline will get your ad maximum attention.

- Include a list of locations where donations are being accepted.

A NOVEL IDEA

Donate your books to the
PECOS LIBRARY
BOOKLOVERS SALE
(We also take cash)

Each year, your donations of new and used books help raise thousands of dollars for the Pecos Library. Money raised through our annual Booklovers Sale goes to support all our activities including new book acquisitions, literacy programs, our authors lecture series and everybody's favorite—the Pecos Bookmobile traveling library.

If you have new books or used volumes in good condition to donate*, please bring them in between March 15 and April 15. If you're giving cash, send in your check any time. Thank you.

PECOS LIBRARY BOOKLOVERS SALE
Thursday & Friday
April 18 & 19—9:00 AM to 8:00 PM
Saturday
April 20—9:00 AM to 5:00 PM

PECOS LIBRARY
15 Butte Drive,
Pecos, NM 87552
505-555-0915

Volunteers needed to assist before and during the sale.

*Donations may be tax deductible.

• Spell out what kinds of goods you want donated. Also mention that you'll accept cash donations.

• Explain how the donations will be used.

For our 35th annual summer theater festival, we're performing three of Shakespeare's greatest plays. Once again, sell-outs are expected for all performances. Order your tickets now— don't miss the chance to see superb performances at the state's oldest continuously run summer theater.

"Shakespeare as it should be done"
Kansas Tribune

SHAKESPEARE
under the Stars

Hamlet – July 9, 10 & 11
A Midsummer Night's Dream – July 23, 24 & 25
Macbeth – August 6, 7 & 8 All performances start at 8:00 PM
All tickets $12.50. Bring a blanket and picnic basket.

EMPORIA SUMMER THEATER
2701 Park Lane, Emporia, KS 66801 • 316-555-9010

Please send tickets for the performances indicated below:

Hamlet
July 9 —— Seats
July 10 —— Seats
July 11 —— Seats

A Midsummer Night's Dream
July 23 —— Seats
July 24 —— Seats
July 25 —— Seats

Macbeth
August 6 —— Seats
August 7 —— Seats
August 8 —— Seats

Total: _____ Seats @ $12.50= $ _____

Please charge to my credit card □ Visa □ MasterCard □ American Express

Card number _____

Signature _____ Expiration date _____

□ I have enclosed a check in the amount of $ _____ .

Do not send cash. Make checks payable to: Emporia Summer Theater

(please print all information)

Name _____

Address _____

City/State/Zip _____

Telephone _____

- If you have quotes or testimonials, use them.

- Organize your coupon to make it easy for customers to order and for your staff to fulfill. A photocopy of the fill-in section of this coupon can be used as the address label for the tickets mailed back to the customer.

We Couldn't Have Done It Without You.

To the thousands of wonderful people who helped out on our annual blood drive, we'd like to express our appreciation. You've helped ensure that we'll be able to meet New Milford's needs for another year.

COMMUNITY BLOOD BANK
1100 Hector Street
New Milford, Connecticut 06776
(203) 555-1111
Member United Way

- Remember to thank people for their support—you'll be more likely to get their help again next time.

- If you keep your public service ads small, local newspapers are more likely to use them.

Press Releases 9

An article about your product or service in a newspaper or magazine, or even a single one-line mention, is more than just "free" advertising. It's believability that you can't buy in a paid advertisement. The vehicle that generally attracts the interest of editors and reporters is a well-written press release—a major tool for public relations.

You can use a press release to announce virtually anything you might include in an ad, but some subjects are more appropriate than others. They must measure up to the "newsworthy" benchmark editors and reporters live by.

Some suggested topics include:
- Public service activity
- Publication of an article or book
- Lecture or speech
- Grand opening of a new location
- Professional citation or recognition
- New product or service
- New employee
- New account or client

Be careful how you present your news. Nothing will send your release into the trash can faster than hyperbole and bold, bragging copy. Report your news professionally, using the system journalists prefer, reporting the "5 W's and an H"—who, what, when, where, why and how—in the first paragraph. If a photograph is available to support your news story, send it along—captioned, of course.

Follow the accepted format. Keep press releases to a single 8 1/2" x 11" sheet of paper. Place your company name and address at the top with the contact name and phone number directly below to the left, and the date to the right. State "For Immediate Release" if you want the piece to be published immediately. If you have a specific date for the release, indicate that by stating "For Release October 3." End the release with the traditional "###" or "-30-". If you absolutely need a second page, place "-More-" at the bottom of the first page.

Involve the press. If you're seeking coverage of an upcoming event, invite the press in writing and give adequate advance notice. Follow up with a personal telephone call to the editor, then speak with the reporter assigned to offer any courtesies that might assist them in covering the story.

Keep at it. For best results, invest your time and effort in a sustained program to keep your name before the public. Develop a list of key publications, editors, reporters and other press contacts. If appropriate, include television and radio stations, the business press, trade journals and virtually any other medium that covers news important to your business or service. Mail or fax your stories to them regularly. After a day or two, call them to see if you can provide additional information or discuss a different slant on the story.

Folk Art Gallery (9-01)

Company Name
Address
City, State Zip

Date

Contact: Martin Livesy
(301) 555-1991

FOR IMMEDIATE RELEASE

MARTIN LIVESY TO LECTURE ON AMERICAN FOLK ART

Noted art historian and author Martin Livesy will conduct a two-hour lecture on American folk art and furnishings on Tuesday, May 6, at 7:30 PM at Annapolis Antiquities. Mr. Livesy will present his own unique viewpoint on the arts and crafts of largely unknown farmers, tradesmen and artisans. The presentation will be illustrated with slides taken by the lecturer.

Author of "American Folk Art," published by Envoy Press, Livesy has an extensive knowledge and appreciation of these works. His discussion will cover the aesthetic form, color, and design subtleties of paintings, sculpture, and many kinds of decorations and furnishings. Livesy will draw on examples of arts and crafts from throughout the United States, demonstrating how multiple cultures influenced the evolution and regional characteristics of these classically American items.

Annapolis Antiquities, widely recognized as a major source of American folk arts and crafts throughout the Mid-Atlantic region, is located on Dock Street along Annapolis' waterfront area. For reservations for Livesy's lecture, call (301) 555-1991. Admission is free, but space is limited.

# # #

• A press release about a guest speaker who has a reputation in their field should be sent to all the print and broadcast media in the area.

• Also send your press release to those on your mailing list, along with a note inviting them to attend.

Company
Address
City, Sate Zip

Date

Contact: Anne Weld
           (218) 555-9740

FOR IMMEDIATE RELEASE

WEMBLEY ENVIRONMENTAL SERVICES SPONSORS REINER COLLEGE
SCHOLARSHIP PROGRAM

An annual scholarship for students in the environmental engineering program
at Reiner College has been funded by a grant from Wembley Environmental
Services of Morton, Minnesota.

In announcing the scholarship program, Carl Wembley, president of Wembly
Environmental Sevices, credited the faculty at Reiner College for awakening
his interest in environmental engineering as a student. "Their inspired
teaching led me to pursue a career in environmental engineering and
ultimately resulted in the success of my own company," he said.

Reiner College faculty will select the student who will receive the $1,000.00
Wembley Environmental Engineering Scholarship each year. Applicants may
apply through the Student Financial Aid Office at Reiner College, P.O. Box
2185, New London, MN 56273. Telephone: 218-555-6391. Or write to
Wembley Environmental Services Inc., 14 Roaring Creek Road, Morton, MN
56270. Telephone: (218) 555-9740.

# # #

- To ensure that proper credit is given to everyone involved, identify the parties in the headline
  whenever possible.

- Include an address and phone number if your release requests a response.

Paint Store (9-03)

Company Name
Address
City, State Zip

Date

Contact: Milton Brickman
(201) 555-2545

FOR IMMEDIATE RELEASE

BRICKMAN PAINTS MAKES IT EASY TO RECYCLE YOUR LEFTOVER PAINTS AND SOLVENTS

Montclair, NJ. It's illegal to dispose of old paints and unused solvents with your regular household trash. Now you can get rid of them in a way that's environmentally responsible and convenient. Brickman Paints has announced that it will provide free recycling of unused paints, stains and paint-related solvents for residents of Essex County the first weekend in November.

Miller Brickman, owner of the Montclair paint store, announced the service in cooperation with the Essex County Environmental Services Department's annual hazardous materials recycling campaign. "Residents should bring paints, stains and solvents in their original containers during special recycling hours," Brickman stated. Proof of residence in Essex County will be required. Store employees will collect and separate the containers as required by environmental regulations. After the weekend, Brickman Paints vehicles will transport the materials to Essex County's hazardous waste handling center.

Brickman Paints, one of the retailers of D.I.Y. brand paints and stains, is located at 130 Watchung Road, Montclair, New Jersey 07043. Recycling hours are scheduled for Friday and Saturday, Nov. 3 and 4, from 10:00 AM to 7:00 PM and from Noon to 4:30 PM on Sunday, Nov. 5. For more information, call 201-555-2543.

#

- A public service program contributes to the community and gets your name in the news.

- Be sure to get your local newspaper to cover the event and encourage them to publish a photograph.

Financial Planner (9-04)

Company Name
Address
City, State Zip

Date

Contact: Sheila Mannes
(318) 555-9900

FOR IMMEDIATE RELEASE

HARVEY STEPHENS NAMED CERTIFIED FINANCIAL PLANNER

Harvey Stephens, account executive with the investment firm of Lindenbach Securities in Shreveport, has completed the required course of study and is now a Certified Financial Planner (CFP). Stephens is qualified to advise clients in planning every aspect of their personal financial programs including savings, investments, insurance, and retirement and estate planning.

Stephens now has a second set of initials after his name, adding CFP to the CPA he earned as a Certified Public Accountant. "Being a CPA and a Certified Financial Planner allows me to serve my clients with a more focused approach to their financial needs," says Stephens. "I can combine my accounting and financial planning skills to optimize the performance of their investments."

Lindenbach Securities is located at 1140 Warrington Place, Suite 1500, Shreveport, LA 71101. Harvey Stephens' telephone number is (318) 555-9900.

A life-long resident of Shreveport, Stephens is married and the father of two. He is a graduate of Louisiana State University, class of 1986.

# # #

- When an employee receives a certification, diploma, or award, that's an excellent time to issue a press release.

- Including personal information in a business release can attract the interest of non-business publications—such as local newspapers and alumni magazines.

Veterinarian (9-05)

Company Name
Address
City, State Zip

Date

Contact: Dr. Lynn Doren
(215) 555-0783

FOR IMMEDIATE RELEASE

FREE BOOKLET AVAILABLE ON HOW TO PURCHASE A PEDIGREED DOG

PHILADELPHIA—A newly published booklet, QUESTIONS AND ANSWERS ABOUT PEDIGREED DOGS, written by veterinarian Dr. Lynn Doren and her staff, offers many tips and helpful hints on acquiring a pedigreed dog.

If you're planning on purchasing a pedigreed dog, you need to do some homework, says Dr. Doren, head of the Mt. Airy Veterinary Clinic in Philadelphia. "If you don't have the right answers to breeders' questions," says Dr. Doren, "you may be turned down even though you're waving your checkbook."

Do you have small children? Many breeders won't sell to you until the puppy is old enough—four to five months—to protect themselves. "Most children see a puppy as another toy, and don't understand how fragile it is." But, according to Dr. Doren, some puppies are sold before they're three months old, because available four and five month old puppies are in short supply.

Do you want a show quality or a pet quality puppy? Even though you may be willing to pay for a show quality dog, many breeders will not sell a high caliber dog to non-show families because they want their puppies to be seen in the show ring. Pet quality pedigreed dogs are no less healthy or attractive, but they have some features that would keep them out of the show ring.

QUESTIONS AND ANSWERS ABOUT PEDIGREED DOGS is available free of charge from the Mt. Airy Veterinary Clinic, 388 E. Griffith Street, Philadelphia, PA 19123. For a copy, call (215) 555-0783.

# # #

Privately published booklets, newsletters, etc., are excellent subjects for press releases.

Use quotes in your press release to give it the appearance of a news story.

Institution Name
Address
City, State Zip

Date

Contact: Roberta Strong
(503) 555-7737

FOR IMMEDIATE RELEASE

EUGENE CLINIC REPORTS IMPROVED SUCCESS RATES
IN TREATING INFERTILITY

Eugene, OR.—Physicians at the Goshen Reproductive Sciences Center have reported encouraging results in the treatment of reproductive disorders in a recently concluded two-year study. Wayne N. Commager, MD., director of the center, described the progress as "very promising for many couples who have experienced difficulty in achieving conception."

"In many cases, couples have credited us with helping them have babies long after they'd given up hope," reported Dr. Commager. He pointed to a variety of new and improved services for diagnosis and treatment for producing the results.

The Goshen Reproductive Sciences Center has expanded the methods used in its Andrology Department to include computerized semen analysis, sperm freezing and immunological infertility testing. Clinical services consist of treatment of male and female infertility, donor insemination, intra-uterine insemination, and in-vitro fertilization.

A free seminar for interested couples will be presented on Wednesday, January 23 from 7:30 to 9:00 PM at the Goshen Avenue YMCA on Willamette St. at Broadway in Eugene. To reserve seats or schedule an appointment call the Goshen Reproductive Sciences Center at (503) 555-7737. The center is open seven days a week, and is located at 4701 East 30th Avenue, Eugene OR 97405.

# # #

- Even the most sensitive issues can be handled effectively in a press release.

- Mention your organization several times to be sure that after a zealous editor trims your release, your name remains.

Hospital (9-07)

Institution Name
Address
City, State Zip

Date

Contact: Cynthia Burwick
(206) 555-0576

FOR IMMEDIATE RELEASE

GLENWOOD MEMORIAL HOSPITAL SPONSORS ANTI-SMOKING CAMPAIGN

Glenwood, WA. In an effort to prevent youngsters from smoking, Glenwood Memorial Hospital is sponsoring a multimedia anti-smoking campaign called "BUTT OUT, GLENWOOD." Programs for elementary, junior high and high school students are being presented with the cooperation of the health department at Glenwood Regional High School.

"A significant number of our patient's illnesses can, unfortunately, be directly attributed to tobacco use," reports Dr. Charles Hopkins, chief of pulmonary medicine at Glenwood Memorial Hospital. "We're making this program a top priority of the hospital."

"BUTT OUT, GLENWOOD" programs include video presentations, guest lecturers, posters and group discussions in its programs.

Additional sponsors for "BUTT OUT, GLENWOOD" are needed. Tax deductible donations should be sent to "BUTT OUT, GLENWOOD," c/o Glenwood Memorial Hospital, 1300 Cascade Avenue, Glenwood, WA 98619. Telephone: (206) 555-0567.

\# \# \#

• Promoting a public service campaign through the media gives your project the visibility needed for a successful program. Take every opportunity to publicize it.

• A request for additional support can be made effectively through press releases such as this one. Be sure your organization's address and phone number are included.

Medical Center, Health Fair (9-08)

Institution Name
Address
City, State Zip

Date

Contact: Judith Kimball
(404) 555-1000

FOR IMMEDIATE RELEASE

ALL SAINTS MEDICAL CENTER HOLDS 19TH ANNUAL HEALTH FAIR

The physicians and health professionals of All Saints Medical Center are hosting their annual health fair for the 19th consecutive year. The fair will run from Thursday through Saturday, September 12 to 14 at the Dalton Mall.

"We're inviting the public to attend this informative event, which is focused on education and prevention," said All Saints Medical Center director Charlene D. Pendell, M.D. "Come take advantage of free health screenings and consultations with our physicians. Find out all you need to know to start living a healthier and happier life."

Health Screening booths include:

1	Blood pressure screening	8	EKG demonstrations
2	Cholesterol screening	9	Cosmetic surgery consultations
3	Vision screening	10	Breast self-exam instruction
4	Nutritional evaluation	11	Consultation on laparoscopic and
5	Skin cancer screening		abdominal surgery
6	Diabetes screening	12	Circulatory disorder consultations
7	Substance abuse, mental health	13	Urology, prostate, impotence consultations
	information	14	Hospital volunteer services

The All Saints Medical Center Health Fair is open from 10:00 AM to 5:00 PM Thursday through Saturday, September 12 to 14 at the Dalton Mall on Highway 71. For more information, contact Health Fair Coordinator Judith Kimball, All Saints Medical Center, 1400 Whitfield Avenue, Dalton, GA 30720. Telephone: (404) 555-1000.

# # #

- In spite of the serious nature of your subject, try to include a quote or two that's upbeat and enthusiastic. It can encourage the reporter reading your release to get behind your event.

- As with any press release, list all pertinent information (the five W's and an H): who, what, when, where, why and how.

Historic Preservation League (9-09)

Association Name
Address
City, State Zip

Date

Contact: Joan Sterling
(609) 555-1676

FOR IMMEDIATE RELEASE

HISTORIC GREENWICH HOUSE TOURS PLANNED

Three of the most well-known homes in historic Greenwich will be open to the public during the first weekend in November. Tours will be conducted by members of the Greenwich Preservation League from 10 A.M. to 5 P.M. on Saturday, November 12, and from Noon to 4 P.M. on Sunday, November 13.

Houses open for the tour include:

- The Pedersen House, a two-story Georgian mansion built in 1770
- The Derr House, a pre-revolutionary farmhouse expanded in the Victorian style during the 1860's
- Evergreen, a Federalist mansion featuring Queen Anne and Chippendale furnishings

The cost for the Historic Greenwich House Tour, including a guided walk of the town's cobblestoned streets, is $20 per person, with proceeds donated to the Greenwich Preservation League. Children under 12 are not permitted. Tours will depart the league's headquarters at 15 Cumberland Street, Greenwich, NJ 08323. For reservations, call (609) 555-1676 Monday through Friday from 9:30 A.M. to 3:30 P.M.

# # #

- Include a brief description of highlights to whet the public's appetite.

- If you have restrictions on who may attend, such as excluding children, be sure to say so.

Volunteer Emergency Corps (9-10)

Organization Name
Address
City, State Zip

Date

Contact: Mike Roman
(508) 555-4200

FOR IMMEDIATE RELEASE

DANVERS VOLUNTEERS SET NEW RESCUE RECORD

Members of the Danvers Volunteer Emergency Corps responded to 2,048 calls for emergency assistance last year, announced Joseph N. McGrath, Corps Commander. The number represented an increase of seven percent over last year when 1,920 calls or "runs" were made by Danvers Volunteers. The breakdown of calls for assistance was:

- 992 traffic accidents
- 257 fires
- 628 household emergencies
- 114 school and sports incidents
- 57 swimming and boating rescues

Asked what the Danvers Volunteer Emergency Corps' requirements are for next year, McGrath said, "People and money." Danvers Township helps underwrite the Emergency Corps. Additional money is required to purchase, upgrade and maintain equipment as well as to provide vital training to volunteers.

A meeting will be held Saturday afternoon, October 12 at 1:30 PM to welcome new volunteers and launch the Fall Fundraising Drive and Apple Cider Sale. All interested parties are welcome to attend at the East Avenue Rescue Station, 1201 Minuteman Road, Danvers. For more information, call (508) 555-4200.

# # #

- In fund-raising press releases, statistics give the reader facts to focus on and relate to.

- Quote an authority or organization head.

Organization
Address
City, State Zip

Date

Contact: Florence Davis
(614) 555-5677

FOR IMMEDIATE RELEASE

ABERDEEN GARDEN CLUB SCHEDULES ANNUAL PARK CLEAN-UP

Volunteers are invited to pitch in during the Annual Park Clean-Up on Saturday, April 12th, sponsored by the Aberdeen Garden Club.

During the day-long event, garden club members and other concerned citizens will rake and prune away the last vestiges of winter throughout the 10-acre park grounds.

"We're going to bag any remaining leaves for recycling," stated Florence Davis, president of the garden club. "Twigs and branches will be ground up and mixed with other mulch material and spread over the park gardens."

In addition to Garden Club members, the 4H Club has agreed to help with the program. Other volunteers are welcome to lend a hand, "even if it's only for an hour or two," said Davis.

Sutherland Tree Service will provide the mulching equipment and donate additional mulch. New annual flowers will be furnished by Aberdeen Garden Supply. Refreshments will be supplied by Marie's Catering Service. Additional donations of flowering perennials and shrubs are also being sought.

Volunteers may start arriving at the Aberdeen Park main gate at 8:30 AM for work assignments. Old clothes and garden gloves are recommended.

# # #

When soliciting volunteers, use a press release to communicate what they'll be expected to do, what to bring, along with any other important details.

Use the same press release to acknowledge support already received from other sources.

Radio and TV Commercials 10

Once the exclusive territory of large companies, you can now generate great awareness for your business on radio or TV at an affordable cost. Thanks to the explosive growth of FM radio and the popularity of cable TV, you can efficiently broadcast your message to masses of listeners or viewers with demographic precision, selecting exactly the audience you want.

Both TV and radio offer you immediacy. Your spot can be on the air in a day or less if necessary. You can use the electronic media to create an instant event, or as an ongoing advertising program to establish and maintain your company's presence.

Regardless of whether you're producing a commercial for TV or radio, someone has to speak for you. Use a professional announcer, satisfied customers, yourself or any combination to deliver the message that will bring business to you. Commercial spots are a fixed time length—10, 15, 20, 30 or 60 seconds. Use the time wisely. Try to say too much and your spot will come across as a race against time. Leave room for emphasis, drama, salesmanship and, very importantly, repetition.

Now for some specific suggestions about each medium.

Radio. This is the medium of the imagination. With radio you can paint a vivid picture in the listener's mind with sound effects, music and some creativity. You can put the listener in your showroom, on a beach in Tahiti or in a handsome new car whizzing down the highway.

The local radio station will usually produce your commercial at little or no cost to you, unless your needs are unusual (such as requiring an actor instead of one of the station's announcers).

Telephone numbers should be repeated two or three times to be sure the listener has a chance to write them down. When giving your address, provide a well known landmark so the listener can visualize where you are located.

TV. This is the medium of action, perfect for demonstrating your product or service. Show the sparkle on your car, the size of your homes or the sincerity of your smile in living color. You can get images from your suppliers, or from still photos and custom videos taped just for your use at your location or in a studio by the TV station. Most TV stations have low-cost production services available to assist advertisers in producing quality commercials.

The challenge with TV commercials is to synchronize the audio and video so they reinforce each other rather than confuse. The same advice about repetition given in the radio section applies here equally.

Restaurant--60-Second Radio Spot (10-01)

MUSIC: Festive Italian music

ANNCR: This year, give Mom our best for Mother's Day. Bring her to Pietro's for Festa Della Mama, our Mother's Day Feast. It's a dining experience your mom will talk about for years to come, and it's especially affordable with Pietro's special price fixed menu, created just for the day. First, pin a complimentary corsage on Mom. Then, dinner starts with a choice of lobster bisque or Pietro's own salad vinaigrette. Mom can select from five mouthwatering entrees, including Chicken Breast Tuscano, Grilled Sirloin, Spinach Fettucine Alfredo, Grilled Lemon Sole, or Veal Marsala ala Pietro. Finish with a special creation from Pastry Chef Gian-Carlo, served with coffee or tea. If all this sounds a little extravagant, relax—Pietro's offers this Mother's Day feast for just $17.95 per person, with a special menu for children. Festa Della Mama...the famous Mother's Day Feast at Pietro's—at 11 Providence Place in Cranston. Sunday, May 10th only, 2 PM to 8 PM. Call for reservations at 401-555-2920. Call Pietro's now, and give Mom our best. That's 401-555-2920.

Use music to establish a mood and an atmosphere of anticipation.

Mention the date of the holiday—the listener may not be aware of it.

Heating and A/C Services--60-Second Radio Spot (10-02)

ANNCR: (Starting in shivering, quivering voice)

When you walk from your dining room to your den does it feel like you're going directly from the warmth of spring to the depths of winter? Does the temperature seem to rise and fall as you walk from room to room? Like many homeowners in central Wisconsin, your heater is just fine. The problem is that it needs to spread the warmth better. Duval Heating can help. We can test your heater's output in each room. Then we'll balance the flow through-out your house. . . adjusting a damper here. . . running a new duct there. . .controlling the distribution of heat for total comfort in every room. Duval can make your home more comfortable in no time. At a price so low, it'll probably pay you back in fuel savings in just a year or two. For a free survey, call Duval Heating at 414-555-9975 today. Then turn down the heat and turn up the comfort throughout your home. That's 414-555-9975 for Duval Heating. We're a such a comfort to have around.

- Remember to sell the benefit, not the features. In this example, heat is merely the feature—comfort is the benefit, and it's reinforced throughout the commercial.

- When describing a problem, use a familiar scenario that listeners can identify with, such as temperature changing from room to room.

Mattress Store--60-Second Radio Spot (10-03)

ANNCR: (Sincere, sympathetic)

After a miserable night on an uncomfortable mattress, what's the best news you could wake up to? After tossing and turning, counting more sheep than there are in New Zealand, what's the one thing you want to hear?

MUSIC: Sousa's American Post March

ANNCR: (Excited, enthusiastic)

Well here it is...news so exciting it may put you right to sleep. The grand opening of Miller Bedding's second store is happening right now. You heard right. Miller Bedding, <u>your</u> source for quality mattresses and box springs from makers like DreamQuest, Whitney & Lamb, and Harmony! And here's even more grand opening news—buy any mattress and box spring set from our special grand opening collection and here's what you'll receive: First, take 50% off the regular price. Second, get a matching bed frame, free. Third, enjoy free delivery. You're practically asleep already, right? We'll even remove your bedding free of charge. Hurry to Miller Bedding's Grand Opening today at 426 West Allen in Waterloo. Or save at our original location at 5th and Main in Cedar Falls. Both stores open Monday through Saturday from 9 to 9. Closed Sunday because with a sale like this, everybody needs a day of rest. Call for more information—319-555-0505. That's Miller Bedding. Sweet dreams.

- Remember the traffic-building power of the words "Grand Opening." In radio, words don't sit on a printed page to be read again and again, so they're repeated throughout for emphasis.

- Use humor cautiously. There's nothing as unsuccessful as a "humorous" commercial that's not amusing.

ANNCR: Tired of flipping through those same dull 7 channels? Call Walker Cable now and we'll give you 49 great reasons to move up to cable TV today. And every one's an exciting new channel! We offer movies, sports, comedy, the arts, science, home shopping, the food channel and gardening and decorating, too! There's always something to watch on Walker Cable. Call Walker Cable now. Basic service costs less than fifty cents a day—about what you're paying for the newspaper. And if you sign up now, you'll receive the Bijou Entertainment Network free for a month. So turn down the radio, pick up the phone and call Walker Cable at (802) 555-1596. That's (802) 555-1596. Call now, and see everything you're missing on TV. Offer ends October 31.

- You can make your price far more attractive by breaking it down to a cost per day, and relating it to a similar bill the prospect is already paying.

- Repeat your phone number to help people remember it, or to give them time to write it down.

Bicycle Store--60-Second Radio Spot (10-05)

SFX*:   Outdoors sounds, birds, etc.

ANNCR: (Friendly, laid back)

How can you tell if a mountain bike has what it takes, when you can only try it out for a minute? How do you know if you can trust it in the woods if you can't ride it out of the parking lot? The answer is you can't, and that's why Ike's Bikes introduces the one hour test ride for the new Pyrenees 2000 mountain bike.

Ike's Bikes invites you to reserve time to put this incredible cycling achievement to the test. Feel the power in your legs transfer to the wheels through the incomparable 21 speed Gizo gearing. Experience the confidence you'll feel when you tear around a steep curve on the Pyrenees 2000. It's waiting for you at Ike's Bikes now. And only Ike's Bikes offers you a test ride on any model we sell.

Come in to Ike's Bikes to see the Pyrenees 2000 and all the other fine bikes and accessories in stock. And reserve your free test ride today. That's Ike's Bikes on the Somerville Circle, Somerville, New Jersey. 908-555-IKES. That's Ike's Bikes. Open every day 8 to 5 including Sundays, Thursdays to 9 PM.

*SFX is the abbreviation for sound effects

- With sound effects, radio can take you anywhere. In this spot, outdoors sounds are used to place the listener in the woods on a mountain bike. Substitute the background of a busy office, alter the copy a little and you have a radio spot for testing a fax machine on the job.

- The strongest demonstration is the one a prospect can give himself. You can probably tailor yours to be self-administered.

ANNCR: In this area, one out of every five homes has radon problems. If your home hasn't been tested, or if you're thinking of buying a new home and want to be assured that it's free of radon, call EnviroTest of Williamsport today. Radon is a potentially harmful radioactive gas which occurs naturally in central Pennsylvania. Invisible and odorless, it can seep through the walls of your home's foundation to endanger you and your family and you'll never know it. EnviroTest uses sensitive detectors to evaluate the air and determine if you have a radon problem. Our laboratories are certified by the Environmental Protection Agency so you know you can trust our results.

We are not radon contractors. Our only interest is in the safety of your home for you and your family. If you do have a problem, EnviroTest will consult with you free of charge on possible solutions. For peace of mind on radon, call EnviroTest at 717-555-4141 now. That's EnviroTest at 717-555-4141. Call now. Your family needs to know if radon is a problem in your home.

- When you're advertising a new or emerging service, be sure to include enough explanation so the listener will understand what you are offering.

- Include statements which support your qualifications, such as certification by a government authority or licensing agency.

SFX*:   Jingling sleigh bells

ANNCR: (Booming voice)

Ho, ho, ho and a Merry Christmas. If you'd like to earn extra
money for college tuition, a winter vacation or special holiday
gifts, celebrate Christmas in July on the job at Maxwell Paper.

We have seasonal part-time openings now for assembling,
packing and wrapping assortments of famous Maxwell gift
papers, ribbons and cards. You'll earn good pay, and have
flexible hours. And no experience is necessary. Every
summer, folks like you work at Maxwell Paper to make their
dreams come true with just a few extra hours' work each day.
You can, too.

Apply in person between 9:30 AM and 2:30 PM Monday
through Friday at Maxwell Paper, 2100 Palmetto Highway in
Savannah. That's between 9:30 AM and 2:30 PM Monday
through Friday.

At Maxwell Paper, Christmas always comes early...and pays
very nicely. See for yourself. Maxwell Paper Company—an
equal opportunity employer.

*SFX is the abbreviation for sound effects.

• Radio can be extremely effective in delivering large numbers of job applicants in a short time.

• Emphasize the days and hours when you're taking applications by repeating the information.

Financial Services Company--60-Second Radio Spot (10-08)

ANNCR: Need money to grow your business? It may be sitting in your accounts receivables right this minute! You heard right. The money you haven't collected yet can fund your future growth. . . with the help of Columbus Capital Corporation. As a Columbus Capital customer, you can establish a line of business credit linked directly to your current accounts receivables. And depending on the value of your business assets, personal commitment and accounts receivables, you can borrow from Columbus Capital for as little as 3 percent over prime. 3 percent over prime to keep your business growing and prospering. Columbus Capital has other creative ideas to keep your business growing, too, including new contract and approved purchase order financing. It's all spelled out in a free booklet—Discover New Ways to Grow with Columbus Capital. For your free copy, or to discuss how Columbus Capital can provide growth financing for your business, call 800-555-3535 today. That's 800-555-3535 to fund your company's future now.

- Use a confident, friendly tone to convince business prospects of your sincerity. Enthusiasm should come through without making your message sound like it's delivered by a carnival barker.

- To reach more business customers on radio, consider sponsoring financial news during evening drive time (rush hour) when more prospects are listening.

Graphic Design Service--30-Second Radio Spot (10-09)

ANNCR:　　　　　　　Does your company have everything it needs except a terrific sales brochure? Do you think the biggest hurdle standing in your way is cost? Listen to this. If you have a basic sales presentation, Bantam Design Services can turn it into a stunning brochure in no time! And best of all, you can afford it. At Bantam Design, we know how to work within your budget. We'll show you how we can deliver a powerful sales tool that will put your company out in front of the competition. Call Bantam Design at 414-555-2105 today. That's Bantam Design at 414-555-2105. Get the brochure you really need, at a price you can afford.

• Stressing affordability and ease ("If you have a basic sales presentation...") make it easy for your audience to pick up the phone.

• The use of strong adjectives ("stunning brochure," "powerful sales tool") adds to the listener's sense of success by using your services.

Office Equipment Dealer--60-Second Radio Spot (10-10)

SFX*:   Fax machine signaling an incoming fax

ANNCR: (Confident, serious manner)

Okay, you've got a fax machine—who doesn't these days? But what's your fax machine doing to save you money…to improve your company's productivity…to give you a competitive edge? Consider what the Maxafax Laser 50 from Huntington Office Machines can do for you. The Maxafax Laser 50 can save you money in so many ways. It uses the same paper as your copier, so there's no special paper to buy.

It scans and remembers up to 30 pages, then sends them to up to 99 fax machines at any time, like late at night—when telephone rates are low.

Your employees will be more productive, too, because there's no need to make a photocopy of the fax in order to write on it, file it, or fax it to another machine.

With Maxafax Laser 50 and Huntington Office Machines on your side, you'll have the competitive communications partners you need. For a demonstration of the new Maxafax Laser 50, call Huntington Business Machines today at (304) 555-1010. Or visit Huntington Business Machines at 1000 Third Avenue in Hoovertown. That number again is (304) 555-1010. The Maxafax Laser 50 from Huntington Business Machines—having just any fax isn't enough today.

*SFX is the abbreviation for sound effects

- To sell someone a product they already have, you have to demonstrate real benefits. And be sure to back it up with proof, such as a demonstration, or a money-back guarantee (or, better yet, both).

- Using sound effects to grab the listener's ear can be very effective when you're advertising in a medium that bombards your prospects with hundreds of messages a day.

Event Planners--60-Second Radio Spot (10-11)

MUSIC: Classical, elegant but lively, perhaps Mozart

WOMAN: How do you turn any business occasion into an extra-special event? You need more than a caterer—you need the corporate event specialists at Premiere Planners. We don't just take orders—we help you ask all the right questions and get all the right answers. . . before you make a single decision. Premiere Planners brings much more than food to the table. We'll help you stimulate a sales force. . . make important customers feel good about your company. . . boost employee morale. Whatever your objectives, we'll help you get the results you want. You can choose your place, our place, or someplace else altogether. Invite 20 guests, 200 guests or even 2,000. Include breakfast, lunch, dinner or all three. At Premiere Planners, we make the occasion. For a tour of our facilities, or a meeting at your location, call (717) 555-1040 and ask for Marilyn. That's (717) 555-1040 for Premiere Planners. The special event specialists.

- While selling your business services, remember to include a list of the benefits a prospect can expect. You could be opening their ears and eyes to possibilities they'd never think of on their own.

- By including a name to call, and changing it for each station your commercial runs on, you can tell how effective the various stations are.

Travel Agency--30-Second Radio Spot (10-12)

ANNCR: (Calm, relaxed)

In smaller companies, everyone has to wear more than one hat. If you wear a hat that says "Meeting Planner," don't lose your head. Relax and call Cecil County Travel for all the help you need. We've planned meetings everywhere from Cecil County to Chicago to Honolulu. Travel, lodging, convention facilities—Cecil County Travel does it all. So if you wear the meeting planner's hat, call Terry at Cecil County Travel at (301) 555-1099. That's (301) 555-1099 for Cecil County Travel. You'll tip your hat to us.

• Keep your radio spot simple. Focus on a single message.

• When trying to establish an image of professionalism, use a relaxed, cool tone of voice. That's how to let the listener know they'll be in good hands with your company.

Courier Service--30-Second Radio Spot (10-13)

SFX*:   Clock ticking loudly

ANNCR: (With tension in voice)

When your package just can't wait, who can you depend on to get it there for you? When it has to be in Long Beach by 2:30 and you can't take it, who's gonna go? Call GoGo Couriers. We go more places in Southern California for same day delivery than any other courier service. From Pasadena to Santa Ana, call GoGo. From Whittier to Santa Monica call GoGo. From Beverly Hills to Garden Grove, call 800-555-GOGO. Call anywhere in Southern California and watch your package GoGo fast! That's GoGo Couriers. . . centrally located in Los Angeles at 2101 Wilshire with branches everywhere. GoGo picks up and delivers like lightning. Call 800-555-GOGO. We get there when you can't.

*SFX is the abbreviation for sound effects

• Asking questions is an effective way to get listener attention. Just make sure you answer quickly and definitively.

• Choose sound effects carefully. Clocks ticking or urban street sounds create tension. Birds chirping are relaxing.

Attorney, Tax--60-Second Radio Spot (10-14)

ANNCR: Nobody knows the Internal Revenue Service better than someone who's worked for it for 45 years. So just imagine how a law firm founded by two former IRS agents can serve your needs. Think about how even your most complex tax issues can be handled with a combined 45 years of experience in interpreting and applying the law. The law firm of Gary and Rudin has the knowledge, experience and reputation that you need to tackle your tax problems. I'm Bill Rudin and I invite you to call on Gary and Rudin to discuss your questions on city, county, state or federal tax laws. Sometimes tax problems can be handled with just a phone call or two. Tom Gary and Bill Rudin have the answers to your questions. If you have a business or personal tax problem and need advice immediately, or if you're an attorney who needs counsel on a complex tax issue, call me — Bill Rudin or my partner Tom Gary at Gary and Rudin — to discuss your needs in strictest privacy. Call Gary and Rudin at 305-555-1489 to set up an appointment. That's 305-555-1489 for Gary and Rudin. Put 45 years' experience at the IRS to work for you.

• If you choose to use your own voice in a commercial, rehearse, rehearse, rehearse then deliver it with as much sincerity as you can muster.

• Talk to listeners as you would talk to someone sitting across the desk from you.

CPA, Tax--30-Second Radio Spot (10-15)

ANNCR: Are you going to pay taxes this year even if you don't really owe a cent? With the changes in the tax laws, you could overpay big and not even know it. Better talk to Scott, first. Scott Tax Filers save thousands of people from making needless overpayments every year. Think about it. It's against the law to pay too little. But who's going to stop you from paying too much? Scott Tax Filers. In Mankuto, Rochester or Austin, call 507-555-SCOT for a free appointment. That's 507-555-7268 for Scott. It really pays.

- A 30-second spot can be more cost effective than a 60-second one because you can run your message with greater frequency.

- If you have a telephone number which spells out a message, also present it in numerical form. Many people find it easier to dial numbers.

ANNCR: Attention, small business owners. In our changing economy, here's something really important to think about. Soon, you could be the victim of your own success. As business increases, you could be in over your head managing accounts, preparing tax forms and spending too little time keeping your business growing.

Act now and call Duncan Accounting Services. We specialize in handling the accounting needs of growing small companies. Duncan Accounting Services will assist you with computerized accounting systems, streamlined for productivity and accuracy. We'll provide training to help your employees handle the work in-house. With Duncan on your side, you'll learn how to minimize your tax liabilities as you grow. We'll work with you to get the most favorable terms when you negotiate purchases, leases and other contracts.

Now that the economy is expanding, seize the moment with the professional accounting help you need. Call Pete Duncan today at 315-555-2535 for a free consultation. That's 315-555-2535. Duncan Accounting Services—for small companies like yours, it's the only way to grow.

- Get the attention of your target audience by addressing it at the beginning of your commercial.

- Tailor your message to the economy. Good—and bad—economic times present potential marketing opportunities.

VIDEO	AUDIO
• SERIES OF STILL PHOTOGRAPHS FROM SALES BROCHURE SHOWING AMENITIES AND ACTIVITIES FOR RETIRED RESIDENTS	Are you retired, but not the retiring type? Enjoy a full life at Normandy Manor...the perfect retirement community for active people like you.
• INCLUDE RESIDENCE INTERIORS, DINING ROOMS, GROUNDS AND TRANSPORTATION	Normandy Manor offers you all the activities and amenities of a fine country club along with the staff and facilities of a community created just for people
• SUPERIMPOSE TITLES OVER PHOTOS—9 HOLE GOLF COURSE, LIGHTED TENNIS COURTS, GOURMET DINING, ETC.	who value their independence! With the security of a complete lifecare program to safeguard your health. Everything's here at Normandy Manor, located just off Baltimore National Pike
• SHOW COMMUNITY ENTRANCE OR AERIAL VIEW	in Normandy Heights.
• SHOW SAVINGS CERTIFICATE	Right now, Normandy Manor is offering an extraordinary value—save $1,500 off the entrance fee if you choose one of our spacious, carefree apartments now.
• SHOW EXTERIOR OF MAIN BUILDING	Visit Normandy Manor and see how enjoyable and active your life can be. Plus get your savings certificate for $1,500 off the entrance fee, today.
• SUPERIMPOSE LOGO AND TELEPHONE NUMBER	For directions and an appointment, call 301-555-1515. That's 301-555-1515 for Normandy Manor...the perfect retirement community for active people like you. Join us and enjoy life to the fullest!

• Your brochure can provide all the on-screen visuals you need for low-cost production. Use the still photographs with camera movement to provide interest.

• As with any advertising medium, local TV stations will recommend the time slots that attract the greatest number of people in your target market.

VIDEO: Camera slowly pans along a row of old, broken-down copying machines

AUDIO: If your copier's suddenly gone gray. If it can't feed itself any more. If you're too embarrassed to show your copies in public, Copy Pro has a deal for you.

VIDEO: Cut to showroom or studio full of new copy machines

AUDIO: Copy Pro is having a trade-in sale on seven terrific copy machines. No matter how old or how run down your copier is, get hundreds of dollars off a new Copy Pro copier. Copy Pro has all the features you want, plus our famous service guarantees to keep you up and running.

VIDEO: Address and phone number

AUDIO: Copy Pro. 2325 Fifth Street in Tulsa. Every day except Sunday, from 9 to 5. Come in or call 918-555-2325. Let's talk trade.

• TV is a terrific medium for generating immediate response to an offer. Use its visual impact to bring your selling proposition to life.

[a] If your own showroom isn't suitable for videotaping, set up your products in a TV studio.

VIDEO: Camera zooms in slowly to focus on close-up of man in bed staring straight up at ceiling. Wide-eyed, wide awake, frightened and worried, occasionally shakes head, tosses and turns.

SFX*:   Endless ticking of loud clock.

AUDIO: It's tax time again. You can't sleep… all you can think about are forms and schedules and W-4's. Who do you owe? What do you owe?

SFX*:   Alarm goes off.

VIDEO: Man sits straight up in bed, eyes staring straight into camera, frozen with fear and lack of sleep.

AUDIO: Wake up to a new day with an appointment at Thomas Charles Tax Service. There's nothing to worry about.

VIDEO: Cut to main sitting in office across desk from tax preparer, whose back is to camera. Sign "Thomas Charles Tax Service" Is behind man.

AUDIO: Just call for an appointment, Thomas Charles Tax Service will take care of everything. We'll prepare your tax return using the most up-to-date computer software. And, if you are owed a refund, we'll file your return electronically to get your refund back fast.

VIDEO   Back to man sleeping peacefully.

SUPER: "Thomas Charles Tax Service" and "800-555-1000"

AUDIO: Call Thomas Charles Tax Service now and rest easy. 1-800-555-1000. That's 1-800-555-1000. Call now.

*SFX is the abbreviation for sound effects

• This is a simple commercial, requiring only two actors and simple sets. Your local TV station can produce it with little cost.

• Don't rely solely on the announcer's voice to communicate your phone number—have it superimposed on the screen with your name.

VIDEO:	Clean white surface into which a wheelchair is pushed. A neckbrace is tossed in, followed by a pair of crutches.
AUDIO:	Injured in an automobile crash...an accident at work? Has a defective product harmed you or someone you love? You may be eligible to collect payment for medical expenses and pain and suffering.
VIDEO:	Law office scene of lawyer discussing case with married couple, one of whom has a neckbrace.
AUDIO:	Talk to one of the expert attorneys at Price and Michaels. The initial consultation is free.
VIDEO:	Superimpose title "Price & Michaels—free initial consultation"
AUDIO:	A Price and Michaels attorney will review your case in our offices, at your home—even at the hospital.
VIDEO:	Superimpose title "Price & Michaels—no fee unless you collect"
AUDIO:	We'll recommend the best course of action. And there's no fee unless you collect.
VIDEO:	Superimpose title "Price & Michaels—1-800-555-2020"
AUDIO:	Call Price and Michaels at 1-800-555-2020. That's 1-800-555-2020. If you've been hurt, we can help.

- While you may do a TV spot using still photographs, live action and real people are more effective. A TV station should be able to produce a commercial like this relatively inexpensively.

- Superimpose key selling points on the screen to reinforce them.

- Repeat your telephone number at least once to assist the listener in recalling or writing it down.

Trade Ads 11

Virtually every field of business or professional practice has widely read trade publications. In its Directory of Business Publications, Standard Rates and Data Service lists more than 6,500 newspapers and magazines in the United States and Canada that reach specific trades and industries. These publications generally fall into one of two readership categories:

• Horizontal publications targeting specific trades or professions such as accountants or dentists. They may be further differentiated by sub-specialties such as tax accountants or orthodontists.

• Vertical publications reaching individual industries such as computers or office products. Readers may be segmented into smaller categories such as software developers or retail stationers.

You'll find trade publications that have national focus, as well as regional, state and city-oriented journals. It's up to you and your marketing objectives to determine how far your message should travel.

As Fairfax Cone, founder of one of America's great ad agencies, once said, "Advertising is what you do when you can't go see somebody." Use your trade advertising to announce events, new products, expanded service, new sales reps, general product line overviews, new catalogs...virtually anything you'd like to tell those somebodies you can't go see.

Include sales reps. If your list of trade representatives is short enough, put it in your ad. If the list is too long, consider enlarging your standard size ad and listing reps by state, city or region. If you want more distributors, invite them to call in your ads.

Use industry jargon. In developing copy for your ad, speak the language of the trade, but do so sparingly. A little jargon helps to reinforce your credibility—too much gets in the way of communication. Use words that establish you as a contemporary, up to date, reliable resource.

Measure results. Many publications offer a service to advertisers for generating leads through a reader response card ("bingo card") at the back of the magazine. This can be a valuable tool for measuring the performance of your ad as well as judging the value of the publication.

Your trade ads are also valuable as sales tools outside their publications. Make reprints for mailing to sales reps and customers, and for distribution at trade shows.

Henley Electronics has excellent connections with our new manufacturers' representative organization:

The Breuer Group

In Ohio, Indiana and Kentucky, the Breuer Group is now representing our comprehensive line of precision Henley electronic components. You'll find them the most knowledgeable rep firm in the tri-state area when it comes to high-sensitivity measuring equipment. For a presentation, information, pricing or specs, call the Breuer Group today.

7 4 0 - 5 5 5 - 1 5 5 9

HENLEY ELECTRONICS, INC.
Represented by the Breuer Group
711 Hollis Blvd., Euclid, Ohio

- If you want to steer customers to a specific rep organization, don't muddy the waters with your address or phone number. Announce their phone number in your ad and leave your number out of it.

- Give the rep firm a boost by stating why they're special.

Baxter & McNally
—the perfect combination

Baxter, the best in brass hardware, locks and security products, is now represented by McNally Associates throughout South Carolina. It's an unbeatable team.

Count on Baxter for uncompromising quality standards established and maintained since 1875. And rely on McNally Associates for equally high standards in service and support.

Now more than ever, we are your one source for the finest in hardware.

McNally Associates

Representing the world's finest hardware manufacturers
3800 West Avenue, Columbia, SC 29203
803-555-1459 • FAX 803-555-1472

- Connect your company's name with your new product line in the headline and continue the connection throughout the ad.

- Clearly inform the reader of the territory your representation covers.

You're never far from

TOTAL ELEKTRONIX!

With 5 locations throughout New England,
Total Elektronix is always nearby to serve you.

Nobody covers the electronics market in New England like Total Elektronix. We represent only the finest electronics manufacturers so you can count on us for the largest selection of quality parts and supplies. You're welcome to call our highly knowledgeable in-house service associates to assist you at any time. And you can depend on Total Elektronix for same day delivery on orders received by 11:00 AM within 100 miles of any of our locations.*

Call Total Elektronix—
the total solution to all your electronics needs.

*All other orders shipped same day for next day delivery.

Capacitors • Components • Connectors • Fuses •
Lamps • Potentiometers • Relays • Resistors •
Semiconductors • Testing Equipment • Wire

TOTAL ELEKTRONIX
New England's largest electronics distributor

Toll-free phone order line: 800-555-1113
Toll-free fax order line: 800-555-6004

477 Congress Avenue,
Portland, ME 04103

935 Elm Street,
Manchester, NH 03101

N. Pearl Street,
Boston, MA 02101

1011 Veterans Parkway,
Providence, RI 02915

755 Main Street,
Hartford, CT 06103

- Dramatize your locations by showing them on a map. If you have a logo which lends itself, use it to pinpoint each location.

- If you have a minimum order requirement for delivery or service, be sure to include it in your ad.

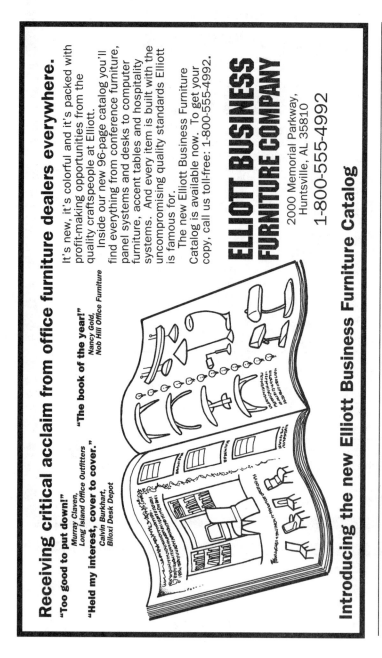

Receiving critical acclaim from office furniture dealers everywhere.

"Too good to put down!"
Murray Claven,
Long Island Office Outfitters

"Held my interest, cover to cover."
Calvin Burkhart,
Biloxi Desk Depot

"The book of the year!"
Nancy Gold,
Nob Hill Office Furniture

It's new, it's colorful and it's packed with profit-making opportunities from the quality craftspeople at Elliott.

Inside our new 96-page catalog you'll find everything from conference furniture, panel systems and desks to computer furniture, accent tables and hospitality systems. And every item is built with the uncompromising quality standards Elliott is famous for.

The new Elliott Business Furniture Catalog is available now. To get your copy, call us toll-free: 1-800-555-4992.

ELLIOTT BUSINESS FURNITURE COMPANY

2000 Memorial Parkway,
Huntsville, AL 35810

1-800-555-4992

Introducing the new Elliott Business Furniture Catalog

- Include a photograph of your catalog featuring the cover and an open section to entice the reader.

- Provide a phone number to invite requests for your catalog.

YOUR ABRASIVES HEADQUARTERS

If you need abrasives for:

grinding or
lapping,
tumbling or
polishing,
blasting or
buffing,
call Dominic
Brothers first

Since 1953, we've been Delaware's leading manufacturer and distributor of quality abrasives and equipment. Hundreds of products in stock for immediate delivery to you:

- Aluminum oxide
- Belts, rolls, wheels, sheets, disks, points
- Buffing compounds
- Burnishing compounds
- Diamond compounds & powders
- Garnet
- Glass beads
- Lapping compounds
- Nut shells
- Polishing compounds
- Pumice
- Quartz
- Rouge
- Silicon carbide
- Steel shot

Call for our full-line catalog!
800-555-5757
Fax your order 24 hours a day, toll-free—800-555-5760

DOMINIC BROTHERS

Manufacturers and distributors of abrasives & supplies since 1953

2100 Kirkwood Highway
Newark, DE 19711

- This headline tells the reader exactly what the company does in just three words, adaptable for virtually any kind of manufacturing or distributing operation.
- Show your product line. If space is limited or the product line is too extensive, show product categories plus major brand names, if applicable.

Yellow Pages 12

It's true—people really do "let their fingers do the walking" in the Yellow Pages®. In a study of Pennsylvania consumers conducted for Bell Atlantic, the following usage statistics emerged:

- 92% used the Yellow Pages at least once a year
- 53% referred to it an average of 1.5 times a week
- 55% purchased as a result
- The average amount spent was $50

Keep in mind that the majority of people looking in the Yellow Pages don't know the slightest thing about you, so you need to communicate as much as you can in the space you buy. What's more, you're fighting for attention in a very cluttered environment.

Size. Before creating an ad, you must make some important decisions regarding size. A regular listing gets you in the book but is unlikely to attract much attention. Statistics show that a bold type listing draws 3 times the interest and a 1 inch ad works 9 times as hard. Make the investment in an even larger display ad and you should generate significant interest from potential customers.

Content. Budget permitting, buy a large enough ad so you can include a simple photograph or artwork to grab the reader's attention. As in any ad, you should include days and hours of operation, address and phone number (fax number if appropriate), credit cards accepted, brand names and products or services available. Keep the information short and sweet; use bullets for emphasis.

Color. You can now have as many as 4 colors in your ad in the Yellow Pages. Research shows that with just the addition of one color (red) to an ad, you can increase impact 17 times over black ink alone. If you can afford to buy an extra color, do so.

Above all else, stand out from the pack. Compare what others have done in the same space and *be different*.

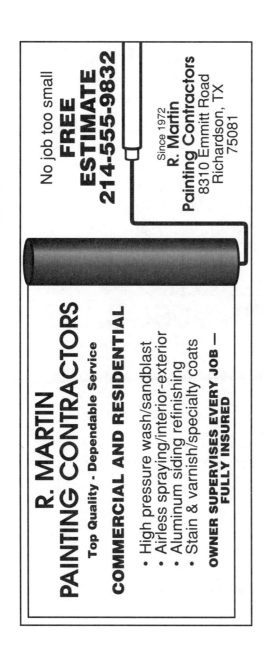

No job too small

FREE ESTIMATE
214-555-9832

Since 1972
R. Martin
Painting Contractors
8310 Emmitt Road
Richardson, TX
75081

R. MARTIN
PAINTING CONTRACTORS
Top Quality - Dependable Service
COMMERCIAL AND RESIDENTIAL

- High pressure wash/sandblast
- Airless spraying/interior-exterior
- Aluminum siding refinishing
- Stain & varnish/specialty coats

OWNER SUPERVISES EVERY JOB —
FULLY INSURED

- Let the reader know what types of jobs you handle (large or small, commercial or residential, etc.).

- Details such as being fully insured and method of supervision will help you get more calls for estimates.

OVER 20 YEARS' EXPERIENCE

WE BEAT ALL COMPETITION

DONALDSON'S

AIR CONDITIONING AND HEATING

Every Job is Satisfaction Guaranteed!

MENTION THIS AD AND GET AN ADDITIONAL 5% DISCOUNT!

WE SELL • SERVICE• INSTALL
- Central Air Conditioning
- Gas Units
- Furnaces
- Water Heaters
- Humidifiers
- Attic Fans
- Oil Burners
- Air Cleaners

Call Burlington's Most Dependable Contractor

781-555-3288

112 E. Fayville Avenue • Burlington, MA 01805

Maintenance Contracts Available
Emergency 24-Hour Service
Financing Available

SALES SERVICE INSTALLATION

FREE ESTIMATE ON ANY JOB

- Draw attention to your ad with a distinctive border.

- Offering a discount for mentioning the ad gives people an added incentive to call, and helps *you* measure effectiveness.

HOME & INSTITUTIONAL MEDICAL EQUIPMENT SALES AND RENTALS

FREE Same Day Delivery and Set-Up... No Waiting!

The widest selection of home medical supplies in the state of Florida

- Hospital beds
- Wheelchairs
- Walkers
- Overbed tables
- Crutches
- Commodes
- Oxygen concentrators
- Trapeze bars
- Whirlpools

We bill Medicare, Medicaid and other third party insurers.

SPECIAL SENIOR CITIZENS DISCOUNT

Visit Our Showroom
Monday-Thursday
9:00 a.m. to 9:00 p.m.
Friday-Sunday
9:00 a.m. to 6:00 p.m.

305-555-5678

1822 Eagle Lake Avenue
Ft. Lauderdale, FL 33306

- If you can offer special services (e.g., "Same day delivery...no waiting!"), be sure to say so.

- List the equipment for which you have the greatest demand. That's what most buyers are looking for.

CELLULAR TELEPHONE SYSTEMS

SALES • RENTALS • SERVICE • INSTALLATION

Authorized Agent for INFONECT Mobile Systems

Dozens of FREE services, including:

- Travel and traffic updates
- Weather reports
- Emergency road service
- Sports scores
- Customer service

250 FREE MINUTES
with your purchase

We'll match the system to your needs

PORTABLE TRANSPORTABLE MOBILE

- On-the-spot activation— no waiting period!
- Corporate/group discounts
- FREE training and consulting

24 HOUR SERVICE AND SUPPORT

Executive Cellular Systems, Inc.
240 Green Tree Place, Suite B
West Point, PA 19486

CALL 215-555-5758

- With new and rapidly-changing technology, an offer of training and consulting (even at a price) is vital.

- If appropriate, be sure to mention that you offer discounts; it will deliver more buyers.

THE BARNARD BROKERAGE

Excellent service made us the Valley's largest commercial insurance brokerage

With our size, we can put together the best package for your business, backed by personal service without equal.

- Property
- Casualty
- Liability
- Fire
- Marine
- Health & Disability
- Workers Compensation
- Bonding Services

21 Ygnacio Valley Drive,
Walnut Creek, CA 94598

Phone **415-555-1900**

Fax **415-555-1988**

- Don't use large size as the sole reason for people to do business with your company. Tell readers why clients have made you the largest.

- Publish your fax number. It will encourage greater response.

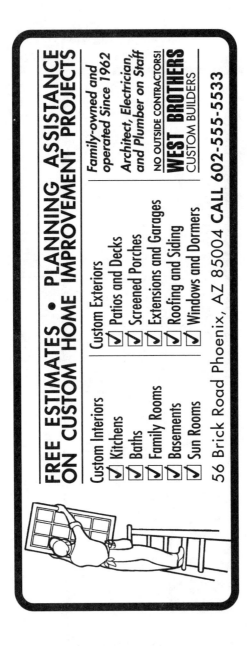

FREE ESTIMATES • PLANNING ASSISTANCE
ON CUSTOM HOME IMPROVEMENT PROJECTS

Custom Interiors
- ✓ Kitchens
- ✓ Baths
- ✓ Family Rooms
- ✓ Basements
- ✓ Sun Rooms

Custom Exteriors
- ✓ Patios and Decks
- ✓ Screened Porches
- ✓ Extensions and Garages
- ✓ Roofing and Siding
- ✓ Windows and Dormers

Family-owned and operated Since 1962

Architect, Electrician, and Plumber on Staff

NO OUTSIDE CONTRACTORS!

WEST BROTHERS
CUSTOM BUILDERS

56 Brick Road Phoenix, AZ 85004 **CALL 602-555-5533**

- Features such as family ownership and length of time in business signify stability and establish confidence.

- In this kind of business, an assurance that all work is done by company employees is a major factor in attracting calls and inquiries.

Every day's a sale day at White Knight ... check our prices before you buy.

We're the city's largest appliance dealer offering sales and service on most major brands.

- Washers
- Dryers
- Freezers
- Trash Compactors
- Refrigerators
- Dishwashers
- Air Conditioners
- Ranges
- Microwaves
- Garbage Disposals

Residential and commercial equipment
Factory trained technicians

Most items in stock for immediate delivery

SALES:
317-555-1490

SERVICE:
317-555-1495

WHITE KNIGHT
APPLIANCE

640 Centennial Ave., Muncie, IN 47303
Showroom open Mon.-Sat. 9 AM-5 PM
Wed. & Fri. 'til 9 PM

Financing available—Major credit cards accepted

• Use your Yellow Pages ad to build traffic and inquiries by inviting people to "check our prices before you buy."

• Listing a separate phone number for service can increase calls dramatically.

Monsieur René's
since 1912

Authentic country French dining in a majestic Victorian mansion on the banks of the Merrimack

Distinguished wine list
Rated five stars by the Concord Record

Breads and pastries baked on premises

LUNCH AND DINNER SERVICE
Tuesday - Sunday
Reservations Suggested
1-603-555-1110

398 Cooper Landing Road, Concord, NH 03301

- Identify the elements that make your service unique.

- Use language and graphics that reflect the image you want to project.

Museum Quality Framing at Reasonable Prices

The Gallery

Our team of art consultants and designers is ready to assist you:

- More than one thousand frame styles to choose from
- Conservation and shadow box framing
- Rice paper and other creative matting
- Open and limited edition lithographs and serigraphs
- Thousands of classic reproduction posters
- Discounts on all posters framed at The Gallery

All major credit cards accepted
Corporate and wholesale accounts welcome

Monday-Saturday 9:30 - 6:00

1376 White Horse Road
Sante Fe, New Mexico 87501
505-555-2960

- If you're targeting an upscale audience, reflect that in your words and images.

- A special border (in this case, a picture frame look) will distinguish you from other ads.

The
LIFETIME
FITNESS
CENTER

Family and Corporate
Membership Discounts

Feel better, look better, be better with
LIFETIME's acclaimed Holistic Fitness
Program. Certified instructors,
nutritionists, and chiropractors
build a program tailored to
your needs.

- **Fitness evaluations**
- **Weight loss programs**
- **Nutritional guidance**
- **Cardiovascular workout room**
- **Free-weight gym**
- **Low and high impact aerobic and
  step classes**
- **Saunas, whirlpools, steam room**
- **Racquetball courts**
- **Rehabilitation and sports medicine
  clinic**

Co-ed facility
Open Daily, 6:00 a.m.-11:00 p.m.
(Hours that suit busy families and execs!)

2200 Church Road
(1/4 mile from the Clayton Mall)
Little Rock, AR 72116

501-555-5657

- By including the words "family" and "corporate," you plant seeds in the readers' minds. It marks you as a facility that caters to "regular" people, not just body-builders.

- A strong graphic design should catch the reader's eye—and underscore the benefits of your service.

Brand name clothing seconds at remarkable prices!

Jill Chamberlain™ fashions for you…
Mugwumps™ for the kids…
many other major brands of
women's and children's
clothing and accessories at
super savings. Everything
imperfect—but you'd
hardly know it! Fresh
bargains arriving daily.

**JUST
ABOUT
PERFECT**

315 Black Horse Road
Raleigh, NC 27650

919-555-4545

Open Monday through
Saturday, 10 AM to 6 PM
Sunday Noon to 5 PM

- Be sure to let the reader know what you're selling.

- Strong graphics make your ad get noticed.

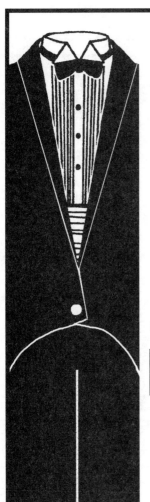

TUXEDO JUNCTION

Largest selection of styles and sizes

Tuxedo sales & rentals for weddings, proms, all occasions
- Esquire
- Marcel Noir
- Earl of Camden
- Mr. Formal

Sizes 3 child to 60 adult
Expert tailoring
Group discounts
Same day service available
All major credit cards accepted

FREE TUXEDO FOR GROOM WITH 5 RENTALS

301-555-8147
Tuxedo Junction
1120 Salisbury Boulevard
Salisbury, MD 21801

- Make your promotional offer stand out by enclosing it in a box.

- If your business can be symbolized by a distinctive graphic, include it in all your advertising to gain attention and continuity.

- Artwork that reflects the nature of the business brings the reader right into your ad.

- List key features/services to give yourself the best chance to sell the prospect.

- People like doing business with establishments that have staying power. Let them know you've been around for a long time.

NUMBER ONE IN LISTINGS

We offer
the greatest
number of
listings in
these areas:

- Automation
- Clerical
- Customer Service
- Data Entry
- Secretarial

No Fees

Ask about our
career re-training
and counseling
program

FIRST CHOICE PERSONNEL

Call 504-555-5678

5237 Steuben Road
(across from Washington
High School)
Metairie, LA 11566

- The use of a graphic device related to your selling approach reinforces the message.

- If you specialize in certain areas, list them. This will help you attract the right kind of customers.

Think how much you dislike electronic phone answering . . . Now put yourself in your customers' shoes!

Starting today . . . give your company

PERSONAL PHONE SERVICE

professional telephone answering and paging

- Personalized, dependable service
- Every call taken promptly by a <u>trained</u> and <u>courteous</u> operator
- 24-hour service available
- Immediate message transmission available, including:
  - Fax transmission
  - Complete message beeper service
  - Phone forwarding
  - A wide range of additional services available, including 800 numbers and mail fulfillment

Call for our FREE BROCHURE

PERSONAL PHONE SERVICE

815A Marietta Drive
Medford, OR 97504
Local Calls: 503-555-4175
Out-of-Town: 800-555-CALL

- The artwork will set the tone for your ad. In this case, a professional looking operator is every bit as important as the words.

- Having your headline hit a nerve with the reader assures strong response.

- With technically oriented products, the more information you provide, the better your chance of receiving an inquiry. Never assume a potential client knows anything about you.

- Business-to-business Yellow Page ads, such as this, can be a lucrative source of new customers.

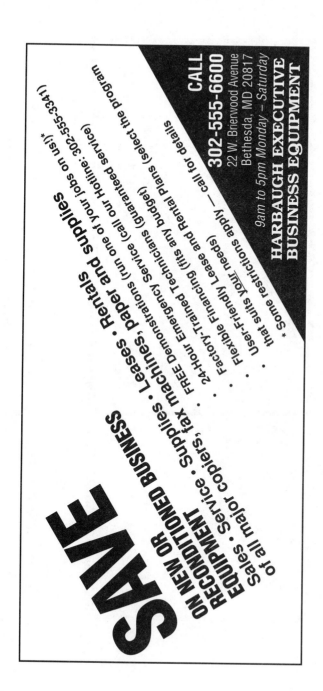

SAVE

ON NEW OR RECONDITIONED OFFICE EQUIPMENT

Sales of all major machines
Service copiers, fax machines, paper
Rentals and supplies

Leases • paper • fax machines • Service copiers' • Sales major

SAVE ON NEW OR RECONDITIONED BUSINESS

Supplies • Leases • paper • fax machines • Service copiers',

Rentals and supplies

FREE Demonstrations Service (guaranteed) (select the program

run one of our Hotline) (service)

call your jobs on us!)* 302-555-3341)

24-Hour-Trained Emergency Technicians any budget) (select the program
FREE Demonstrations Service (guaranteed) (g)
Factory Financing (fits any Rental plans)
Flexible Financing Lease (needs) — call for details
User-Friendly your needs) apply
   that suits restrictions apply
*   Some restrictions

CALL
302-555-6600

22 W. Brierwood Avenue
Bethesda, MD 20817

9am to 5pm Monday – Saturday

HARBAUGH EXECUTIVE
BUSINESS EQUIPMENT

- Service is the key to attracting and holding customers in equipment-oriented businesses. Concentrate on giving the potential buyer a sense of security about yours. Phrases such as "24-hr. emergency service" will help insure that fingers stop on your ad.

- Adjectives sell. "Flexible financing" and "User-friendly lease" make rather ordinary items seem special. (Just leave out the descriptive words to see how important they are.)

DERMATOLOGY

For Children and Adults
Geriatric Specialization

- Skin diseases and surgery
- Skin cancer screening and management
- Skin ulcers and wrinkle treatment
- Varicose vein correction

SKINCARE CENTER

Albert Markham, M.D.
Yvonne Yeo, M.D.
Lance Delaney, M.D.

82 Blair Mill Run
Ferguson, MO 63136

Call for Appointment:
314-555-3678

- Don't make prospective patients guess at your specialty. Make it clear.
- Senior citizens prefer service providers who understand their special problems. Indicate a geriatric practice where applicable.

POWERFUL
PRESENTATIONS
for all occasions
Events staged for audiences of 10 to 10,000.
Slides, film, video and live productions
designed and produced.
Complete turnkey packages available
including equipment rental, set-up
and operation at locations worldwide.
In-house systems design, installation and training.
References available in all major industries.
CALL FOR FREE DEMONSTRATION—
719-555-0522

Rocky Mountain AV
5525 Academy Blvd.,
Colorado Springs, CO 80910

• List your services to show you can provide whatever the prospect wants.

• A free demonstration permits you to sell face-to-face with your strongest asset, a quality product.

Employee benefits & pension plans... is your company competitive?

Pension Plan

Major Medical Plan

Are you losing employees to other companies because your benefits programs aren't competitive? Are you paying more than you need and receiving less than you deserve? We can help you find the answers by comparing your employee benefits and pension programs with other companies:

☑ in your field
☑ in your region
☑ of comparable size

Free expert review and analysis

ST. JAMES ACTUARIES

Employee Benefits Specialists
1520 Edwards Place, Ames, IA 50010
515-555-0999

- Use your headline to raise compelling questions which you have the resources to answer.

- Offer a free review to increase response.

The Finest Address for Furnished Office Space in the Silver Spring Area

SILVER SPRING
Executive Suites

2000 Georgia Avenue,
Silver Spring, MD 20910
301-555-2727

PROJECT A QUALITY IMAGE FOR VISITING CLIENTS AND CUSTOMERS WITH HANDSOME OFFICE SPACE IN OUR EXECUTIVE QUARTERS, STAFFED BY SUPPORT PERSONNEL WITH FORTUNE 500 EXPERIENCE.

- PROFESSIONAL RECEPTION AND SECRETARIAL STAFF
- PERSONALIZED TELEPHONE ANSWERING & VOICE MAIL
- 24 HOUR ACCESS
- CONFERENCE AND SEMINAR ROOMS WITH AUDIO-VISUAL EQUIPMENT
- COMPLETE SUPPORT SERVICES
- SHORT OR LONG TERM LEASES AVAILABLE
- FREE PARKING
- SUPERB SILVER SPRING LOCATION

- You're surrounded by competition in the Yellow Pages. State your competitive advantage clearly and compellingly.

- If available, use a second color to add emphasis and make your ad stand out.

- Focus on the major reason for dealing with your company (in this case, fast delivery).

- If you specialize in a well known brand, feature the manufacturer's logo in your ad and for recognition and credibility. You may also be able to collect cooperative advertising funds from the manufacturer.

When Speed and Accuracy are Important . . .

CARTER RADIOLOGY ASSOCIATES P.A.

Complete range of services available:

- X-ray
- Ultrasound (Color Doppler)
- MRI
- Cat Scan
- Low Dose Mammography (ACR approved)
- Fluoroscopy

CALL 701-555-5551

for Same Day Appointments and Same Day Reporting to Physician

Early morning, evening and weekend appointments available

Carter Radiology Associates P.A.

3407 Soblar Highway
(Across from Cinema 12)
Bismark, ND 58502

Medicare and Most Insurance Plans Accepted
All Major Credit Cards Accepted

- Some advertisements are best directed at a dual audience (as in this situation, to physicians as well as patients). Keep in mind the two audiences and use copy that both can relate to.

- Focus on how you are different from the competition, such as lower prices, highest quality and, in this example, speed and accuracy.

Caring help for teens.

Specializing in the emotional problems of teenagers since 1978.

- **Depression & anxiety**
- **Relationship problems**
- **Substance abuse**
- **Poor self esteem, shyness**
- **Fears & phobias**
- **Eating Disorders**

Caring short term treatment in strictest confidence

Convenient hours, day and evening

FREE evaluation

Most insurance plans accepted

Call now:

George Elwood, PhD.,
Director

**THE
ELWOOD
CLINIC**

2100 Carrington Avenue
Walla Walla, WA 99362
509-555-6413
Licensed Psychologists

509-555-6413

- In a category with many other practitioners, put your area of specialization in the headline to make it easy for readers to spot your ad.

- Even with professional services, offering something free increases response (in this case, a free evaluation).

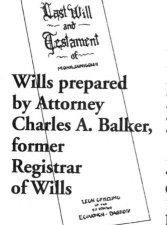

Don't let someone else make decisions for you. Plan your estate now to make sure every detail is handled according to your wishes. For expert advice and preparation, call Attorney Charles A. Balker today.

Wills prepared by Attorney Charles A. Balker, former Registrar of Wills

- **Living Wills**
- **Living Trusts**
- **Durable Powers of Attorney**
- **Last Will & Testaments**
- **Other related services including Decedent Estates**

307-555-5796

Charles A. Balker, Esq.
14 Big Sky Plaza
Newcastle, WY 82701

- If you have special experience or background (as in this case, Former Registrar of Wills) that makes you uniquely qualified, feature it in your ad.

- Even a small ad can stand out if you organize it well.

Guide to Typefaces Used in the Ads

The world of fonts, or typefaces, is vast. There are at least 15,000 fonts currently available for use with personal computers. For graphics professionals and anyone who wants to exercise some freedom and creativity, there is a font to produce any desired effect. However, practically speaking, the great majority of people will normally use the fonts that come with their computer's operating system or Web browser.

While we have taken advantage of a large library of fonts in creating the ads in this book, we recognize that many readers who have a much more limited library of fonts will benefit from this index of suggested font substitutions.

In the first column are the names of the actual fonts that were used in each advertisement, brochure, etc.

In the second column is a suggestion for a substitute font from a library that might be found on an "average" PC.

The third column shows the absolute, simplest form of substitution, by picking from one of the two biggest font families, Times or Arial (Helvetica). The families Times New Roman and Arial are found on practically all PCs. The equivalent families, Times and Helvetica, are found on all Macintoshes. Together, these two font families are used in the overwhelming majority of printed publications in most of the world. The Times family is the premier example of a serif font, while the Arial, or Helvetica, family is the premier example of a sans-serif font.

Fonts come in weights, such as Light, Medium, Book, Demi, Bold, and Extra Bold. There are various terms to indicate italic versions of the fonts, such as Oblique, Kursiv, Slanted, or Italic. With most word processing software, it is possible to make a font "bold" or "italic" with the touch of a style button. Invoking both styles gives you "bold italic." When substituting fonts, this is an expedient way to achieve the desired result, and we have indicated in braces (e.g., {Italic}) when to apply this style to a font. However, if you have the ability to select the actual bold or italic font (e.g., Helvetica Oblique), it is more accurate to do so.

Some of this book's items do not require any particular font (a radio script, for example, can be written on any word processor in any appropriate font), but a substitution from among the Times or Helvetica families is always a safe bet.

Actual Font Used in Book	Substitute Font, Typical PC	Simplest Substitute Font
Ad No. 1-01		
Memphis Bold	Rockwell (Bold)	Times New Roman (Times)
Futura Condensed	Century Gothic	Arial (Helvetica)
Futura Condensed Extra Bold	Century Gothic {Bold}	Arial (Helvetica)
Memphis Medium	Rockwell	Times New Roman (Times)
Memphis Medium Italic	Rockwell {Italic}	Times New Roman (Times)
Memphis Extra Bold	Rockwell Extra Bold	Times New Roman (Times)
Ad No. 1-02		
Trump Mediaeval Bold	Perpetua {Bold}	Times New Roman (Times)
Franklin Gothic	Franklin Gothic	Arial (Helvetica)
Frankiln Gothic Heavy	Frankiln Gothic Heavy	Arial (Helvetica)
Franklin Gothic Heavy Oblique	Franklin Gothic Heavy {Italic}	Arial (Helvetica)
Trump Mediaeval Italic	Perpetua {Italic}	Times New Roman (Times)
Trump Mediaeval	Perpetua	Times New Roman (Times)
Ad No. 1-03		
Futura Condensed Light	Century Gothic	Arial (Helvetica)
Futura Condensed Extra Bold	Century Gothic {Bold}	Arial (Helvetica)
Futura Extra Bold	Century Gothic {Bold}	Arial (Helvetica)
Century Old Style	Century Schoolbook	Times New Roman (Times)
Futura Heavy	Century Gothic {Bold}	Arial (Helvetica)
Futura	Century Gothic	Arial (Helvetica)
Ad No. 1-04		
Clearface Black	Gloucester MT {Bold}	Times New Roman (Times)
Futura Condensed	Century Gothic	Arial (Helvetica)
Futura Heavy	Century Gothic {Bold}	Arial (Helvetica)
Ad No. 1-05		
Bookman Medium	Bookman Old Style	Times New Roman (Times)
Helvetica Black	Arial Black (Helvetica Black)	Arial (Helvetica)
Ad No. 1-06		
Helvetica Neue Black 95	Arial Black	Arial (Helvetica)
Helvetica Condensed Bold	Arial Narrow {Bold}	Arial (Helvetica)
Helvetica Condensed Light	Arial Narrow	Arial (Helvetica)
Helvetica Condensed Black	Arial Narrow {Bold}	Arial (Helvetica)
Helvetica Condensed Light Oblique	Arial Narrow {Italic}	Arial (Helvetica)
Helvetica Neue Black Condensed	Arial Narrow {Bold}	Arial (Helvetica)
Ad No. 1-07		
Adobe Garamond Semibold	Garamond {Bold}	Times New Roman (Times)
Trump Mediaeval Bold	Perpetua {Bold}	Times New Roman (Times)
Helvetica Black	Arial Black (Helvetica Black)	Arial (Helvetica)
Trump Mediaeval Bold Italic	Perpetua {Bold Italic}	Times New Roman (Times)
Ad No. 1-08		
Optima Bold	Verdana {Bold}	Arial (Helvetica)
Helvetica Condensed	Arial Narrow	Arial (Helvetica)
Helvetica Condensed Bold	Arial Narrow {Bold}	Arial (Helvetica)
Helvetica Black	Arial Black (Helvetica Black)	Arial (Helvetica)
Optima	Verdana	Arial (Helvetica)
Ad No. 1-09		
Futura Bold	Century Gothic {Bold}	Arial (Helvetica)
Futura Bold Oblique	Century Gothic {Bold Italic}	Arial (Helvetica)
Futura Condensed Extra Bold	Century Gothic {Bold}	Arial (Helvetica)
Century Old Style	Century Schoolbook	Times New Roman (Times)
Futura	Century Gothic	Arial (Helvetica)
Futura Extra Bold	Century Gothic {Bold}	Arial (Helvetica)

Actual Font Used in Book	Substitute Font, Typical PC	Simplest Substitute Font
Ad No. 1-10		
Memphis Bold	Rockwell (Bold)	Times New Roman (Times)
Univers 65 Bold	Franklin Gothic Demi	Arial (Helvetica)
Univers 65 Bold Oblique	Franklin Gothic Demi {Italic}	Arial (Helvetica)
Univers 75 Black Oblique	Franklin Gothic Heavy {Italic}	Arial (Helvetica)
Univers 55 Oblique	Franklin Gothic Medium {Italic}	Arial (Helvetica)
Univers 55	Franklin Gothic Medium	Arial (Helvetica)
Ad No. 1-11		
Optima Bold	Verdana {Bold}	Arial (Helvetica)
Optima Oblique	Verdana {Italic}	Arial (Helvetica)
Helvetica Black	Arial Black (Helvetica Black)	Arial (Helvetica)
Optima	Verdana	Arial (Helvetica)
Ad No. 1-12		
Century Old Style Bold	Century Schoolbook {Bold}	Times New Roman (Times)
Optima Bold	Verdana {Bold}	Arial (Helvetica)
Century Old Style	Century Schoolbook	Times New Roman (Times)
Century Old Style Italic	Century Schoolbook {Italic}	Times New Roman (Times)
Optima Oblique	Verdana {Italic}	Arial (Helvetica)
Optima	Verdana	Arial (Helvetica)
Ad No. 1-13		
Cheltenham Bold	Baskerville Old Face {Bold}	Times New Roman (Times)
Cheltenham Bold Italic	Baskerville Old Face {Bold Italic}	Times New Roman (Times)
Cheltenham	Baskerville Old Face	Times New Roman (Times)
Franklin Gothic Heavy	Franklin Gothic Heavy	Arial (Helvetica)
Cheltenham Book Italic	Baskerville Old Face {Bold Italic}	Times New Roman (Times)
Ad No. 1-14		
Adobe Garamond Bold	Garamond {Bold}	Times New Roman (Times)
Optima Bold	Verdana {Bold}	Arial (Helvetica)
Optima Bold Oblique	Verdana {Bold Italic}	Arial (Helvetica)
Optima Oblique	Verdana {Italic}	Arial (Helvetica)
Optima	Verdana	Arial (Helvetica)
Ad No. 1-15		
Century Old Style	Century Schoolbook	Times New Roman (Times)
Helvetica Inserat Roman	Impact	Arial (Helvetica)
Century Old Style Italic	Century Schoolbook {Italic}	Times New Roman (Times)
Ad No. 2-01		
Aachen Bold	Rockwell Extra Bold	Times New Roman (Times)
Goudy Bold	Goudy Old Style {Bold}	Times New Roman (Times)
Goudy	Goudy Old Style	Times New Roman (Times)
Goudy Italic	Goudy Old Style {Italic}	Times New Roman (Times)
Ad No. 2-02		
Optima Bold	Verdana {Bold}	Arial (Helvetica)
Ad No. 2-03		
Avant Garde Demi	Century Gothic {Bold}	Arial (Helvetica)
Goudy Bold	Goudy Old Style {Bold}	Times New Roman (Times)
Goudy	Goudy Old Style	Times New Roman (Times)
Goudy Italic	Goudy Old Style {Italic}	Times New Roman (Times)
Ad No. 2-04		
Souvenir Demi	Lucida Casual {Bold}	Times New Roman (Times)
Helvetica Black	Arial Black (Helvetica Black)	Arial (Helvetica)
Ad No. 2-05		
Century Old Style	Century Schoolbook	Times New Roman (Times)

Actual Font Used in Book	Substitute Font, Typical PC	Simplest Substitute Font
Ad No. 2-06		
Memphis Medium	Rockwell	Times New Roman (Times)
Memphis Bold	Rockwell (Bold)	Times New Roman (Times)
Ad No. 2-07		
Franklin Gothic Demi	Franklin Gothic Demi	Arial (Helvetica)
Bodoni	Modern No. 20	Times New Roman (Times)
Franklin Gothic	Franklin Gothic	Arial (Helvetica)
Bodoni Poster	Poster Bodoni ATT	Times New Roman (Times)
Ad No. 2-08		
Palatino	Book Antiqua	Times New Roman (Times)
Palatino Bold	Book Antiqua {Bold}	Times New Roman (Times)
Palatino Italic	Book Antiqua {Italic}	Times New Roman (Times)
Avant Garde Demi	Century Gothic {Bold}	Arial (Helvetica)
Ad No. 2-09		
Memphis Bold	Rockwell (Bold)	Times New Roman (Times)
Futura Extra Bold	Century Gothic {Bold}	Arial (Helvetica)
Memphis Light	Rockwell	Times New Roman (Times)
Memphis Medium	Rockwell	Times New Roman (Times)
Ad No. 2-10		
Avant Garde Condensed Demi	Century Gothic {Bold}	Arial (Helvetica)
Korinna Bold	Lucida Casual {Bold}	Times New Roman (Times)
Korinna	Lucida Casual	Times New Roman (Times)
Ad No. 2-11		
Helvetica Light	Arial	Arial (Helvetica)
Helvetica Black	Arial Black (Helvetica Black)	Arial (Helvetica)
Helvetica	Arial (Helvetica)	Arial (Helvetica)
Ad No. 2-12		
Helvetica Condensed Bold	Arial Narrow {Bold}	Arial (Helvetica)
Machine	Impact	Arial (Helvetica)
Helvetica Bold	Arial (Helvetica) {Bold}	Arial (Helvetica)
Helvetica Italic	Arial (Helvetica) {Italic}	Arial (Helvetica)
Helvetica Condensed Bold	Arial Narrow {Bold}	Arial (Helvetica)
Helvetica	Arial (Helvetica)	Arial (Helvetica)
Ad No. 2-13		
Helvetica Condensed	Arial Narrow	Arial (Helvetica)
Helvetica Condensed Black	Arial Narrow {Bold}	Arial (Helvetica)
Helvetica Black	Arial Black (Helvetica Black)	Arial (Helvetica)
Ad No. 2-14		
Adobe Garamond	Garamond	Times New Roman (Times)
Adobe Garamond Bold	Garamond {Bold}	Times New Roman (Times)
Helvetica Bold	Arial (Helvetica) {Bold}	Arial (Helvetica)
Helvetica	Arial (Helvetica)	Arial (Helvetica)
Ad No. 2-15		
Futura Condensed Light	Century Gothic	Arial (Helvetica)
Helvetica Extra Compressed	Impact	Arial (Helvetica)
Helvetica Light	Arial	Arial (Helvetica)
Helvetica	Arial (Helvetica)	Arial (Helvetica)
Ad No. 2-16		
Helvetica Black	Arial Black (Helvetica Black)	Arial (Helvetica)
Machine Bold	Impact {Bold}	Arial (Helvetica)
Helvetica Bold	Arial (Helvetica) {Bold}	Arial (Helvetica)
Helvetica Italic	Arial (Helvetica) {Italic}	Arial (Helvetica)
Helvetica	Arial (Helvetica)	Arial (Helvetica)

Actual Font Used in Book	Substitute Font, Typical PC	Simplest Substitute Font
Ad No. 2-17		
Helvetica Condensed Black	Arial Narrow {Bold}	Arial (Helvetica)
Helvetica Black	Arial Black (Helvetica Black)	Arial (Helvetica)
Helvetica Bold	Arial (Helvetica) {Bold}	Arial (Helvetica)
Helvetica Italic	Arial (Helvetica) {Italic}	Arial (Helvetica)
Helvetica	Arial (Helvetica)	Arial (Helvetica)
Ad No. 3-01 through 3-11 (All of Chapter 3)		
(No specific fonts required. Any word processor font will be acceptable for sending ads to the newspaper. The newspaper will set the type in its own desired font.)		
Ad No. 4-01 through 4-08 (All of Chapter 4)		
(No specific fonts required. Any word processor font will be acceptable.)		
Ad No. 5-01		
Helvetica Condensed Bold	Arial Narrow {Bold}	Arial (Helvetica)
Helvetica Condensed Black	Arial Narrow {Bold}	Arial (Helvetica)
Freestyle Script	Bradley Hand ITC	Times New Roman (Times)
Helvetica	Arial (Helvetica)	Arial (Helvetica)
Courier	Courier New	Times New Roman (Times)
Ad No. 5-02		
Adobe Garamond Bold Italic	Garamond {Bold Italic}	Times New Roman (Times)
Souvenir Demi	Lucida Casual {Bold}	Times New Roman (Times)
New Century Schoolbook Bold Italic	Century Schoolbook {Bold Italic}	Times New Roman (Times)
Bookman Medium Italic	Bookman Old Style {Italic}	Times New Roman (Times)
Souvenir Light Italic	Lucida Casual {Italic}	Times New Roman (Times)
Souvenir	Lucida Casual	Times New Roman (Times)
Souvenir Medium	Lucida Casual	Times New Roman (Times)
Souvenir Medium Italic	Lucida Casual {Italic}	Times New Roman (Times)
Ad No. 5-03		
Avant Garde Condensed Demi	Century Gothic {Bold}	Arial (Helvetica)
Cheltenham Bold	Baskerville Old Face {Bold}	Times New Roman (Times)
Helvetica Condensed		
Cheltenham	Baskerville Old Face	Times New Roman (Times)
Helvetica	Arial (Helvetica)	Arial (Helvetica)
Ad No. 5-04		
Aachen Bold	Rockwell Extra Bold	Times New Roman (Times)
Goudy Bold	Goudy Old Style {Bold}	Times New Roman (Times)
Goudy Bold Italic	Goudy Old Style {Bold Italic}	Times New Roman (Times)
Goudy	Goudy Old Style	Times New Roman (Times)
Goudy Italic	Goudy Old Style {Italic}	Times New Roman (Times)
Helvetica	Arial (Helvetica)	Arial (Helvetica)
Ad No. 5-05		
Palatino Bold	Book Antiqua {Bold}	Times New Roman (Times)
Palatino Bold Italic	Book Antiqua {Bold Italic}	Times New Roman (Times)
Palatino	Book Antiqua	Times New Roman (Times)
Ad No. 5-05		
Bookman Bold Italic	Bookman Old Style {Bold Italic}	Times New Roman (Times)
Ad No. 5-06		
Futura	Century Gothic	Arial (Helvetica)
Souvenir	Lucida Casual	Times New Roman (Times)
Souvenir Medium	Lucida Casual	Times New Roman (Times)
Souvenir Medium Italic	Lucida Casual {Italic}	Times New Roman (Times)
Futura Extra Bold	Century Gothic {Bold}	Arial (Helvetica)
Ad No. 5-06		
Souvenir	Lucida Casual	Times New Roman (Times)
Souvenir Medium	Lucida Casual	Times New Roman (Times)
Futura Extra Bold	Century Gothic {Bold}	Arial (Helvetica)

Actual Font Used in Book	Substitute Font, Typical PC	Simplest Substitute Font
Ad No. 5-06		
Souvenir	Lucida Casual	Times New Roman (Times)
Souvenir Medium	Lucida Casual	Times New Roman (Times)
Ad No. 5-07		
Times	Times (Times New Roman)	Times New Roman (Times)
Helvetica	Arial (Helvetica)	Arial (Helvetica)
Ad No. 5-08		
Cheltenham Bold	Baskerville Old Face {Bold}	Times New Roman (Times)
New Century Schoolbook Bold	Century Schoolbook {Bold}	Times New Roman (Times)
Optima Bold	Verdana {Bold}	Arial (Helvetica)
Cheltenham	Baskerville Old Face	Times New Roman (Times)
New Century Schoolbook Italic	Century Schoolbook {Italic}	Times New Roman (Times)
Optima	Verdana	Arial (Helvetica)
Helvetica	Arial (Helvetica)	Arial (Helvetica)
Ad No. 5-09		
Adobe Garamond Bold	Garamond {Bold}	Times New Roman (Times)
Futura Condensed Bold	Century Gothic {Bold}	Arial (Helvetica)
Futura	Century Gothic	Arial (Helvetica)
Futura Book	Century Gothic	Arial (Helvetica)
Futura Heavy	Century Gothic {Bold}	Arial (Helvetica)
Helvetica	Arial (Helvetica)	Arial (Helvetica)
Ad No. 5-10		
Adobe Garamond Bold	Garamond {Bold}	Times New Roman (Times)
Aachen Bold	Rockwell Extra Bold	Times New Roman (Times)
Times	Times (Times New Roman)	Times New Roman (Times)
Helvetica	Arial (Helvetica)	Arial (Helvetica)
Ad No. 5-10		
Adobe Garamond Bold	Garamond {Bold}	Times New Roman (Times)
Aachen Bold	Rockwell Extra Bold	Times New Roman (Times)
Times	Times (Times New Roman)	Times New Roman (Times)
Helvetica	Arial (Helvetica)	Arial (Helvetica)
Ad No. 5-11		
Eurostile Bold	Eurostile {Bold}	Arial (Helvetica)
Galliard Bold	Footlight MT Light {Bold}	Times New Roman (Times)
Eurostile	Eurostile	Arial (Helvetica)
Galliard	Footlight MT Light	Times New Roman (Times)
Americana Extra Bold	Wide Latin	Times New Roman (Times)
Times	Times (Times New Roman)	Times New Roman (Times)
Ad No. 5-12		
Aachen Bold	Rockwell Extra Bold	Times New Roman (Times)
Clearface Regular	Gloucester MT	Times New Roman (Times)
Freestyle Script	Bradley Hand ITC	Times New Roman (Times)
Helvetica	Arial (Helvetica)	Arial (Helvetica)
Ad No. 5-12		
Aachen Bold	Rockwell Extra Bold	Times New Roman (Times)
Clearface Regular	Gloucester MT	Times New Roman (Times)
Ad No. 5-12		
Clearface Black	Gloucester MT {Bold}	Times New Roman (Times)
Clearface Regular	Gloucester MT	Times New Roman (Times)
Clearface Heavy	Gloucester MT {Bold}	Times New Roman (Times)
Clearface Regular Italic	Gloucester MT {Italic}	Times New Roman (Times)
Helvetica	Arial (Helvetica)	Arial (Helvetica)
Freestyle Script	Bradley Hand ITC	Times New Roman (Times)
Aachen Bold	Rockwell Extra Bold	Times New Roman (Times)

Actual Font Used in Book	Substitute Font, Typical PC	Simplest Substitute Font
Ad No. 5-13		
Adobe Garamond	Garamond	Times New Roman (Times)
Adobe Garamond Bold	Garamond {Bold}	Times New Roman (Times)
Adobe Garamond Italic	Garamond {Italic}	Times New Roman (Times)
Futura Bold	Century Gothic {Bold}	Arial (Helvetica)
Futura	Century Gothic	Arial (Helvetica)
Futura Book	Century Gothic	Arial (Helvetica)
Futura Extra Bold	Century Gothic {Bold}	Arial (Helvetica)
Helvetica	Arial (Helvetica)	Arial (Helvetica)
Ad No. 5-14		
Century Old Style Bold	Century Schoolbook {Bold}	Times New Roman (Times)
Century Old Style	Century Schoolbook	Times New Roman (Times)
Helvetica Neue Black Cond. Obl.	Arial Narrow {Bold Italic}	Arial (Helvetica)
Century Old Style Italic	Century Schoolbook {Italic}	Times New Roman (Times)
Helvetica Black	Arial Black (Helvetica Black)	Arial (Helvetica)
Helvetica	Arial (Helvetica)	Arial (Helvetica)
Times	Times (Times New Roman)	Times New Roman (Times)
Times Bold	Times (Times New Roman) Bold	Times New Roman (Times)
Ad No. 5-15		
Optima	Verdana	Arial (Helvetica)
Optima Bold	Verdana {Bold}	Arial (Helvetica)
Optima Bold Oblique	Verdana {Bold Italic}	Arial (Helvetica)
Helvetica	Arial (Helvetica)	Arial (Helvetica)
Ad No. 5-16		
Cooper Black Italic	Cooper Black {Italic}	Times New Roman (Times)
Helvetica Black	Arial Black (Helvetica Black)	Arial (Helvetica)
Helvetica	Arial (Helvetica)	Arial (Helvetica)
Helvetica Bold	Arial (Helvetica) {Bold}	Arial (Helvetica)
Helvetica Bold Italic	Arial {Bold Italic}	Arial (Helvetica)
Times	Times (Times New Roman)	Times New Roman (Times)
Ad No. 5-17		
Friz Quadrata	Goudy Old Style	Times New Roman (Times)
Palatino	Book Antiqua	Times New Roman (Times)
Helvetica	Arial (Helvetica)	Arial (Helvetica)
Palatino Bold	Book Antiqua {Bold}	Times New Roman (Times)
Ad No. 5-18		
Benguiat Bold	Footlight MT Light {Bold}	Times New Roman (Times)
Souvenir Demi	Lucida Casual {Bold}	Times New Roman (Times)
Benguiat	Footlight MT Light	Times New Roman (Times)
Machine	Impact	Arial (Helvetica)
Souvenir	Lucida Casual	Times New Roman (Times)
Souvenir Bold	Lucida Casual {Bold}	Times New Roman (Times)
Souvenir Medium	Lucida Casual	Times New Roman (Times)
Souvenir Medium Italic	Lucida Casual {Italic}	Times New Roman (Times)
Helvetica	Arial (Helvetica)	Arial (Helvetica)
Ad No. 5-19		
Adobe Garamond Bold Italic	Garamond {Bold Italic}	Times New Roman (Times)
Kabel Book	Eras Demi ITC	Arial (Helvetica)
Kabel Demi	Eras Demi ITC	Arial (Helvetica)
Kabel Medium	Eras Light ITC	Arial (Helvetica)
Helvetica	Arial (Helvetica)	Arial (Helvetica)

Actual Font Used in Book	Substitute Font, Typical PC	Simplest Substitute Font
Ad No. 5-20		
Memphis Bold Italic	Rockwell {Bold Italic}	Times New Roman (Times)
Futura	Century Gothic	Arial (Helvetica)
Futura Heavy	Century Gothic {Bold}	Arial (Helvetica)
Memphis Medium Italic	Rockwell {Italic}	Times New Roman (Times)
Futura Extra Bold	Century Gothic {Bold}	Arial (Helvetica)
Helvetica	Arial (Helvetica)	Arial (Helvetica)
Ad No. 5-21		
Helvetica Black Italic	Arial Black {Italic}	Arial (Helvetica)
Palatino Bold	Book Antiqua {Bold}	Times New Roman (Times)
Palatino	Book Antiqua	Times New Roman (Times)
Times	Times (Times New Roman)	Times New Roman (Times)
Times Bold	Times (Times New Roman) Bold	Times New Roman (Times)
Palatino Italic	Book Antiqua {Italic}	Times New Roman (Times)
Ad No. 5-22		
Franklin Gothic Demi	Franklin Gothic Demi	Arial (Helvetica)
Bodoni	Modern No. 20	Times New Roman (Times)
Franklin Gothic	Franklin Gothic	Arial (Helvetica)
Franklin Gothic Heavy Oblique	Franklin Gothic Heavy {Italic}	Arial (Helvetica)
Bodoni Poster	Poster Bodoni ATT	Times New Roman (Times)
Franklin Gothic Bold Italic	Franklin Gothic Demi {Italic}	Arial (Helvetica)
Times	Times (Times New Roman)	Times New Roman (Times)
Helvetica	Arial (Helvetica)	Arial (Helvetica)
Ad No. 5-23		
Korinna Bold	Lucida Casual {Bold}	Times New Roman (Times)
Helvetica Condensed Black	Arial Narrow {Bold}	Arial (Helvetica)
Helvetica Condensed Black Italic	Arial Narrow {Bold Italic}	Arial (Helvetica)
Helvetica	Arial (Helvetica)	Arial (Helvetica)
Ad No. 5-24		
Adobe Garamond	Garamond	Times New Roman (Times)
Adobe Garamond Bold	Garamond {Bold}	Times New Roman (Times)
Helvetica	Arial (Helvetica)	Arial (Helvetica)
Times	Times (Times New Roman)	Times New Roman (Times)
Adobe Garamond Italic	Garamond {Italic}	Times New Roman (Times)
Adobe Garamond Bold Italic	Garamond {Bold Italic}	Times New Roman (Times)
Ad No. 5-25		
American Typewriter	Courier New	Times New Roman (Times)
American Typewriter Bold	Courier New {Bold}	Times New Roman (Times)
Times	Times (Times New Roman)	Times New Roman (Times)
Helvetica	Arial (Helvetica)	Arial (Helvetica)
Ad No. 5-26		
Kabel Bold	Eras Bold ITC	Arial (Helvetica)
Kabel Demi	Eras Demi ITC	Arial (Helvetica)
Bodoni Poster	Poster Bodoni ATT	Times New Roman (Times)
Helvetica	Arial (Helvetica)	Arial (Helvetica)
Ad No. 5-27		
Helvetica Condensed Black	Arial Narrow {Bold}	Arial (Helvetica)
Helvetica Black	Arial Black (Helvetica Black)	Arial (Helvetica)
Palatino Bold	Book Antiqua {Bold}	Times New Roman (Times)
Helvetica	Arial (Helvetica)	Arial (Helvetica)
Times	Times (Times New Roman)	Times New Roman (Times)
Helvetica Bold	Arial (Helvetica) {Bold}	Arial (Helvetica)

Actual Font Used in Book	Substitute Font, Typical PC	Simplest Substitute Font
Ad No. 5-28		
New Century Schoolbook Bold	Century Schoolbook {Bold}	Times New Roman (Times)
Helvetica Black	Arial Black (Helvetica Black)	Arial (Helvetica)
Helvetica Black Italic	Arial Black {Italic}	Arial (Helvetica)
Helvetica	Arial (Helvetica)	Arial (Helvetica)
Helvetica Bold Italic	Arial {Bold Italic}	Arial (Helvetica)
Ad No. 5-29		
Century Old Style Bold	Century Schoolbook {Bold}	Times New Roman (Times)
Bookman Bold	Bookman Old Style {Bold}	Times New Roman (Times)
Bookman Medium	Bookman Old Style	Times New Roman (Times)
Bookman Medium	Bookman Old Style	Times New Roman (Times)
Franklin Gothic Heavy	Franklin Gothic Heavy	Arial (Helvetica)
Century Old Style	Century Schoolbook	Times New Roman (Times)
Helvetica	Arial (Helvetica)	Arial (Helvetica)
Times	Times (Times New Roman)	Times New Roman (Times)
Times Bold	Times (Times New Roman) Bold	Times New Roman (Times)
Ad No. 5-30		
Bookman Demi	Bookman Old Style {Bold}	Times New Roman (Times)
Friz Quadrata Bold	Goudy Old Style {Bold}	Times New Roman (Times)
Bodoni Bold Italic	Modern No. 20 {Bold Italic}	Times New Roman (Times)
Bookman	Bookman Old Style	Times New Roman (Times)
Bookman Bold	Bookman Old Style {Bold}	Times New Roman (Times)
Friz Quadrata	Goudy Old Style	Times New Roman (Times)
Helvetica	Arial (Helvetica)	Arial (Helvetica)
Times	Times (Times New Roman)	Times New Roman (Times)
Ad No. 5-31		
Memphis Bold	Rockwell (Bold)	Times New Roman (Times)
Futura Bold Oblique	Century Gothic {Bold Italic}	Arial (Helvetica)
Memphis Medium	Rockwell	Times New Roman (Times)
Memphis Extra Bold	Rockwell Extra Bold	Times New Roman (Times)
Helvetica	Arial (Helvetica)	Arial (Helvetica)
Times	Times (Times New Roman)	Times New Roman (Times)
Times Bold	Times (Times New Roman) Bold	Times New Roman (Times)
Ad No. 5-32		
Adobe Garamond	Garamond	Times New Roman (Times)
Adobe Garamond Italic	Garamond {Italic}	Times New Roman (Times)
Helvetica Black	Arial Black (Helvetica Black)	Arial (Helvetica)
Helvetica Black Italic	Arial Black {Italic}	Arial (Helvetica)
Helvetica	Arial (Helvetica)	Arial (Helvetica)
Ad No. 5-33		
Adobe Garamond	Garamond	Times New Roman (Times)
Futura Bold	Century Gothic {Bold}	Arial (Helvetica)
Futura Condensed Bold	Century Gothic {Bold}	Arial (Helvetica)
Times	Times (Times New Roman)	Times New Roman (Times)
Helvetica	Arial (Helvetica)	Arial (Helvetica)
Futura	Century Gothic	Arial (Helvetica)
Futura Condensed Extra Bold Oblique	Century Gothic {Bold Italic}	Arial (Helvetica)
Ad No. 5-34		
Benguiat Bold	Footlight MT Light {Bold}	Times New Roman (Times)
Palatino	Book Antiqua	Times New Roman (Times)
Palatino Bold	Book Antiqua {Bold}	Times New Roman (Times)

Actual Font Used in Book	Substitute Font, Typical PC	Simplest Substitute Font
Ad No. 5-35		
Helvetica Black	Arial Black (Helvetica Black)	Arial (Helvetica)
New Century Schoolbook	Century Schoolbook	Times New Roman (Times)
Memphis Extra Bold	Rockwell Extra Bold	Times New Roman (Times)
Helvetica	Arial (Helvetica)	Arial (Helvetica)
Helvetica Bold	Arial (Helvetica) {Bold}	Arial (Helvetica)
Ad No. 5-36		
Stone Serif	Book Antiqua	Times New Roman (Times)
Stone Serif Bold	Book Antiqua {Bold}	Times New Roman (Times)
Futura Bold	Century Gothic {Bold}	Arial (Helvetica)
Umbra	Gill Sans MT Shadow	Arial (Helvetica)
Helvetica	Arial (Helvetica)	Arial (Helvetica)
Ad No. 5-37		
Futura Book	Century Gothic	Arial (Helvetica)
Helvetica Black	Arial Black (Helvetica Black)	Arial (Helvetica)
Helvetica	Arial (Helvetica)	Arial (Helvetica)
Helvetica Bold	Arial (Helvetica) {Bold}	Arial (Helvetica)
Ad No. 5-38		
Avant Garde Medium	Century Gothic	Arial (Helvetica)
Franklin Gothic Bold	Franklin Gothic Demi	Arial (Helvetica)
Franklin Gothic	Franklin Gothic	Arial (Helvetica)
Franklin Gothic Heavy	Franklin Gothic Heavy	Arial (Helvetica)
Franklin Gothic Heavy Italic	Franklin Gothic Heavy {Italic}	Arial (Helvetica)
Helvetica	Arial (Helvetica)	Arial (Helvetica)
Times	Times (Times New Roman)	Times New Roman (Times)
Times Bold	Times (Times New Roman) Bold	Times New Roman (Times)
Ad No. 5-39		
Bookman Demi	Bookman Old Style {Bold}	Times New Roman (Times)
Helvetica Condensed Bold	Arial Narrow {Bold}	Arial (Helvetica)
Helvetica	Arial (Helvetica)	Arial (Helvetica)
Bookman	Bookman Old Style	Times New Roman (Times)
Times	Times (Times New Roman)	Times New Roman (Times)
Times Bold	Times (Times New Roman) Bold	Times New Roman (Times)
Ad No. 5-40		
American Typewriter	Courier New	Times New Roman (Times)
Helvetica Black	Arial Black (Helvetica Black)	Arial (Helvetica)
Helvetica Condensed Black Italic	Arial Narrow {Bold Italic}	Arial (Helvetica)
Helvetica	Arial (Helvetica)	Arial (Helvetica)
Times	Times (Times New Roman)	Times New Roman (Times)
Times Bold	Times (Times New Roman) Bold	Times New Roman (Times)
Helvetica Bold	Arial (Helvetica) {Bold}	Arial (Helvetica)
Ad No. 5-41		
Adobe Garamond	Garamond	Times New Roman (Times)
Adobe Garamond Bold Italic	Garamond {Bold Italic}	Times New Roman (Times)
Futura Condensed Extra Bold	Century Gothic {Bold}	Arial (Helvetica)
Garamond Bold Condensed	Garamond	Times New Roman (Times)
Futura	Century Gothic	Arial (Helvetica)
Ad No. 5-42		
Adobe Garamond	Garamond	Times New Roman (Times)
Adobe Garamond Bold	Garamond {Bold}	Times New Roman (Times)
Adobe Garamond Italic	Garamond {Italic}	Times New Roman (Times)

Actual Font Used in Book	Substitute Font, Typical PC	Simplest Substitute Font
Ad No. 5-43		
Souvenir Demi	Lucida Casual {Bold}	Times New Roman (Times)
Souvenir	Lucida Casual	Times New Roman (Times)
Futura Extra Bold	Century Gothic {Bold}	Arial (Helvetica)
Times	Times (Times New Roman)	Times New Roman (Times)
Helvetica	Arial (Helvetica)	Arial (Helvetica)
Ad No. 5-44		
Franklin Gothic Demi	Franklin Gothic Demi	Arial (Helvetica)
Galliard Bold	Footlight MT Light {Bold}	Times New Roman (Times)
Franklin Gothic Demi Oblique	Franklin Gothic Demi {Italic}	Arial (Helvetica)
Franklin Gothic	Franklin Gothic	Arial (Helvetica)
Times	Times (Times New Roman)	Times New Roman (Times)
Helvetica	Arial (Helvetica)	Arial (Helvetica)
Times Bold	Times (Times New Roman) Bold	Times New Roman (Times)
Ad No. 5-45		
Aachen Bold	Rockwell Extra Bold	Times New Roman (Times)
Bodoni Bold	Modern No. 20 {Bold}	Times New Roman (Times)
Bodoni Bold Italic	Modern No. 20 {Bold Italic}	Times New Roman (Times)
Bodoni	Modern No. 20	Times New Roman (Times)
Ad No. 5-46		
Adobe Garamond	Garamond	Times New Roman (Times)
Futura Book	Century Gothic	Arial (Helvetica)
Futura Heavy	Century Gothic {Bold}	Arial (Helvetica)
Adobe Garamond Bold	Garamond {Bold}	Times New Roman (Times)
Times Bold	Times (Times New Roman) Bold	Times New Roman (Times)
Times	Times (Times New Roman)	Times New Roman (Times)
Ad No. 5-47		
Adobe Garamond	Garamond	Times New Roman (Times)
Adobe Garamond Bold	Garamond {Bold}	Times New Roman (Times)
Helvetica	Arial (Helvetica)	Arial (Helvetica)
Ad No. 6-01		
Cheltenham Bold	Baskerville Old Face {Bold}	Times New Roman (Times)
Cheltenham	Baskerville Old Face	Times New Roman (Times)
Cooper Black	Cooper Black	Times New Roman (Times)
Helvetica	Arial (Helvetica)	Arial (Helvetica)
Ad No. 6-02		
Avant Garde Bold	Century Gothic {Bold}	Arial (Helvetica)
Kabel Bold	Eras Bold ITC	Arial (Helvetica)
Souvenir	Lucida Casual	Times New Roman (Times)
Souvenir Medium	Lucida Casual	Times New Roman (Times)
Souvenir Medium Italic	Lucida Casual {Italic}	Times New Roman (Times)
Ad No. 6-03		
Adobe Garamond	Garamond	Times New Roman (Times)
Adobe Garamond Bold	Garamond {Bold}	Times New Roman (Times)
Adobe Garamond Bold Italic	Garamond {Bold Italic}	Times New Roman (Times)
Adobe Garamond Semibold	Garamond {Bold}	Times New Roman (Times)
Franklin Gothic Heavy	Franklin Gothic Heavy	Arial (Helvetica)
Ad No. 6-04		
Melior Bold	Lucida Fax {Bold}	Times New Roman (Times)
Helvetica Ultra Compressed	Impact	Arial (Helvetica)
Melior	Lucida Fax	Times New Roman (Times)
Stencil	Stencil	Times New Roman (Times)

Actual Font Used in Book	Substitute Font, Typical PC	Simplest Substitute Font

Ad No. 6-05

Souvenir Demi	Lucida Casual {Bold}	Times New Roman (Times)
Souvenir Demi Italic	Lucida Casual {Bold Italic}	Times New Roman (Times)
Souvenir	Lucida Casual	Times New Roman (Times)
Souvenir Medium	Lucida Casual	Times New Roman (Times)
Souvenir Medium Italic	Lucida Casual {Italic}	Times New Roman (Times)

Ad No. 6-06

Avant Garde Demi	Century Gothic {Bold}	Arial (Helvetica)
Cheltenham Bold	Baskerville Old Face {Bold}	Times New Roman (Times)
Cheltenham	Baskerville Old Face	Times New Roman (Times)
Helvetica Black	Arial Black (Helvetica Black)	Arial (Helvetica)
Helvetica	Arial (Helvetica)	Arial (Helvetica)
Helvetica Bold	Arial (Helvetica) {Bold}	Arial (Helvetica)

Ad No. 6-07

Souvenir Demi	Lucida Casual {Bold}	Times New Roman (Times)
Machine Bold	Impact {Bold}	Arial (Helvetica)
Souvenir	Lucida Casual	Times New Roman (Times)

Ad No. 6-08

Avant Garde Extra Light	Century Gothic	Arial (Helvetica)
Korinna Bold	Lucida Casual {Bold}	Times New Roman (Times)
Optima Bold	Verdana {Bold}	Arial (Helvetica)
Optima Oblique	Verdana {Italic}	Arial (Helvetica)
Optima	Verdana	Arial (Helvetica)

Ad No. 6-09

Adobe Garamond	Garamond	Times New Roman (Times)
Adobe Garamond Bold	Garamond {Bold}	Times New Roman (Times)
Adobe Garamond Bold Italic	Garamond {Bold Italic}	Times New Roman (Times)
Adobe Garamond Semibold	Garamond {Bold}	Times New Roman (Times)
Spire	Onyx	Times New Roman (Times)

Ad No. 6-10

Souvenir Demi	Lucida Casual {Bold}	Times New Roman (Times)
Souvenir Demi Italic	Lucida Casual {Bold Italic}	Times New Roman (Times)
Franklin Gothic		
Souvenir Light Italic	Lucida Casual {Italic}	Times New Roman (Times)
Souvenir	Lucida Casual	Times New Roman (Times)
Times	Times (Times New Roman)	Times New Roman (Times)

Ad No. 6-11

Souvenir Demi	Lucida Casual {Bold}	Times New Roman (Times)
Souvenir	Lucida Casual	Times New Roman (Times)
Futura Extra Bold	Century Gothic {Bold}	Arial (Helvetica)

Ad No. 6-12

Aachen Bold	Rockwell Extra Bold	Times New Roman (Times)
Helvetica Condensed	Arial Narrow	Arial (Helvetica)
Helvetica Condensed Black	Arial Narrow {Bold}	Arial (Helvetica)
Helvetica Ultra Compressed	Impact	Arial (Helvetica)
Helvetica	Arial (Helvetica)	Arial (Helvetica)
Helvetica Bold	Arial (Helvetica) {Bold}	Arial (Helvetica)

Ad No. 6-13

New Century Schoolbook Bold	Century Schoolbook {Bold}	Times New Roman (Times)
New Century Schoolbook Bold Italic	Century Schoolbook {Bold Italic}	Times New Roman (Times)
Friz Quadrata	Goudy Old Style	Times New Roman (Times)
Helvetica Black	Arial Black (Helvetica Black)	Arial (Helvetica)
New Century Schoolbook	Century Schoolbook	Times New Roman (Times)
Helvetica	Arial (Helvetica)	Arial (Helvetica)

Actual Font Used in Book	Substitute Font, Typical PC	Simplest Substitute Font
Ad No. 6-14		
Clearface Black	Gloucester MT {Bold}	Times New Roman (Times)
Clearface Black Italic	Gloucester MT {Bold Italic}	Times New Roman (Times)
Clearface Regular	Gloucester MT	Times New Roman (Times)
Clearface Heavy	Gloucester MT {Bold}	Times New Roman (Times)
Clearface Italic	Gloucester MT {Italic}	Times New Roman (Times)
Ad No. 6-15		
Souvenir Demi	Lucida Casual {Bold}	Times New Roman (Times)
Souvenir Demi Italic	Lucida Casual {Bold Italic}	Times New Roman (Times)
Helvetica Condensed Black	Arial Narrow {Bold}	Arial (Helvetica)
Souvenir	Lucida Casual	Times New Roman (Times)
Ad No. 6-16		
Helvetica Condensed Black	Arial Narrow {Bold}	Arial (Helvetica)
Helvetica Black	Arial Black (Helvetica Black)	Arial (Helvetica)
Helvetica	Arial (Helvetica)	Arial (Helvetica)
Ad No. 6-17		
Clearface Bold	Gloucester MT {Bold}	Times New Roman (Times)
Cheltenham Bold Italic	Baskerville Old Face {Bold Italic}	Times New Roman (Times)
Clearface Black	Gloucester MT {Bold}	Times New Roman (Times)
Clearface	Gloucester MT	Times New Roman (Times)
Ad No. 6-18		
Futura Condensed Bold	Century Gothic {Bold}	Arial (Helvetica)
Futura Condensed Extra Bold	Century Gothic {Bold}	Arial (Helvetica)
Linotext	French Script MT	Times New Roman (Times)
Palatino	Book Antiqua	Times New Roman (Times)
Ad No. 6-19		
Adobe Garamond	Garamond	Times New Roman (Times)
Adobe Garamond Bold	Garamond {Bold}	Times New Roman (Times)
Adobe Garamond Italic	Garamond {Italic}	Times New Roman (Times)
Zapf Dingbats	Wingdings	(None Applicable)
Ad No. 7-01		
Machine Bold	Impact {Bold}	Arial (Helvetica)
Souvenir	Lucida Casual	Times New Roman (Times)
Souvenir Medium	Lucida Casual	Times New Roman (Times)
Souvenir Medium Italic	Lucida Casual {Italic}	Times New Roman (Times)
Helvetica	Arial (Helvetica)	Arial (Helvetica)
Ad No. 7-02		
Adobe Garamond	Garamond	Times New Roman (Times)
Adobe Garamond Bold	Garamond {Bold}	Times New Roman (Times)
Adobe Garamond Italic	Garamond {Italic}	Times New Roman (Times)
Futura Extra Bold	Century Gothic {Bold}	Arial (Helvetica)
Ad No. 7-03		
Helvetica	Arial (Helvetica)	Arial (Helvetica)
Helvetica Black	Arial Black (Helvetica Black)	Arial (Helvetica)
Helvetica Neue Black Condensed	Arial Narrow {Bold}	Arial (Helvetica)
Helvetica Bold	Arial (Helvetica) {Bold}	Arial (Helvetica)
Helvetica Condensed Bold	Arial Narrow {Bold}	Arial (Helvetica)
Memphis Extra Bold	Rockwell Extra Bold	Times New Roman (Times)
Ad No. 7-04		
Bookman Demi	Bookman Old Style {Bold}	Times New Roman (Times)
Bookman	Bookman Old Style	Times New Roman (Times)
Helvetica Neue Black Condensed	Arial Narrow {Bold}	Arial (Helvetica)
Americana Extra Bold	Wide Latin	Times New Roman (Times)
Helvetica	Arial (Helvetica)	Arial (Helvetica)
Helvetica Bold	Arial (Helvetica) {Bold}	Arial (Helvetica)
Helvetica Italic	Arial (Helvetica) {Italic}	Arial (Helvetica)

Actual Font Used in Book	Substitute Font, Typical PC	Simplest Substitute Font
Ad No. 7-05		
Century Old Style Bold	Century Schoolbook {Bold}	Times New Roman (Times)
Futura Condensed Bold	Century Gothic {Bold}	Arial (Helvetica)
Futura Condensed Light	Century Gothic	Arial (Helvetica)
Century Old Style	Century Schoolbook	Times New Roman (Times)
Ad No. 7-06		
Korinna	Lucida Casual	Times New Roman (Times)
Korinna Bold	Lucida Casual {Bold}	Times New Roman (Times)
Tiffany Demi	Baskerville Old Face	Times New Roman (Times)
Tiffany Heavy Italic	Baskerville Old Face {Italic}	Times New Roman (Times)
Ad No. 8-01		
Avant Garde Medium	Century Gothic	Arial (Helvetica)
Souvenir	Lucida Casual	Times New Roman (Times)
Souvenir Medium	Lucida Casual	Times New Roman (Times)
Times	Times (Times New Roman)	Times New Roman (Times)
Ad No. 8-02		
Bookman Demi	Bookman Old Style {Bold}	Times New Roman (Times)
Helvetica Condensed Bold Italic	Arial Narrow {Bold Italic}	Arial (Helvetica)
Helvetica Condensed Black	Arial Narrow {Bold}	Arial (Helvetica)
Helvetica Condensed Black Oblique	Arial Narrow {Bold Italic}	Arial (Helvetica)
Helvetica	Arial (Helvetica)	Arial (Helvetica)
Helvetica Bold	Arial (Helvetica) {Bold}	Arial (Helvetica)
Ad No. 8-03		
Adobe Garamond Bold	Garamond {Bold}	Times New Roman (Times)
Eurostile Bold	Eurostile {Bold}	Arial (Helvetica)
Futura Book Oblique	Century Gothic {Italic}	Arial (Helvetica)
Futura	Century Gothic	Arial (Helvetica)
Futura HeavyOblique	Century Gothic {Italic}	Arial (Helvetica)
Eurostile Oblique	Eurostile {Italic}	Arial (Helvetica)
Ad No. 8-04		
Arnold Boecklin	Harrington	Times New Roman (Times)
Korinna Bold	Lucida Casual {Bold}	Times New Roman (Times)
Prestige Elite Bold	Couirer New	Times New Roman (Times)
Korinna Kursiv Bold	Lucida Casual {Bold Italic}	Times New Roman (Times)
Korinna Kursiv Regular	Lucida Casual {Italic}	Times New Roman (Times)
Korinna	Lucida Casual	Times New Roman (Times)
Ad No. 8-05		
Helvetica Condensed Bold	Arial Narrow {Bold}	Arial (Helvetica)
Helvetica Condensed Black	Arial Narrow {Bold}	Arial (Helvetica)
Umbra	Gill Sans MT Shadow	Arial (Helvetica)
Helvetica	Arial (Helvetica)	Arial (Helvetica)
Helvetica Bold	Arial (Helvetica) {Bold}	Arial (Helvetica)
Ad No. 8-06		
Benguiat Bold	Footlight MT Light {Bold}	Times New Roman (Times)
Palatino	Book Antiqua	Times New Roman (Times)
Palatino Bold	Book Antiqua {Bold}	Times New Roman (Times)
Times	Times (Times New Roman)	Times New Roman (Times)
Ad No. 8-07		
Cheltenham Bold	Baskerville Old Face {Bold}	Times New Roman (Times)
Futura Book	Century Gothic	Arial (Helvetica)
VAG Rounded Thin	Arial Rounded MT Bold	Arial (Helvetica)
Helvetica	Arial (Helvetica)	Arial (Helvetica)

Actual Font Used in Book	Substitute Font, Typical PC	Simplest Substitute Font
Ad No. 8-08		
Benguiat Bold	Footlight MT Light {Bold}	Times New Roman (Times)
Freestyle Script	Bradley Hand ITC	Times New Roman (Times)
Helvetica	Arial (Helvetica)	Arial (Helvetica)
Helvetica Bold	Arial (Helvetica) {Bold}	Arial (Helvetica)
Ad No. 8-09		
Eurostile Bold	Eurostile {Bold}	Arial (Helvetica)
Eurostile Demi	Eurostile {Bold}	Arial (Helvetica)
Eurostile	Eurostile	Arial (Helvetica)
Helvetica Bold	Arial (Helvetica) {Bold}	Arial (Helvetica)
Ad No. 8-10		
Benguiat Bold	Footlight MT Light {Bold}	Times New Roman (Times)
Optima Bold	Verdana {Bold}	Arial (Helvetica)
Optima Bold Oblique	Verdana {Bold Italic}	Arial (Helvetica)
Optima	Verdana	Arial (Helvetica)
Ad No. 8-11		
Adobe Garamond	Garamond	Times New Roman (Times)
Adobe Garamond Bold	Garamond {Bold}	Times New Roman (Times)
Garamond Bold Condensed	Garamond	Times New Roman (Times)
Ad No. 8-12		
Memphis Bold	Rockwell (Bold)	Times New Roman (Times)
Futura Condensed Extra Bold	Century Gothic {Bold}	Arial (Helvetica)
Memphis Medium	Rockwell	Times New Roman (Times)
Memphis Extra Bold	Rockwell Extra Bold	Times New Roman (Times)
Ad No. 8-13		
Friz Quadrata Bold	Goudy Old Style {Bold}	Times New Roman (Times)
Bauhaus Light	Eurostile	Arial (Helvetica)
Bauhaus Medium	Eurostile {Bold}	Arial (Helvetica)
Friz Quadrata	Goudy Old Style	Times New Roman (Times)
Ad No. 8-14		
Helvetica Condensed Bold	Arial Narrow {Bold}	Arial (Helvetica)
Helvetica Condensed Black	Arial Narrow {Bold}	Arial (Helvetica)
Helvetica Condensed Black Italic	Arial Narrow {Bold Italic}	Arial (Helvetica)
Helvetica Black Italic	Arial Black {Italic}	Arial (Helvetica)
Machine	Impact	Arial (Helvetica)
Helvetica	Arial (Helvetica)	Arial (Helvetica)
Ad No. 8-15		
Futura Condensed Extra Bold Oblique	Century Gothic {Bold Italic}	Arial (Helvetica)
Futura	Century Gothic	Arial (Helvetica)
Futura Heavy	Century Gothic {Bold}	Arial (Helvetica)
Futura Heavy Oblique	Century Gothic {Bold Italic}	Arial (Helvetica)
Ad No. 8-16		
Clearface Black	Gloucester MT {Bold}	Times New Roman (Times)
Clearface Black Italic	Gloucester MT {Bold Italic}	Times New Roman (Times)
Clearface Regular	Gloucester MT	Times New Roman (Times)
Clearface Heavy	Gloucester MT {Bold}	Times New Roman (Times)
Futura Extra Bold	Century Gothic {Bold}	Arial (Helvetica)
Ad No. 8-17		
Memphis Bold	Rockwell (Bold)	Times New Roman (Times)
Memphis Extra Bold	Rockwell Extra Bold	Times New Roman (Times)
Memphis Medium	Rockwell	Times New Roman (Times)

Actual Font Used in Book	Substitute Font, Typical PC	Simplest Substitute Font
Ad No. 8-18		
Helvetica Black	Arial Black (Helvetica Black)	Arial (Helvetica)
Helvetica Black Italic	Arial Black {Italic}	Arial (Helvetica)
Helvetica	Arial (Helvetica)	Arial (Helvetica)
Helvetica Bold	Arial (Helvetica) {Bold}	Arial (Helvetica)
Ad No. 8-19		
Kabel Medium	Eras Light ITC	Arial (Helvetica)
Kabel Ultra	Eras Ultra ITC	Arial (Helvetica)
Times	Times (Times New Roman)	Times New Roman (Times)
Ad No. 8-20		
Futura Condensed Extra Bold	Century Gothic {Bold}	Arial (Helvetica)
Helvetica Extra Compressed	Impact	Arial (Helvetica)
Futura Extra Bold	Century Gothic {Bold}	Arial (Helvetica)
Helvetica	Arial (Helvetica)	Arial (Helvetica)
Helvetica Bold	Arial (Helvetica) {Bold}	Arial (Helvetica)
Ad No. 8-21		
Souvenir Demi	Lucida Casual {Bold}	Times New Roman (Times)
Souvenir Demi Italic	Lucida Casual {Bold Italic}	Times New Roman (Times)
Souvenir	Lucida Casual	Times New Roman (Times)
Kabel Ultra	Eras Ultra ITC	Arial (Helvetica)
Ad No. 8-22		
Palatino	Book Antiqua	Times New Roman (Times)
Palatino Bold	Book Antiqua {Bold}	Times New Roman (Times)
Palatino Italic	Book Antiqua {Italic}	Times New Roman (Times)
Ad No. 8-23		
Korinna Bold	Lucida Casual {Bold}	Times New Roman (Times)
Souvenir Demi Italic	Lucida Casual {Bold Italic}	Times New Roman (Times)
Korinna	Lucida Casual	Times New Roman (Times)
Ad No. 8-24		
Avant Garde Condensed Book	Century Gothic	Arial (Helvetica)
Avant Garde Demi	Century Gothic {Bold}	Arial (Helvetica)
Avant Garde Demi Oblique	Century Gothic {Bold Italic}	Arial (Helvetica)
Memphis Medium	Rockwell	Times New Roman (Times)
Ad No. 8-25		
Adobe Caslon Ornaments	Not Applicable	Times New Roman (Times)
Benguiat Bold	Footlight MT Light {Bold}	Times New Roman (Times)
Century Old Style Bold	Century Schoolbook {Bold}	Times New Roman (Times)
New Century Schoolbook	Century Schoolbook	Times New Roman (Times)
Futura Extra Bold	Century Gothic {Bold}	Arial (Helvetica)
New Century Schoolbook Bold Italic	Century Schoolbook {Bold Italic}	Times New Roman (Times)
New Century Schoolbook Italic	Century Schoolbook {Italic}	Times New Roman (Times)
New Century Schoolbook Bold	Century Schoolbook {Bold}	Times New Roman (Times)
Ad No. 8-26		
Palatino	Book Antiqua	Times New Roman (Times)
Palatino Bold	Book Antiqua {Bold}	Times New Roman (Times)
Palatino Bold Italic	Book Antiqua {Bold Italic}	Times New Roman (Times)
Ad No. 8-27		
Futura Condensed Bold	Century Gothic {Bold}	Arial (Helvetica)
Helvetica Black	Arial Black (Helvetica Black)	Arial (Helvetica)
Helvetica Bold	Arial (Helvetica) {Bold}	Arial (Helvetica)
Helvetica	Arial (Helvetica)	Arial (Helvetica)
Helvetica Bold Italic	Arial {Bold Italic}	Arial (Helvetica)

Actual Font Used in Book	Substitute Font, Typical PC	Simplest Substitute Font
Ad No. 8-28		
Stone Serif	Book Antiqua	Times New Roman (Times)
Stone Serif Bold	Book Antiqua {Bold}	Times New Roman (Times)
Futura Bold	Century Gothic {Bold}	Arial (Helvetica)
Futura Book	Century Gothic	Arial (Helvetica)
Ad No. 8-29		
Helvetica Black	Arial Black (Helvetica Black)	Arial (Helvetica)
Kabel Ultra	Eras Ultra ITC	Arial (Helvetica)
Helvetica	Arial (Helvetica)	Arial (Helvetica)
Ad No. 8-30		
Futura Bold	Century Gothic {Bold}	Arial (Helvetica)
Clearface Black	Gloucester MT {Bold}	Times New Roman (Times)
Clearface Black Italic	Gloucester MT {Bold Italic}	Times New Roman (Times)
Clearface Heavy	Gloucester MT {Bold}	Times New Roman (Times)
Clearface Italic	Gloucester MT {Italic}	Times New Roman (Times)
Clearface Regular	Gloucester MT	Times New Roman (Times)
Ad No. 8-31		
Adobe Garamond	Garamond	Times New Roman (Times)
Adobe Garamond Bold	Garamond {Bold}	Times New Roman (Times)
Ad No. 8-32		
Souvenir Demi	Lucida Casual {Bold}	Times New Roman (Times)
Souvenir	Lucida Casual	Times New Roman (Times)
Souvenir Bold	Lucida Casual {Bold}	Times New Roman (Times)
Souvenir Medium	Lucida Casual	Times New Roman (Times)
Futura Bold Oblique	Century Gothic {Bold Italic}	Arial (Helvetica)
Ad No. 8-33		
Avant Garde Demi	Century Gothic {Bold}	Arial (Helvetica)
Cheltenham Bold	Baskerville Old Face {Bold}	Times New Roman (Times)
Avant Garde	Century Gothic	Arial (Helvetica)
Cheltenham Bold Italic	Baskerville Old Face {Bold Italic}	Times New Roman (Times)
Cheltenham	Baskerville Old Face	Times New Roman (Times)
Ad No. 8-34		
Stone Serif	Book Antiqua	Times New Roman (Times)
Stone Serif Bold	Book Antiqua {Bold}	Times New Roman (Times)
Century Old Style Bold	Century Schoolbook {Bold}	Times New Roman (Times)
Century Old Style	Century Schoolbook	Times New Roman (Times)
Helvetica Condensed		
Ad No. 8-35		
Century Old Style Bold	Century Schoolbook {Bold}	Times New Roman (Times)
Avant Garde	Century Gothic	Arial (Helvetica)
Century Old Style	Century Schoolbook	Times New Roman (Times)
Ad No. 8-36		
Cheltenham Bold	Baskerville Old Face {Bold}	Times New Roman (Times)
Cheltenham	Baskerville Old Face	Times New Roman (Times)
Helvetica Extra Compressed	Impact	Arial (Helvetica)
Helvetica Black	Arial Black (Helvetica Black)	Arial (Helvetica)
Ad No. 8-37		
Helvetica Condensed	Arial Narrow	Arial (Helvetica)
Helvetica Condensed Bold	Arial Narrow {Bold}	Arial (Helvetica)
Helvetica Condensed Black	Arial Narrow {Bold}	Arial (Helvetica)
Helvetica	Arial (Helvetica)	Arial (Helvetica)
Helvetica Bold	Arial (Helvetica) {Bold}	Arial (Helvetica)
Helvetica Bold Italic	Arial {Bold Italic}	Arial (Helvetica)
Helvetica Black	Arial Black (Helvetica Black)	Arial (Helvetica)

Actual Font Used in Book	Substitute Font, Typical PC	Simplest Substitute Font
Ad No. 8-38		
Friz Quadrata Bold	Goudy Old Style {Bold}	Times New Roman (Times)
Helvetica Black	Arial Black (Helvetica Black)	Arial (Helvetica)
Friz Quadrata	Goudy Old Style	Times New Roman (Times)
Ad No. 8-39		
Helvetica	Arial (Helvetica)	Arial (Helvetica)
Helvetica Black	Arial Black (Helvetica Black)	Arial (Helvetica)
Helvetica Bold	Arial (Helvetica) {Bold}	Arial (Helvetica)
Helvetica Bold Italic	Arial {Bold Italic}	Arial (Helvetica)
Ad No. 8-40		
Adobe Garamond	Garamond	Times New Roman (Times)
Adobe Garamond Bold	Garamond {Bold}	Times New Roman (Times)
Adobe Garamond Bold Italic	Garamond {Bold Italic}	Times New Roman (Times)
Adobe Garamond Italic	Garamond {Italic}	Times New Roman (Times)
Bookman Medium	Bookman Old Style	Times New Roman (Times)
Ad No. 8-41		
Century Old Style Bold	Century Schoolbook {Bold}	Times New Roman (Times)
Century Old Style	Century Schoolbook	Times New Roman (Times)
Futura Extra Bold	Century Gothic {Bold}	Arial (Helvetica)
Ad No. 8-42		
Bookman	Bookman Old Style	Times New Roman (Times)
Helvetica Black	Arial Black (Helvetica Black)	Arial (Helvetica)
Ad No. 8-43		
Adobe Garamond Bold	Garamond {Bold}	Times New Roman (Times)
Helvetica Black	Arial Black (Helvetica Black)	Arial (Helvetica)
Helvetica	Arial (Helvetica)	Arial (Helvetica)
Helvetica Bold	Arial (Helvetica) {Bold}	Arial (Helvetica)
Ad No. 8-44		
Futura Bold Oblique	Century Gothic {Bold Italic}	Arial (Helvetica)
Futura Condensed Extra Bold	Century Gothic {Bold}	Arial (Helvetica)
Futura	Century Gothic	Arial (Helvetica)
Futura Heavy	Century Gothic {Bold}	Arial (Helvetica)
Ad No. 8-45		
Palatino	Book Antiqua	Times New Roman (Times)
Palatino Bold	Book Antiqua {Bold}	Times New Roman (Times)
Ad No. 8-46		
Galliard Bold	Footlight MT Light {Bold}	Times New Roman (Times)
Helvetica Condensed Bold	Arial Narrow {Bold}	Arial (Helvetica)
Galliard	Footlight MT Light	Times New Roman (Times)
Galliard Italic	Footlight MT Light {Italic}	Times New Roman (Times)
Ad No. 8-47		
Clearface Bold	Gloucester MT {Bold}	Times New Roman (Times)
Clearface Black	Gloucester MT {Bold}	Times New Roman (Times)
Clearface Regular	Gloucester MT	Times New Roman (Times)
Ad No. 8-48		
Helvetica Condensed	Arial Narrow	Arial (Helvetica)
Futura Condensed Bold	Century Gothic {Bold}	Arial (Helvetica)
Helvetica Condensed Black	Arial Narrow {Bold}	Arial (Helvetica)
Helvetica Black	Arial Black (Helvetica Black)	Arial (Helvetica)
Helvetica	Arial (Helvetica)	Arial (Helvetica)
Ad No. 8-49		
Eurostile Bold	Eurostile {Bold}	Arial (Helvetica)
Trump Mediaeval Bold	Perpetua {Bold}	Times New Roman (Times)
Trump Mediaeval	Perpetua	Times New Roman (Times)

Actual Font Used in Book	Substitute Font, Typical PC	Simplest Substitute Font
d No. 8-50		
odoni Poster	Poster Bodoni ATT	Times New Roman (Times)
alatino	Book Antiqua	Times New Roman (Times)
alatino Bold	Book Antiqua {Bold}	Times New Roman (Times)
d No. 8-51		
ptima Bold	Verdana {Bold}	Arial (Helvetica)
one Serif Bold Italic	Book Antiqua {Bold Italic}	Times New Roman (Times)
ptima Oblique	Verdana {Italic}	Arial (Helvetica)
ptima	Verdana	Arial (Helvetica)
alatino Bold	Book Antiqua {Bold}	Times New Roman (Times)
d No. 8-52		
ookman Demi	Bookman Old Style {Bold}	Times New Roman (Times)
entury Old Style	Century Schoolbook	Times New Roman (Times)
entury Old Style Italic	Century Schoolbook {Italic}	Times New Roman (Times)
d No. 8-53		
dobe Garamond	Garamond	Times New Roman (Times)
dobe Garamond Bold	Garamond {Bold}	Times New Roman (Times)
ptima Bold	Verdana {Bold}	Arial (Helvetica)
d No. 8-54		
elvetica Neue Heavy 85	Arial Black	Arial (Helvetica)
heltenham Bold	Baskerville Old Face {Bold}	Times New Roman (Times)
elvetica	Arial (Helvetica)	Arial (Helvetica)
elvetica Bold	Arial (Helvetica) {Bold}	Arial (Helvetica)
d No. 8-55		
dobe Garamond Alternate	Garamond	Times New Roman (Times)
ptima Bold	Verdana {Bold}	Arial (Helvetica)
ptima	Verdana	Arial (Helvetica)
d No. 8-56		
entury Old Style Bold	Century Schoolbook {Bold}	Times New Roman (Times)
entury Old Style	Century Schoolbook	Times New Roman (Times)
entury Old Style Italic	Century Schoolbook {Italic}	Times New Roman (Times)
elvetica Compressed	Impact	Arial (Helvetica)
d No. 8-57		
one Informal	Book Antiqua	Times New Roman (Times)
one Informal Bold	Book Antiqua {Bold}	Times New Roman (Times)
one Informal Italic	Book Antiqua {Italic}	Times New Roman (Times)
one Informal Semibold	Book Antiqua {Bold}	Times New Roman (Times)
d No. 8-58		
ookman	Bookman Old Style	Times New Roman (Times)
elvetica Black	Arial Black (Helvetica Black)	Arial (Helvetica)
d No. 8-59		
elvetica Black	Arial Black (Helvetica Black)	Arial (Helvetica)
entury Old Style	Century Schoolbook	Times New Roman (Times)
d No. 8-60		
learface Black	Gloucester MT {Bold}	Times New Roman (Times)
learface Regular	Gloucester MT	Times New Roman (Times)
learface Heavy	Gloucester MT {Bold}	Times New Roman (Times)
learface Regular Italic	Gloucester MT {Italic}	Times New Roman (Times)
ranklin Gothic Heavy	Franklin Gothic Heavy	Arial (Helvetica)
d No. 8-61		
imes	Times (Times New Roman)	Times New Roman (Times)
elvetica Condensed Black	Arial Narrow {Bold}	Arial (Helvetica)
entury Old Style	Century Schoolbook	Times New Roman (Times)
entury Old Style Italic	Century Schoolbook {Italic}	Times New Roman (Times)
elvetica Black	Arial Black (Helvetica Black)	Arial (Helvetica)

Actual Font Used in Book	Substitute Font, Typical PC	Simplest Substitute Font
Ad No. 8-62		
Century Old Style Bold	Century Schoolbook {Bold}	Times New Roman (Times)
Friz Quadrata Bold	Goudy Old Style {Bold}	Times New Roman (Times)
Century Old Style	Century Schoolbook	Times New Roman (Times)
Century Old Style Italic	Century Schoolbook {Italic}	Times New Roman (Times)
Ad No. 8-63		
Adobe Garamond	Garamond	Times New Roman (Times)
Adobe Garamond Bold	Garamond {Bold}	Times New Roman (Times)
Adobe Garamond Bold Italic	Garamond {Bold Italic}	Times New Roman (Times)
Helvetica Black	Arial Black (Helvetica Black)	Arial (Helvetica)
Times	Times (Times New Roman)	Times New Roman (Times)
Helvetica Bold	Arial (Helvetica) {Bold}	Arial (Helvetica)
Ad No. 8-64		
Adobe Garamond	Garamond	Times New Roman (Times)
Adobe Garamond Bold	Garamond {Bold}	Times New Roman (Times)
Ad No. 8-65		
Franklin Gothic	Franklin Gothic	Arial (Helvetica)
Avant Garde	Century Gothic	Arial (Helvetica)
Helvetica Black	Arial Black (Helvetica Black)	Arial (Helvetica)
Palatino	Book Antiqua	Times New Roman (Times)
Ad No. 8-66		
Helvetica Neue Black 95	Arial Black	Arial (Helvetica)
Adobe Garamond	Garamond	Times New Roman (Times)
Adobe Garamond Bold	Garamond {Bold}	Times New Roman (Times)
Korinna Bold	Lucida Casual {Bold}	Times New Roman (Times)
Korinna	Lucida Casual	Times New Roman (Times)
Ad No. 8-67		
Adobe Garamond	Garamond	Times New Roman (Times)
Adobe Garamond Bold	Garamond {Bold}	Times New Roman (Times)
Adobe Garamond Semibold	Garamond {Bold}	Times New Roman (Times)
Helvetica Black	Arial Black (Helvetica Black)	Arial (Helvetica)
Ad No. 8-68		
Aachen Bold	Rockwell Extra Bold	Times New Roman (Times)
Bodoni Bold	Modern No. 20 {Bold}	Times New Roman (Times)
Bodoni Bold Italic	Modern No. 20 {Bold Italic}	Times New Roman (Times)
Bodoni	Modern No. 20	Times New Roman (Times)
Times	Times (Times New Roman)	Times New Roman (Times)
Ad No. 8-69		
Century Old Style Bold	Century Schoolbook {Bold}	Times New Roman (Times)
Helvetica Black	Arial Black (Helvetica Black)	Arial (Helvetica)
Century Old Style	Century Schoolbook	Times New Roman (Times)
Ad No. 8-70		
Franklin Gothic Demi	Franklin Gothic Demi	Arial (Helvetica)
Century Old Style Italic	Century Schoolbook {Italic}	Times New Roman (Times)
Century Old Style	Century Schoolbook	Times New Roman (Times)
Franklin Gothic		
Ad No. 8-71		
Souvenir Demi	Lucida Casual {Bold}	Times New Roman (Times)
Souvenir Light Italic	Lucida Casual {Italic}	Times New Roman (Times)
Souvenir	Lucida Casual	Times New Roman (Times)
Kabel Ultra	Eras Ultra ITC	Arial (Helvetica)
Ad No. 8-72		
Bookman Demi	Bookman Old Style {Bold}	Times New Roman (Times)
Helvetica Black	Arial Black (Helvetica Black)	Arial (Helvetica)
Helvetica	Arial (Helvetica)	Arial (Helvetica)

Actual Font Used in Book	Substitute Font, Typical PC	Simplest Substitute Font
Ad No. 8-73		
Trump Mediaeval Bold Italic	Perpetua {Bold Italic}	Times New Roman (Times)
Memphis Medium	Rockwell	Times New Roman (Times)
Memphis Extra Bold	Rockwell Extra Bold	Times New Roman (Times)
Ad No. 8-74		
Franklin Gothic Demi	Franklin Gothic Demi	Arial (Helvetica)
Franklin Gothic	Franklin Gothic	Arial (Helvetica)
Frankiln Gothic Heavy	Frankiln Gothic Heavy	Arial (Helvetica)
Ad No. 8-75		
Aachen Bold	Rockwell Extra Bold	Times New Roman (Times)
Century Old Style Bold	Century Schoolbook {Bold}	Times New Roman (Times)
Century Old Style	Century Schoolbook	Times New Roman (Times)
Ad No. 8-76		
Galliard Bold	Footlight MT Light {Bold}	Times New Roman (Times)
Freestyle Script	Bradley Hand ITC	Times New Roman (Times)
Helvetica Black	Arial Black (Helvetica Black)	Arial (Helvetica)
Helvetica	Arial (Helvetica)	Arial (Helvetica)
Helvetica Bold	Arial (Helvetica) {Bold}	Arial (Helvetica)
Ad No. 8-77		
Berkeley Bold	Gloucester MT {Bold}	Times New Roman (Times)
Berkeley Book	Gloucester MT	Times New Roman (Times)
Berkeley Book Italic	Gloucester MT {Italic}	Times New Roman (Times)
Ad No. 9-01 through 9-11 (All of Chapter 9)		
No specific fonts required. Any word processor font will be acceptable for sending press releases to news organizations.)		
Ad No. 10-01 through 10-20 (All of Chapter 10)		
No specific fonts required. Any word processor font will be acceptable for radio and television scripts.)		
Ad No. 11-01		
Memphis Bold	Rockwell (Bold)	Times New Roman (Times)
Memphis Light	Rockwell	Times New Roman (Times)
Memphis Medium	Rockwell	Times New Roman (Times)
Memphis Extra Bold	Rockwell Extra Bold	Times New Roman (Times)
Ad No. 11-02		
Cheltenham Bold	Baskerville Old Face {Bold}	Times New Roman (Times)
Cheltenham Bold Italic	Baskerville Old Face {Bold Italic}	Times New Roman (Times)
Cheltenham	Baskerville Old Face	Times New Roman (Times)
Cheltenham Book Italic	Baskerville Old Face {Bold Italic}	Times New Roman (Times)
Ad No. 11-03		
Helvetica Condensed Bold	Arial Narrow {Bold}	Arial (Helvetica)
Helvetica Condensed Black	Arial Narrow {Bold}	Arial (Helvetica)
Machine	Impact	Arial (Helvetica)
Ad No. 11-04		
Franklin Gothic Demi	Franklin Gothic Demi	Arial (Helvetica)
Franklin Gothic Demi Oblique	Franklin Gothic Demi {Italic}	Arial (Helvetica)
Machine	Impact	Arial (Helvetica)
Franklin Gothic	Franklin Gothic	Arial (Helvetica)
Franklin Gothic Heavy	Franklin Gothic Heavy	Arial (Helvetica)
Ad No. 11-05		
Helvetica Condensed Black	Arial Narrow {Bold}	Arial (Helvetica)
Ad No. 12-01		
Avant Garde Demi	Century Gothic {Bold}	Arial (Helvetica)
Helvetica Black	Arial Black (Helvetica Black)	Arial (Helvetica)
Helvetica	Arial (Helvetica)	Arial (Helvetica)

Actual Font Used in Book	Substitute Font, Typical PC	Simplest Substitute Font
Ad No. 12-02		
Franklin Gothic Demi	Franklin Gothic Demi	Arial (Helvetica)
Prestige Elite Bold	Couirer New	Times New Roman (Times)
Clearface Black	Gloucester MT {Bold}	Times New Roman (Times)
Franklin Gothic	Franklin Gothic	Arial (Helvetica)
Franklin Gothic Book Oblique	Franklin Gothic Book (Italic)	Arial (Helvetica)
Ad No. 12-03		
Futura	Century Gothic	Arial (Helvetica)
Futura Heavy	Century Gothic {Bold}	Arial (Helvetica)
Futura Extra Bold	Century Gothic {Bold}	Arial (Helvetica)
Trump Mediaeval Bold	Perpetua {Bold}	Times New Roman (Times)
Ad No. 12-04		
Clearface Black	Gloucester MT {Bold}	Times New Roman (Times)
Helvetica Extra Compressed	Impact	Arial (Helvetica)
Helvetica Black	Arial Black (Helvetica Black)	Arial (Helvetica)
Ad No. 12-05		
Eurostile Bold	Eurostile {Bold}	Arial (Helvetica)
Memphis Bold	Rockwell (Bold)	Times New Roman (Times)
Memphis Bold Italic	Rockwell {Bold Italic}	Times New Roman (Times)
Memphis Medium	Rockwell	Times New Roman (Times)
Ad No. 12-06		
Futura Condensed	Century Gothic	Arial (Helvetica)
Futura	Century Gothic	Arial (Helvetica)
Futura Heavy	Century Gothic {Bold}	Arial (Helvetica)
Futura Heavy Oblique	Century Gothic {Bold Italic}	Arial (Helvetica)
Helvetica Extra Compressed	Impact	Arial (Helvetica)
Ad No. 12-07		
Glypha Bold	Rockwell Bold	Times New Roman (Times)
Helvetica Black	Arial Black (Helvetica Black)	Arial (Helvetica)
Helvetica	Arial (Helvetica)	Arial (Helvetica)
Ad No. 12-08		
Adobe Garamond	Garamond	Times New Roman (Times)
Adobe Garamond Bold	Garamond {Bold}	Times New Roman (Times)
Adobe Garamond Bold Italic	Garamond {Bold Italic}	Times New Roman (Times)
Adobe Garamond Italic	Garamond {Italic}	Times New Roman (Times)
Ad No. 12-09		
Friz Quadrata Bold	Goudy Old Style {Bold}	Times New Roman (Times)
Friz Quadrata	Goudy Old Style	Times New Roman (Times)
Ad No. 12-10		
Kabel Bold	Eras Bold ITC	Arial (Helvetica)
Souvenir Demi	Lucida Casual {Bold}	Times New Roman (Times)
Souvenir Demi Italic	Lucida Casual {Bold Italic}	Times New Roman (Times)
Souvenir	Lucida Casual	Times New Roman (Times)
Ad No. 12-11		
Souvenir Demi	Lucida Casual {Bold}	Times New Roman (Times)
Cooper Black	Cooper Black	Times New Roman (Times)
Souvenir	Lucida Casual	Times New Roman (Times)
Ad No. 12-12		
Benguiat Bold	Footlight MT Light {Bold}	Times New Roman (Times)
Benguiat	Footlight MT Light	Times New Roman (Times)

Actual Font Used in Book	Substitute Font, Typical PC	Simplest Substitute Font
Ad No. 12-13		
Franklin Gothic Demi	Franklin Gothic Demi	Arial (Helvetica)
Franklin Gothic Demi Oblique	Franklin Gothic Demi {Italic}	Arial (Helvetica)
Franklin Gothic		
Franklin Gothic Heavy	Franklin Gothic Heavy	Arial (Helvetica)
Franklin Gothic Heavy Oblique	Franklin Gothic Heavy {Italic}	Arial (Helvetica)
Ad No. 12-14		
Helvetica Condensed Black	Arial Narrow {Bold}	Arial (Helvetica)
Helvetica Black	Arial Black (Helvetica Black)	Arial (Helvetica)
Ad No. 12-15		
Helvetica Neue Medium 66	Arial	Arial (Helvetica)
Benguiat Bold	Footlight MT Light {Bold}	Times New Roman (Times)
Helvetica	Arial (Helvetica)	Arial (Helvetica)
Helvetica Bold	Arial (Helvetica) {Bold}	Arial (Helvetica)
Helvetica Italic	Arial (Helvetica) {Italic}	Arial (Helvetica)
Ad No. 12-16		
Avant Garde Condensed Book	Century Gothic	Arial (Helvetica)
Prestige Elite Bold	Courier New	Times New Roman (Times)
Helvetica	Arial (Helvetica)	Arial (Helvetica)
Helvetica Bold	Arial (Helvetica) {Bold}	Arial (Helvetica)
Helvetica Italic	Arial (Helvetica) {Italic}	Arial (Helvetica)
Ad No. 12-17		
Bookman Demi	Bookman Old Style {Bold}	Times New Roman (Times)
Helvetica Condensed	Arial Narrow	Arial (Helvetica)
Helvetica Condensed Bold	Arial Narrow {Bold}	Arial (Helvetica)
Helvetica Condensed Oblique	Arial Narrow {Italic}	Arial (Helvetica)
Helvetica Condensed Black	Arial Narrow {Bold}	Arial (Helvetica)
Helvetica Bold	Arial (Helvetica) {Bold}	Arial (Helvetica)
Ad No. 12-18		
Franklin Gothic Demi	Franklin Gothic Demi	Arial (Helvetica)
Galliard Bold	Footlight MT Light {Bold}	Times New Roman (Times)
Franklin Gothic		
Franklin Gothic Heavy	Franklin Gothic Heavy	Arial (Helvetica)
Ad No. 12-19		
Helvetica Condensed Bold	Arial Narrow {Bold}	Arial (Helvetica)
Helvetica Black	Arial Black (Helvetica Black)	Arial (Helvetica)
Bodoni Poster	Poster Bodoni ATT	Times New Roman (Times)
Helvetica	Arial (Helvetica)	Arial (Helvetica)
Ad No. 12-20		
Aachen Bold	Rockwell Extra Bold	Times New Roman (Times)
Optima Bold	Verdana {Bold}	Arial (Helvetica)
Optima Oblique	Verdana {Italic}	Arial (Helvetica)
Optima	Verdana	Arial (Helvetica)
Ad No. 12-21		
Cheltenham Bold	Baskerville Old Face {Bold}	Times New Roman (Times)
Friz Quadrata Bold	Goudy Old Style {Bold}	Times New Roman (Times)
Cheltenham	Baskerville Old Face	Times New Roman (Times)
Ad No. 12-22		
Helvetica Condensed Bold	Arial Narrow {Bold}	Arial (Helvetica)

Actual Font Used in Book	Substitute Font, Typical PC	Simplest Substitute Font
Ad No. 12-23		
Century Old Style Bold	Century Schoolbook {Bold}	Times New Roman (Times)
Optima Bold	Verdana {Bold}	Arial (Helvetica)
Optima Oblique	Verdana {Italic}	Arial (Helvetica)
Optima	Verdana	Arial (Helvetica)
Ad No. 12-24		
Franklin Gothic Demi	Franklin Gothic Demi	Arial (Helvetica)
Souvenir Demi	Lucida Casual {Bold}	Times New Roman (Times)
Souvenir	Lucida Casual	Times New Roman (Times)
Ad No. 12-25		
Adobe Garamond	Garamond	Times New Roman (Times)
Adobe Garamond Bold	Garamond {Bold}	Times New Roman (Times)

Title Index

ndex by Subject

Bottled water company,
business card (2-08), 59
Box manufacturer, direct mail
(5-37), 219
Brochures, 1
attorney (1-12), 36
binder manufacturer (1-09), 27
computer consultant (1-05), 15
conference center (1-07), 21
CPA (1-11), 33
environmental organization
(1-15), 45
mailing services (1-04), 12
medical group (1-13), 39
plant nursery (1-03), 9
plastics molding company (1-06), 18
printer (1-08), 24
public relations firm (1-10), 30
real estate, commercial (1-14), 42
remodeling contractor
(1-01, 1-02), 3, 6
Business cards, 49
antique shop (2-06), 57
bathroom remodeling store
(2-03), 53
bottled water company (2-08), 59
computer consultant (2-14), 66
computer programmer (2-09), 60
liquor store (2-01), 51
marketing consultant (2-15), 67
painting contractor (2-04), 54
party planner (2-10), 61
plastics molding company (2-13), 65
premium incentives (2-11), 63
real estate broker (2-07), 58
restaurant (2-05), 55
security services (2-12), 64
travel agent, corporate (2-17), 70
veterinarian (2-02), 52
video producer (2-16), 69

Business broker, classified ad (3-04), 76
Business school, direct mail (5-09, 5-10),
122, 125
Business writing consultant, direct mail
(5-29), 191

C

Cable TV service, radio commercial
(10-04), 390
Cars and trucks
cleaning, direct mail (5-16), 147
custom vans, direct mail (5-20), 159
dealer, newspaper ad (8-01), 293
washing
commercial, newspaper ad
(8-30), 322
high school, flier (6-17), 277
Carpet cleaning service, direct mail
(5-13), 138
Caster manufacturer, direct mail
(5-39), 225
Caterer, newspaper ad (8-40), 332
Cellular phone manufacturer,
newspaper ad (8-03), 295
Cellular phone store
newspaper ad (8-21), 313
Yellow Pages ad (12-04), 420
Chain manufacturer, direct mail
(5-43), 239
Children's
gift shop, direct mail (5-19), 156
gymnastics, direct mail (5-21), 162
Chiropractor, direct mail (5-08), 119
Church
candy sale, flier (6-18), 278
flea market, newspaper ad
(8-73), 365
Classified ads, 71
administrative assistant (3-02), 74
apartment rental (3-03), 75

environmental testing service
(6-06), 266
eyeglass store (6-05), 263
furniture store (6-12), 272
garden supply, lawnmower sale
(6-10), 270
gas station (6-13), 273
hardware store (6-11), 271
high school, car wash (6-17), 277
ice cream shop (6-02), 260
kitchen supplies (6-15), 275
lingerie store (6-09), 269
merchants' association (6-03), 261
photo processor (6-07), 267
real estate, office complex
(6-08), 268
stationery store, sale (6-16), 276
Flea market (8-73), 365
Floor covering
manufacturer, newspaper ad
(8-15), 307
store, newspaper ad (8-05), 297
Florist
direct mail (5-34), 210
newspaper ad (8-06), 298
Yellow Pages ad (12-13), 429
Folk art gallery, press release (9-01), 373
Framing shop, Yellow Pages ad
(12-09), 425
Furniture
manufacturer, trade ad (11-04), 412
store, flier (6-12), 272

G

Garden club
newspaper ad (8-71), 363
press release (9-11), 383
Garden supply, lawnmower sale, flier
(6-10), 270
Gas station, flier (6-13), 273

Golf equipment dealer, cover letter
(4-01), 86
Gourmet gift baskets, direct mail
(5-30), 196
Graphic design service
radio commercial (10-09), 395
newspaper ad (8-35, 8-36), 327, 328

H

Hardware store, flier (6-11), 271
Health club, direct mail (5-01), 97
Health foundation, direct mail
(5-47), 254
Heating and air conditioning services
direct mail (5-11), 128
radio commercial (10-02), 388
Yellow Pages ad,(12-02), 418
Historic preservation league, press
release (9-09), 381
Home remodeler, Yellow Pages ad
(12-06), 422
Hospital
anti-smoking, press release
(9-07), 379
physician referral, newspaper ad
(8-49), 341

I

Ice cream shop, flier (6-02), 260
Image ads, 281
advertising agency (7-05), 288
book store (7-02), 285
corporation, charity drive
(7-04), 287
printer (7-01), 282
secretarial school (7-03), 286
women's clothing store (7-06), 289
Insurance agency
personal lines
cover letter (4-02), 87

cable TV service (10-04), 390
courier service (10-13), 399
CPA
   accounting systems (10-16), 402
   tax (10-15), 401
environmental testing services
   (10-06), 392
event planner (10-11), 397
financial services company
   (10-08), 394
graphic design service (10-09), 395
heating and air conditioning services
   (10-02), 388
manufacturer, help wanted
   (10-07), 393
mattress store (10-03), 389
office equipment dealer (10-10), 396
restaurant (10-01), 387
travel agency (10-12), 398
Real estate (see also Real estate broker)
   apartments, newspaper ad
      (8-65), 357
   commercial, brochure (1-14), 42
   corporate facility, newspaper ad
      (8-69), 361
   grand opening, newspaper ad
      (8-67), 359
   office park
      direct mail (5-45), 245
      flier (6-08), 268
      newspaper ad (8-68), 360
   houses, newspaper ad (8-66), 358
Real estate broker (see also Real estate)
   business card (2-07), 58
   direct mail (5-22, 5-23), 165, 170
   newspaper ad (8-70), 362
Real estate management, direct mail
   (5-07), 116
Remodeling contractor
   brochure (1-01, 1-02), 3, 6
Restaurant
   business card (2-05), 55

direct mail (5-03), 103
newspaper ad (8-25), 317
radio commercial (10-01), 387
Yellow Pages ad (12-08), 424
Retirement community, TV commercial
   (10-17), 403

S

Sales representative, trade ad (11-01,
   11-02), 409, 410
Sales trainer, classified ad (3-07), 79
Sandwich shop/music store, direct mail
   (5-02), 100
Sauna manufacturer, direct mail
   (5-36), 216
Secretarial school, image (7-03), 286
Security services, business card
   (2-12), 64
Software sales, classified ad (3-10), 82
Sporting goods store
   direct mail (5-18), 153
   newspaper ad (8-14), 306
Stationery store, sale, flier (6-16), 276
Summer theater, newspaper ad
   (8-76), 368
Surveying supplies, direct mail
   (5-44), 242
Symphony, flier (6-19), 279

T

Telephone answering service
   newspaper ad (8-32), 24
   Yellow Pages ad (12-15), 431
Testing equipment company, newspaper
   ad (8-44), 336
Trade ads
   abrasives company (11-05), 413
   electronics supply company
      (11-03), 411
   furniture company (11-04), 412
   sales representative (11-01, 11-02),
      409, 410